ANTONIO CARLUCCIO
THE COLLECTION

ANTONIO CARLUCCIO

THE COLLECTION

Photography by Alastair Hendy

Illustrations by Katie Horwich

quadrille

Notes

All spoon measures are level unless otherwise stated:
1 tsp = 5ml spoon; 1 tbsp = 15ml spoon.

Egg sizes are given where they are critical, otherwise use medium eggs, preferably organic or free-range. Anyone who is pregnant or in a vulnerable health group should avoid sauces that use raw egg whites or lightly cooked eggs.

Use fresh herbs, sea salt and freshly ground black pepper unless otherwise suggested.

If using the zest of citrus fruit, buy organic, unwaxed fruit.

Timings are for fan-assisted ovens. If using a conventional oven, increase the temperature by 15°C (1 Gas mark). Use an oven thermometer to check the temperature.

CONTENTS

Introduction

This collection of recipes celebrates my lifetime's dedication to food in general, and to the food of my homeland, *La Bella Italia*, in particular. In all the 18 books that I have had published, the majority of my recipes reflect the authenticity of the food from Italy's 20 diverse regions. Those recipes that are entirely my own creation similarly keep to my passion for regional Italian cookery, something which has always fascinated me.

Real Italian food is all about simplicity and flavour. It is about fish straight from the water, meat reared and butchered with skill, wine made with local grapes and matured in ancient barrels, organic vegetables just dug from fertile fields and ripe fruit picked off the tree. The simplicity of the recipes relies on one thing – the finest and freshest ingredients available.

What Italian food is not so known for is change, or at least not radical change! Yet these days I find that many chefs – Italian and non-Italian alike –tinker with it. I'm not sure why this is. As far as I'm concerned, Italian food doesn't need to be changed, it just needs to be cooked properly with excellent authentic ingredients.

The classic Italian repertoire contains many thousands of delightful recipes, not to mention the countless recipes that hail from extremely localised regions in Italy. My self-imposed task has always been to make this food accessible to as wide an audience as possible. Over the last 30 years I have done, and still do, a lot of work – through books, television, articles and talks – to get this message across. Judging from the feedback of readers and the good judgement of critics I know I have done a good job, of which I am proud.

The recipes contained within this collection demonstrate the quintessential simplicity and exceptional flavours of Italian regional food and reflect my keen interest and appreciation of the culture and cooking of the whole of Italy. I urge you to cook from these pages and discover the benefits of the cuisine I believe to be the best in the world.

Have fun and *buon appetito*!

ANTIPASTI

RAVANELLI AL BALSAMICO
RADISHES WITH BALSAMIC VINEGAR

500g small fresh, round radishes
6 tbsp extra virgin olive oil
2 tbsp balsamic vinegar (preferably 5 years old)
3 spring onions, white part only, extremely
  finely chopped
salt and pepper

Clean the radishes, leaving two or three central leaves at the top. Make four incisions with a sharp knife laterally, without cutting right through, to increase penetration of the flavourings.

In a bowl, mix the radishes with the oil, vinegar, spring onions and some salt and pepper to taste.

Eat with Fettunta (p28) or grissini.

Serves 4

Radishes are mainly eaten raw or as part of a salad. Here is a salad using them on their own. The dish can be served as an appetiser, with drinks, or as a nibble at the beginning of the meal.

BAGNA CAUDA
HOT GARLIC AND ANCHOVY DIP

16 garlic cloves
milk, for covering
300g anchovy fillets (preferably salted and rinsed),
  or 30 anchovy fillets in oil, drained
300g butter (preferably Alpine), cut into pieces
200ml extra virgin olive oil
100ml double cream
selection of raw vegetables such as celery, Jerusalem
  artichokes, small globe artichokes, cardoons, peppers,
  cucumber, fennel, radicchio and asparagus
a little beaten egg (optional)

Put the garlic cloves into a small pan, cover with milk and cook extremely slowly over a very low heat until the garlic is soft. Remove from the heat and crush the garlic into the milk until the mixture becomes creamy. Add the anchovies and let them dissolve, stirring, over a very low heat. When everything is amalgamated, add the butter and olive oil and stir gently to combine. Finally add the cream.

Pour the bagna cauda into little fondue dishes, or into one single one, and keep warm over a lighted candle. Now, one by one, dip the tips of the vegetable pieces into it, and eat with country bread. Repeat this until you have finished everything or you are satisfied! At the end, you can stir a spoonful of beaten egg into the last of the sauce and let it coagulate. This will be the last wonderful morsel.

Serves 6 or more

" The Piedmontese love garlic and anchovy, and this is a wonderful combination of both, to be served in a fondue dish in the middle of the table, or in little individual pots each with a candle underneath. My recipe is milder than usual – the garlic isn't too pungent – so that everyone can enjoy it. "

GIARDINIERA
MIXED PICKLES

1.5 litres strong white wine vinegar
150g caster sugar
10 bay leaves
10 whole peppercorns
10 cloves
30g salt
300g carrots, cut into rounds
300g celeriac, cut into 5cm cubes
2 stalks of Swiss chard leaves, cut into 10cm chunks
500g firm and fleshy red peppers, de-seeded and
    cut into strips
300g cauliflower, cut into small florets
300g green (French) beans, halved
150ml olive oil

Put the vinegar in a very large stainless-steel pot and add the sugar, bay leaves, peppercorns, cloves and salt, and stir this mixture well. Add the carrot, celeriac and Swiss chard, and boil for 15 minutes. Then add the peppers, cauliflower and beans. When it starts to boil again, cook for another 15–20 minutes.

Remove from the heat and add the olive oil, mix well and divide between sterilised jars. Use the bay leaves to decorate the inside of the glass jars: do this when the jar is half full. Use a very clean fork to put the leaves into place – never use your hands unless you are wearing rubber gloves. Seal in the normal way when everything has cooled down.

Makes 2 litres

" There is no decent antipasto in northern Italy, especially in Piedmont, which does not include a pickled element, something like gherkin, onion, mushrooms, olives or peppers in vinegar. Giardiniera is a mixture of garden vegetables pickled for this purpose. The intention is to balance other, more fatty items of the antipasto, but above all to tease the stomach juices for the dishes following. "

SALICORNIA SOTT'ACETO
PICKLED SAMPHIRE

600g fresh samphire
500ml strong white wine vinegar
100g caster sugar
a few bay leaves
a few dill springs
1 tbsp juniper berries

Wash the samphire in several changes of cold water.

In a large pan, bring the vinegar, sugar and herb and spice flavourings to the boil. Add the samphire and cook for 10 minutes. (Salt is not needed because the samphire is very salty indeed.) Remove from the heat, leave to cool and bottle in a clean, airtight jar. You can use it straightaway.

Fills a 1kg jar

CETRIOLO IN AGRODOLCE
SWEET-AND-SOUR CUCUMBER

2 short cucumbers, peeled, de-seeded and cut into
   batons of 8–10cm long (about 800g cleaned weight)
1 tbsp finely chopped dill
2 tbsp extra virgin olive oil
1 tsp caster sugar
1 tbsp white wine vinegar
salt and pepper

Put all the ingredients into a ceramic bowl and leave to marinate for 1 hour in the fridge. Stir from time to time to coat every piece and then serve.

Serves 4

A dish to nibble or to serve at a party with aperitifs – perhaps together with rapanelli, or radishes, as a little crudité to have while you are waiting for a meal. The Italian short cucumbers are less watery than their longer counterparts, so they can absorb the marinating ingredients better.

FRITTELLE DI POMODORI SECCHI
DRIED TOMATO FRITTERS

16 sun-dried tomatoes
olive oil, for shallow-frying

Batter
1 egg, beaten
2 tbsp plain flour
½ tsp baking powder
a little milk (optional)
salt and pepper

Put your tomatoes in a bowl, and cover with water. Leave to de-salt and rehydrate for about 2 hours. They should plump up to a wrinkly equivalent of the original. Drain well, discarding the water.

Beat the egg, flour and baking powder together in a medium-sized bowl, adding a little milk if necessary to obtain a smooth, thick batter. Season with salt and pepper.

Pour enough olive oil into a frying pan to cover the base generously and heat gently. Using a fork, dip the tomatoes in the batter, making sure they are coated well. Allow any excess batter to drip off. Shallow-fry in the hot oil in batches until golden, about 3 minutes on each side.

Drain on kitchen paper and serve either warm or cold.

Serves 4

A good way to serve these tomato fritters, with drinks, say, would be as part of a platter with the spinach balls opposite. Just don't forget the paper napkins!

POLPETTINE DI SPINACI
SPINACH BALLS

500g spinach, cleaned and tough stalks removed
salt and pepper
2 eggs, beaten
a pinch of freshly grated nutmeg
1 garlic clove, finely puréed
100g fresh white breadcrumbs
50g Parmesan, grated
olive oil, for shallow-frying

Wash the spinach, put it in a pan of salted boiling water and blanch for 2 minutes or so, then drain. Squeeze out as much water as you can, using your hands or pressing in a sieve, then chop the leaves finely.

Put the spinach in a medium bowl and stir in the beaten eggs, a pinch of salt, some pepper, the nutmeg, garlic, breadcrumbs and Parmesan. Mix well until you achieve a binding consistency. If the mixture is too wet, add an extra tablespoon of breadcrumbs.

Pour enough olive oil into a frying pan to cover the base generously, and heat gently.

Roll the mixture into little balls the size of walnuts. Shallow-fry the spinach balls in the hot olive oil until golden, about 4–5 minutes per side. Drain on kitchen paper and serve either warm or cold.

Makes 24 little balls

❝ Some 25 years ago I invented the recipe for these little spinach balls for a chapter on finger food in a book published by *The Sunday Times*. Since then I have used them in all sorts of ways, most significantly in a vegetarian pasta dish (p108). They are very simple to make and very jolly. ❞

OLIVE FARCITE ALL'ASCOLANA
DEEP-FRIED STUFFED OLIVES

50 Ascoli olives
olive oil, for deep-frying
plain white flour, for coating
2 eggs, beaten
dried breadcrumbs, for coating

Filling
3 tbsp olive oil
50g butter
100g lean pork, finely minced
100g lean veal, finely minced
50g boneless chicken, minced
salt and pepper
3 tbsp dry Marsala or Sherry
1 small black truffle, diced
few drops of truffle oil
30g Parma ham, finely chopped
3 tbsp finely chopped parsley
½ tsp freshly grated nutmeg
finely grated zest of 1 lemon
1 egg, beaten
50g Parmesan, freshly grated
a little milk (if needed)

To make the filling, heat the olive oil and butter in a pan. Add the minced meats and fry, stirring, for 5–6 minutes until well browned. Season with salt and pepper, add the Marsala or Sherry and let bubble to reduce. Take off the heat and cool, then transfer to a food processor.

Add the truffle and truffle oil, ham, parsley, nutmeg and lemon zest. Process briefly to mix, then add the egg and grated cheese, and whiz to combine. The mixture should be firm enough to use as a stuffing but not too dry; soften with a drop or two of milk if necessary.

Starting from the top, cut each olive in a spiral fashion to reach and lose the stone inside, keeping the spiral intact. Take a little of the filling and enclose it in the olive spiral, pressing a little to regain the original shape.

Finish and cook the olives a few at a time. Heat the olive oil for deep-frying in a suitable pan. Dip the olives in a little flour, then into the beaten egg, and then roll them in the breadcrumbs. Deep-fry for 2–3 minutes until brown, then drain on kitchen paper. Serve hot as an antipasto, with little lemon wedges if you like.

PATE DI OLIVE NERE
BLACK OLIVE PASTE

500g firm black olives, pitted
500g salted capers, soaked and drained
4 anchovy fillets in oil, drained
1 tsp pepper
1 small chilli, chopped (optional)
pinch of chopped oregano (optional)
125ml extra virgin olive oil

Put all the ingredients except the oil into a liquidiser. With the motor running, add the oil a little at a time until you have a spreadable paste. No salt is necessary because the olives, capers and anchovies are already salted. If you do include the chilli, reduce the amount of black pepper.

Makes 400g

" This makes a welcome spread for crostini or served with bread as an antipasto. The pâté can also be made with green olives, although the anchovies should then be replaced with ground almonds. "

CIPOLLE DI TROPEA E PECORINO

BAKED RED ONIONS STUFFED WITH PECORINO

4 large Tropea onions (or equivalent)
salt and pepper
4 tbsp olive oil, plus extra to drizzle
50g smoked pancetta, very finely chopped
100g fresh, young pecorino cheese, diced

Preheat the oven to 200°C/Gas 6. Peel off the papery onion skins. Cut a slice off the top of each onion to reveal all the inner circles, then, using a melon baller, excavate everything apart from the 3 or 4 outer layers, leaving an onion casing; reserve the flesh. Boil the onion casings in salted water for 10–12 minutes. Drain and cool.

Meanwhile, chop the excavated onion flesh finely. Fry in the olive oil with the pancetta and lots of black pepper until soft.

Mix the fried onions with the diced cheese and use to fill the onion cavities. Stand the onions in a baking dish, drizzle with olive oil and bake for 20 minutes. Serve as a starter.

Serves 4

" The onions of Tropea can be eaten raw in salads, or cooked. I decided to cook them with pecorino here, combining two wonderful Calabrian ingredients. "

FRITTELLA PALERMITANA

ARTICHOKES, PEAS AND BROAD BEANS FROM PALERMO

4–5 small young artichokes
90ml olive oil
1 large onion, thinly sliced
150g shelled fresh peas
150g shelled fresh broad beans
1 tsp salted capers, soaked and drained
salt and pepper
300ml water

Prepare the artichokes by removing the stalks and outer leaves. Small young artichokes have hardly any choke and should need very little preparation. Cut the artichokes into quarters.

Heat the olive oil in a saucepan, add the onion and fry briefly, until softened. Add the peas, broad beans, artichokes, capers and some salt and pepper, then pour in the water and stir well. Put the lid on the pan and cook over a medium heat for about 20 minutes or until the vegetables are tender, stirring from time to time.

Serves 2 as a main course or 4 as an accompaniment

Made when the new season's vegetables have just appeared, this dish is the epitome of springtime in Sicily. A speciality of Palermo, it is extremely simple to make. Sometimes a teaspoon of white wine vinegar is added after the vegetables have been cooked. Without the vinegar it can be used as a pasta sauce.

CARCIOFI ALLA BRACE

ROAST ARTICHOKES

12 young purpled-leaved artichokes
6 tbsp extra virgin olive oil
1 tbsp very finely chopped parsley
salt and pepper
1 lemon, cut into wedges

Cut off and discard the spiky tops of the artichokes, leaving only 5cm of stem. Beat them on a hard surface to loosen the tight inside leaves.

Mix the oil with the parsley and drop a little of this into the centre of each artichoke, adding salt and pepper as well. 'Close' the artichokes by pressing with your hand, and put them on the barbecue grill over the charcoal (be careful it's not too hot). Turn them a quarter every 5 minutes. After 20 minutes, they are ready.

Eat the artichokes by discarding the burnt and tough outer leaves – the centre will be heavenly! Serve with lemon wedges.

Serves 4

" During a visit to one of our tomato suppliers near Naples I was invited to an impromptu lunch. On the menu were artichokes, just cut from the fields, to be cooked on a small metal charcoal grill which had already been lit. The artichokes were 'beaten' to open the leaves a little in order to season them well inside, and they were put on the grill. The flavour still lingers on my palate! "

ASPARAGI AL BURRO E PARMIGIANO
ASPARAGUS WITH BUTTER AND PARMESAN

1kg green or white asparagus spears
85g unsalted butter
85g Parmesan cheese, freshly shaved or grated
salt and pepper to taste

Cut off the tough ends of the asparagus and peel the lower stems, discarding all the stringy parts. Boil in lightly salted water until tender (test with a pointed knife after 10–15 minutes). Drain and leave to cool.

Melt the butter in a pan. Drain the asparagus and divide between the serving plates. Pour over the melted butter, and add salt, a good twist of freshly ground black pepper and the Parmesan (either in shavings or grated).

Serves 4

" This is perhaps the simplest way to prepare and eat asparagus. The combination of the melted butter and the nuttiness of the Parmesan is a simple one, but nonetheless very, very good. In Lombardy, some people serve fried eggs on top – but it's up to you! "

ZUCCHINI E FAGIOLINI ALLA MENTA
COURGETTES AND GREEN BEANS WITH MINT

200g green (French) beans, trimmed
300g small courgettes, trimmed and
    quartered lengthways
salt and pepper
3 garlic cloves, roughly sliced
bunch of fresh mint leaves
6 tbsp extra virgin olive oil
1 tbsp white wine vinegar or the juice of ½ lemon

In a large pan, cook the beans and courgettes in boiling salted water until al dente, probably about 15 minutes. Drain both and when still warm put in a bowl. Add the garlic, mint and olive oil, season with salt and pepper to taste and mix in the vinegar or lemon juice.

Leave at room temperature, uncovered, for at least half an hour to allow the vegetables absorb the flavours. The longer you leave them to infuse, the darker, softer and more garlicky they will become.

Serve with some good country bread.

Serves 4

The Italians tend to cook their vegetables more than other people – and certainly don't serve them almost raw as the French would. They need to be at the most al dente, or 'to the tooth'. To test, stick the tip of a sharp knife into the vegetable: if it offers resistance, cook a little longer; if there is little resistance, it should be ready. But ultimately it is all a matter of taste…

" This dish is a favourite of mine and
can be eaten either as an antipasto or as
an accompaniment for various dishes. "

ROTOLINI DI MELANZANE, PEPERONI E ZUCCHINI
AUBERGINE, PEPPER AND COURGETTE ROLLS

Aubergines
2 large aubergines
olive oil flavoured with garlic
salt and pepper
2 buffalo mozzarella
16 large basil leaves

Peppers
2 yellow peppers, chargrilled
2 red peppers, chargrilled
olive oil
16 anchovy fillets in oil, drained
2 tbsp chopped flat-leaf parsley

Courgettes
3 courgettes, trimmed
salt and pepper
olive oil, for brushing
12 soft, sun-dried tomatoes
12 basil leaves

Preheat the oven to 200°C/Gas 6.

Top and tail the aubergines and cut them lengthways, into slices about 5mm thick. Brush both sides of each slice with the garlic oil, season with salt and pepper, and bake in the preheated oven for 10 minutes.

Cut the mozzarella into thick slices first and then into fingers. Lay a basil leaf on each slice of aubergine, put the mozzarella finger on top, add salt and pepper to taste, and roll up, using a toothpick to secure.

After you have grilled the peppers and blackened each side of them, let them cool. Skin them and discard the seeds and stalks. Divide them each into four fillets and brush with olive oil. Place an anchovy fillet in the middle and put a layer of parsley on top. Roll up and secure with a toothpick.

Cut the courgettes in thin slices lengthways, then blanch them in plenty of boiling salted water for about 5 minutes, until soft and pliable. Drain, and leave to cool. Brush with oil, put a piece of sun-dried tomato and a basil leaf at one end of each slice, and roll. Secure with a toothpick. Serve at drinks parties or as a snack.

Makes 16 rolls

PEPERONI ARROSTO
ROASTED PEPPERS
Illustrated overleaf

4 firm and fleshy yellow and red sweet peppers

Dressing
2 garlic cloves, coarsely chopped
3 tbsp extra virgin olive oil
1 tbsp coarsely chopped flat-leaf parsley
salt

Roast the peppers on a barbecue, turning them over frequently with tongs, until the skins are blackened and blistered. Depending on the flame, this can take quite a while. Don't be afraid of allowing them to become black; they're better overcooked than too raw – but you don't want them to turn to ash!

Alternatively, roast the peppers in a preheated oven at 200°C/Gas 6 for about 30–45 minutes. However, while this method is a little less labour-intensive, the flavour is not quite so good.

When the peppers are ready, put them in a dish to cool a little. I don't think they need to be put in a plastic bag or covered, despite the advice of many other chefs. When cool enough to handle, rub the skins off with your hands and discard, then slice the peppers in half and remove the stalks, inner membranes and seeds.

Cut the pepper flesh lengthways into narrow strips and place in a dish. Add the dressing ingredients and mix, seasoning with salt to taste. You can eat the dish straightaway, or leave it to become cold – but it is at its best the next day, when the flavours have had a bit of time to mingle.

Serves 4

These roasted peppers are most delicious when prepared over a barbecue, but they can also be cooked in the oven. They are great as an antipasto, but can also be served with roast meats, fish or combined with anchovies and olives to make a pasta sauce.

CASTAGNE AL BURRO
BUTTERED CHESTNUTS

500g last season's dried chestnuts (preferably Italian)
30g lardo (salt-cured pork belly)
200g Alpine butter, cut into 1cm cubes
salt

Soak the chestnuts in plenty of water overnight.

The next day, remove any brown pieces of skin remaining, and put the chestnuts in a pan with a lid. Cover completely with water and add a piece of lardo, which will give flavour but also 'shininess' to the dish. Cook slowly on a low heat with the lid on for at least 2 hours, or until the liquid has been absorbed and the chestnuts are brown and soft. Remove the lardo, and serve the chestnuts hot with a few cubes of butter on top and a pinch of salt. It should all be eaten before the butter starts to melt.

Serves 4–6

" A while back I was in Settimo Vittone in Piedmont at the Trattoria dell'Angelo, famous for its warm and cold antipasti. My whole family was there, one of those occasions where everybody sits together at one long, jolly table. After we had eaten huge amounts of first courses, all of a sudden the pièce de résistance arrived – cooked chestnuts with plenty of cubes of butter melting on top. I ate so many that I couldn't manage the next three courses! "

FUNGHI AL FUNGHETTO
SAUTEED MUSHROOMS

600g fresh ceps or other wild mushrooms, cleaned
8 tbsp olive oil
2 garlic cloves, finely chopped
salt and pepper
2 tbsp chopped oregano
squeeze of lemon juice

Slice the mushrooms. Heat the olive oil in a sauté pan and sauté the mushrooms over a high heat with the garlic until softened, seasoning them with some salt and pepper. Add the oregano, with a squeeze of lemon juice, and serve immediately.

Serves 4

CANEDERLI DI FUNGHI
MUSHROOM DUMPLINGS

1 small onion, finely chopped
20g butter
1 garlic clove, finely chopped
1 tbsp coarsely chopped parsley
375g wild mushrooms (ceps or chanterelles),
    cleaned and cut into small chunks
salt and pepper
6 stale bread rolls, cut into small cubes
300ml milk
3 tbsp plain white flour
4 eggs, beaten
fresh breadcrumbs (if needed)

Fry the onion in the butter until soft, then add the garlic and parsley and fry for a further minute. Add the mushrooms and some salt and pepper, and continue to fry until everything is soft.

Soften the bread cubes in the milk, then squeeze most of the milk out. Add them to the mushrooms with the flour and eggs, then add salt and pepper to taste. If the mixture looks too liquid, mix in some breadcrumbs.

Shape the mixture into balls (about the size of a golf ball) with your hands, and immerse them in lightly boiling water until they float to the surface. Scoop them out and eat them with melted butter.

Serves 4

Canederli are dumplings made using stale bread and any sort of flavouring ingredient you can imagine. Basically, the idea is to make a ball a little larger than a golf ball, which is either boiled in water or stock, or boiled then fried. It can be eaten by itself with some melted butter or sauce, or can accompany main dishes that have a sauce. If you can't find wild mushrooms, use the equivalent weight of cultivated mushrooms along with some dried ceps.

FETTUNTA
TUSCAN TOASTED BREAD

8 slices of Tuscan or good country bread
1 garlic clove
6 tbsp Tuscan extra virgin olive oil
salt and pepper

Toast the bread on both sides, then gently rub with
the garlic. Drizzle over the olive oil, sprinkle with salt
and pepper and eat warm.

Serves 4

" From fetta (slices) and unta (oiled),
this is exactly what it says. The Tuscans
eat it with antipasti or by itself as a snack.
In Lazio and other parts of the South it is
called bruschetta. "

CROSTINI DI FUNGHI
WILD MUSHROOM CROSTINI

400g mixed wild mushrooms (whatever you can get)
2 garlic cloves, 1 finely chopped
1 small red chilli, finely chopped
8 tbsp olive oil
1 tbsp coarsely chopped parsley
1 tbsp marjoram leaves
salt and pepper
4 large slices of Pugliese or good country bread

Clean the mushrooms thoroughly and cut into cubes.

Fry the finely chopped garlic and chilli in 6 tablespoons
of the olive oil, and before the garlic starts to colour,
add the mushrooms. Sauté or stir-fry them briefly for a
few minutes only so that they retain their crisp texture.
Add the parsley, marjoram and some salt and pepper.

Meanwhile, toast the slices of bread on both sides,
then rub them very slightly with the whole garlic clove.
Brush with the remaining olive oil and top with the
mushrooms. Serve immediately.

Serves 4

When you're buying mushrooms,
whether wild or cultivated, make sure
they look fresh, not withered. Wild
mushrooms should be cooked and eaten
on the day they're picked but can
stand a day in the fridge if necessary.
Cultivated mushrooms will keep for
three days in the fridge, as long as
they're in a paper bag. To prepare, cut
out any decayed parts and wipe them
clean with a damp cloth.

❝ This Italian dish is extremely popular because of its versatility: it can be served as a snack or antipasto, or with drinks. Crostini can be topped with chicken liver paté, a mixture of tomato, mozzarella and basil, or grilled vegetables. This version using wild mushrooms is exceptionally good – even if you can't get hold of any wild mushrooms and have to use cultivated instead. ❞

MOZZARELLA IN CARROZZA
FRIED MOZZARELLA SANDWICH

2 thick slices of good country white bread,
   crusts removed
a little milk
1 large slice of buffalo mozzarella
plain flour, for dusting
salt
2 eggs, beaten
olive oil, for shallow-frying

Dip the slices of bread in milk for a few seconds but
do not soak them. Drain, then place the mozzarella
on one piece of bread and put the other on top to make
a sandwich. Dip in flour seasoned with salt, then the
eggs. Shallow-fry in a good quantity of oil for 5 minutes
until golden, turning once. Serve immediately with
a little dipping sauce of passata and chopped basil.

Serves 1

❝ Originally from Naples and generally
from Campania, this dish has spread all
over Italy and is to be found mostly in bars
as a lunchtime snack. It is delicious when
freshly made and still crisp. ❞

FOCACCIA ALL'AGLIO SELVATICO
WILD GARLIC FOCACCIA BREAD

45g fresh yeast
700ml lukewarm water
85ml extra virgin olive oil, plus extra for oiling
30g fine salt
1.25kg Italian '00' flour
300g fine semolina

Topping
150g wild garlic leaves and flowers
100ml extra virgin olive oil
100g shelled almonds, finely crushed
salt and pepper
15kg coarse salt

For the focaccia itself, dissolve the yeast in a little
of the lukewarm water – about 50ml – then mix with
the oil and salt. Mix this into the flour and semolina
to make a dough. Set aside in a warm place and cover
with a clean cloth. Leave to rise until doubled in size,
about 1 hour.

Meanwhile, prepare the topping by coarsely liquidising
the garlic leaves (reserving the flowers if you like),
together with the olive oil. Add the almonds, season
to taste with salt and pepper and mix together.

Preheat the oven 220°C/Gas 7.

Take the dough and knead to remove any air bubbles.
Spread the dough out on an oiled 60 x 40cm baking
tray. It should cover the whole tray and not be higher
than 2cm. With the tips of your fingers make dimples
in the surface of the dough. Bake in the preheated oven
for 20 minutes.

When brown and crisp, remove from the oven. Spread
the wild garlic mixture, the flowers if you like, and the
coarse salt on the top. Return to the oven for 2 more
minutes. Serve warm or cold – either is delicious.

Serves 10

" Romans like frittatas, and this one is said to be an aphrodisiac
thanks to the mint! I love it for its fresh taste and simplicity.
A frittata is a substantial omelette browned on both sides and
not folded, as a French omelette would be. "

FRITTATA ALLA MENTA
OMELETTE WITH MINT AND PECORINO

12 very fresh eggs
200g very fresh sheep's milk ricotta cheese
4 tbsp coarsely chopped mint, plus extra leaves
   to garnish
50g pecorino cheese, grated
salt and pepper
6 tbsp olive oil

Beat the eggs in a large bowl, then add the ricotta and mix together until evenly blended. Add the mint, pecorino and salt and pepper to taste. Mix together well.

Heat the olive oil in a non-stick pan, then pour in the frittata mixture. Cook over a medium heat, without stirring, for about 5 minutes until browned underneath. Then slide the frittata out onto a large plate, before inverting it back into the pan and browning the other side.

Slide the frittata out onto a warm plate and garnish with a few mint leaves. Serve cut into wedges as a snack, or as a light main course accompanied by a simple tomato salad.

Serves 4–6

FRITTATA DI CARDI E PROSCIUTTO
FRITTATA OF CARDOON AND PROSCIUTTO

500g cardoons (cleaned weight)
salt and pepper
6 tbsp olive oil
10 eggs, beaten
60g pecorino cheese (or Parmesan), grated
150g prosciutto, cut into thin slices, then rolled
   and cut into small strips
1 small chilli, finely chopped
bunch of parsley, coarsely chopped

Cut the cardoons into 1cm thick slices. Blanch these in boiling salted water for 10 minutes. Drain well. This can be done in advance.

When ready to cook, put the olive oil in a big frying pan, add the cardoons and warm them up over a gentle heat by stirring them from time to time.

Meanwhile, season the eggs with salt and pepper to taste. Add the grated cheese to the seasoned eggs, along with the prosciutto, chilli and parsley. Mix together well and add to the pan with the cardoons. Proceed to make an Italian omelette, which is cooked to golden and set on both sides.

Serves 4–5

UOVA TONNATE
TUNA-STUFFED EGGS

6 large eggs
150g canned tuna in oil, drained and finely chopped
12 salted capers, soaked, drained and finely chopped
1 gherkin (optional), finely sliced

Mayonnaise
2 eggs yolks
salt and pepper
1 tsp French mustard
100ml olive oil (not extra virgin)
juice of ½ lemon

Put the eggs in a small pan of cold water, bring to the boil and hard-boil for 15 minutes. Drain and leave to cool.

To make the mayonnaise, beat the egg yolks with a pinch of salt and the mustard in a bowl until creamy. Slowly pour in a little of the olive oil, whisking constantly until amalgamated. Keep adding the oil a little at a time, whisking all the while, until the mixture has thickened and all the oil has been used. Now add the lemon juice and mix well. Taste for seasoning and cover until needed.

Peel the eggs and cut in half. Remove the yolks, place in a bowl and, with a fork, reduce to a pulp. Mix this with the tuna, capers (reserving some to use as a garnish) and enough mayonnaise to be able to form balls the size of the original yolks. Place these in the holes of the halved egg whites.

Arrange the eggs in bowls, cover with some more mayonnaise and serve topped with the gherkin slices, if using, and reserved caper pieces.

Serves 4–6

" I can't count the number of times I have surprised guests with this dish, which may be simple but holds plenty of flavour. If you are in a hurry you can buy a good mayonnaise, but it is much better (and not difficult) to make it yourself. You can do it! "

POLPETTE DI TONNO E PATATE
POTATO AND TUNA CAKES

550g potatoes, peeled
salt and pepper
250g canned tuna in oil, drained and finely chopped
30g salted capers, soaked, drained and chopped
4 tbsp chopped flat-leaf parsley
3 eggs
100g dried breadcrumbs
olive oil, for shallow-frying

Cut the potatoes into walnut-sized pieces and boil in a saucepan of salted water until soft, about 20 minutes. Drain well, then mash and cool.

Put the mashed potato in a bowl. Add the tuna, capers, parsley and some pepper along with 2 of the eggs, and mix well.

Shape the mixture with your hands into cakes 8cm wide and 3cm deep. Beat the third egg in a bowl. Dip the cakes in the egg then coat with the breadcrumbs.

Pour enough olive oil into a large frying pan to cover the base generously and heat gently. Shallow-fry the cakes until golden, about 5 minutes per side. Drain on kitchen paper and serve either warm or cold.

Makes 10 little cakes

❝ This recipe uses freshly boiled and mashed potato, but can also be made using leftover mashed potato. Canned tuna, preferably in olive oil, should always be at the ready in a well-stocked Italian larder. ❞

LAVARELLO E TROTA MARINATE
MARINATED LAKE FISH OR TROUT

1 lake bream or trout fillet cut from a large fish, about 600g, very thinly sliced
2 tbsp very finely chopped flat-leaf parsley

Marinade
4 tbsp extra virgin olive oil
juice of 2 lemons
finely grated zest of ½ lemon
1 tsp caster sugar
1 tbsp finely grated horseradish
salt and pepper

To make the marinade, beat together the oil, lemon juice and zest, sugar, horseradish and salt and pepper to taste. Lay the slices of fish on a non-metallic plate.

Spread the marinade over the fish and leave for a couple of hours, then turn the fish over and cover with the marinade that has not been absorbed.

Sprinkle with the parsley and serve with good country bread or grissini.

Serves 4

Only extremely fresh fish are suitable for this uncooked dish. The fillets are 'cooked' by the acid of the lemon juice in the marinade. This modern way of serving fish in Italy is generally known as carpaccio. Tuna and swordfish can also be prepared like this and, if you omit the horseradish, so can fresh boned anchovies.

CALAMARI FRITTI
DEEP-FRIED SQUID

400g squid bodies and tentacles, cleaned (see below)
olive or groundnut oil, for deep-frying
50g semolina flour
50g plain flour
salt and pepper

Wash the squid and dry on kitchen paper. Cut the bodies into rings about 1.5cm thick.

Meanwhile, gently heat the oil in a deep frying pan. You will need enough oil to enable the individual pieces of squid to float, at least 5cm deep.

Mix the flours together in a medium bowl, and season with salt and pepper. Toss the squid pieces in the flour, shaking off any surplus.

Put a few pieces of floured squid into the hot oil at a time and deep-fry until golden brown, about 4–5 minutes. Drain well on kitchen paper. Serve immediately.

Serves 4

BACCALA CON PEPERONI ALLA GRIGLIA
BACCALA WITH GRILLED PEPPERS

800g baccalà (salt cod), de-salted
1 large, fleshy red pepper
8 tbsp olive oil
1 red chilli, finely chopped
80g pitted black olives
2 tbsp coarsely chopped flat-leaf parsley

Cook the baccalà in boiling water for 20 minutes or more, depending on thickness, until soft.

Meanwhile, chargrill the red pepper until the skin blackens. When it has cooled to the touch, peel away the skin, de-seed and cut the flesh into strips.

Drain the baccalà and reduce the flesh to flakes, getting rid of any bones. I keep the skin as I like it, but you can get rid of that too, if you prefer. Add the olive oil and chilli, the olives and parsley, and mix well. Serve topped with the grilled red peppers.

Serves 4

Most squid come ready cleaned these days, but if your fishmonger hasn't done it, simply pull the tentacles and head from the body of the squid. There will be an eye, viscera and ink sac attached to the head, which you should cut off and discard. Cut the hard little beak from the middle of the tentacles at the top, and pull the quill from the body, discarding both. Wash and dry everything well.

" I came across this baccalà speciality in Matera. I have replaced the peperoni cruschi with grilled strips of pepper, which may not be quite authentic, but they are easier to prepare and equally tasty. To de-salt baccalà, soak the chunks of meaty fish, skin-side up, in cold water for 24 hours, changing the water a couple of times. "

COZZE RIPIENE
STUFFED MUSSELS

1kg large black mussels, cleaned (p173)
1 tbsp olive oil
2 garlic cloves, finely chopped
pepper
1 quantity of filling from Sardine Ripiene (opposite)
1 egg, beaten
breadcrumbs, for coating
olive oil, for deep-frying

Place the cleaned mussels in a large pan with the olive oil and garlic. Cook with a lid on for a few minutes, shaking the pan from time to time to allow the mussels to open. When they have all opened, season with pepper and leave to cool.

Remove the mussels from their shells and enclose each one in a little of the sardine filling. Put back in the shell and then close the shell, leaving a little filling showing. Dip the mussels in the beaten egg and then into the breadcrumbs. Deep-fry in olive oil until golden.

Serves 4

SARDINE RIPIENE
STUFFED SARDINES

12 very fresh large sardines
1 egg, beaten
breadcrumbs, for coating
olive oil, for deep-frying

Filling
2 bread rolls, made into breadcrumbs
a little milk
60g extremely fresh mortadella, diced
2 eggs
55g Parmesan, grated
1 garlic clove, very finely chopped
2 tbsp finely chopped flat-leaf parsley
salt and pepper

Cut the heads off the sardines and bone them, leaving them attached down the back. Set aside.

Prepare the filling: soak the breadcrumbs in a little milk to cover, then squeeze out the excess liquid. Mix the breadcrumbs with all the remaining filling ingredients and season to taste.

Use the filling to stuff the sardines, then close each like a sandwich. Dip them in the beaten egg and then in the breadcrumbs. Deep-fry in olive oil until golden. Serve.

Serves 4

ACCIUGHE IN SALSA VERDE
ANCHOVIES IN GREEN SAUCE

300g anchovy fillets in oil (Italian or Spanish are the best)

Salsa verde
2 tbsp white wine vinegar
2 large slices good country bread, crusts removed
bunch of flat-leaf parsley, stalks removed and
    very finely chopped
1 small chilli, finely chopped
1 garlic clove, puréed
10 cornichons (mini gherkins), very finely chopped
15 salted capers, soaked, drained and very finely
    chopped
extra virgin olive oil, as required

Drain the anchovies and put a layer of them in the base of a narrow, medium-sized ceramic container.

To make the salsa verde, pour the vinegar into a bowl, add the bread and soak for a few minutes. Remove and squeeze dry, then finely chop. Put into another bowl with the parsley, chilli, garlic, cornichons and capers, and mix well, adding enough olive oil to achieve a sauce-like consistency.

Cover the anchovies with a layer of salsa verde, then top with another layer of anchovies. Repeat until all the anchovies are covered with sauce. Add enough olive oil to cover everything, and refrigerate for a day, after which the anchovies are ready to eat. Keep refrigerated for up to a week.

Makes a 300g batch

" Italians normally use parsley, basil or rocket as the green base for a salsa verde, a sauce that is often made with rather unorthodox ingredients by non-Italian chefs. When you come home and feel a little peckish for something salty, these anchovies on toasted bread are miraculous. "

SARDINE FARCITE AL FORNO
BAKED SARDINES
Illustrated overleaf

6 tbsp olive oil
2 garlic cloves, very finely chopped
4 tbsp finely chopped parsley
1 tbsp finely chopped basil
5 sage leaves, finely chopped
1 small chilli, very finely chopped
25g pine nuts
30g raisins
salt and pepper
juice of 1 lemon
8 very fresh sardines, boned and butterflied
30g dried breadcrumbs

Preheat the oven to 220°C/Gas 7 and oil a baking sheet with some of the olive oil.

In a bowl, mix the garlic, herbs, chilli, pine nuts and raisins with salt and pepper to taste. Add 1 tablespoon of the olive oil, a few drops of lemon juice and mix together well.

Lay four of the sardines skin-side down next to each other on the prepared baking sheet. Distribute the mixture on top of them, sprinkle with a few drops of lemon juice and sandwich with the remaining sardines skin-side up. Sprinkle with breadcrumbs and drizzle over the remaining olive oil. Bake for 10–12 minutes, until just starting to brown.

Serve hot, sprinkled with the remaining lemon juice, or cold arranged on lemon slices.

Serves 4

Traditionally this dish is made with fresh anchovies, however as they are hard to come by I have substituted small sardines. If you are able to find fresh anchovies then I urge you to use them as their flavour is fantastic.

" Nothing can surpass the taste of freshly caught
sardines. This typical Sicilian recipe, with its raisins
and pine nuts, has echoes of its Arabic origin. "

PIATTO DI SALAMI MISTI E PROSCIUTTO
AIR-DRIED MEAT PLATTER

PATE DI FEGATINI DI POLLO
CHICKEN LIVER PATE

a few slices each of Felino salami, Napoli salami and
  Calabrian hot sausage
a few slices of Parma ham, bresaola (beef) or mortadella
grissini, crostini or unsalted crackers

Display the meats 'artistically' on a platter, and bring
through to the guests to help themselves. Usually
grissini, crostini or unsalted crackers are eaten with
the meats. It is important that they are unsalted
because the preserved meats contain salt.

The most significant thing about this dish is that you
don't need to cook at home, as everything is available
from a good delicatessen.

Per person (multiply as needed)

66 Italians love preserved meat, particularly
pork, which comes in all sorts of shapes,
sizes and tastes. Salami, prosciutto and
the exceptional dried and cured beef,
bresaola, are often displayed on platters
and accompanied by pickled vegetables
like mushrooms, gherkins, onions and
olives — which can all be bought in any
good supermarket or Italian delicatessen. 99

500g chicken livers
4 tbsp olive oil
1 tbsp each of finely chopped sage and parsley
1 garlic clove, puréed
salt and pepper
1 tbsp each of good brandy and sweet Sherry
150g unsalted butter

Line a suitably sized terrine dish, or 4–6 individual
ramekins, with greaseproof paper or cling film.

Using a paring knife, clean the livers by cutting away
any green patches and membrane, removing the fibres
around the centre of each. Wash and dry well, then
roughly chop.

Fry the livers in the oil over a medium heat with the
sage, parsley, garlic, and some salt and pepper for
about 10 minutes, turning, until still pink in the
middle. Remove from the heat and leave to cool.

Blend the mixture in a food processor, adding the
brandy and the Sherry to the machine while operating,
for 3–4 minutes, until you have a rough paste. Return
the paste to the pan, add the butter and melt over a
low heat until the liver mixture becomes very
homogenised – a couple of minutes.

Pour the pâté into the terrine dish or individual
ramekins, and smooth on top. Allow to rest and cool
in the fridge for a couple of hours until solid. Eat spread
on crostini.

Makes about 600g

This recipe originally comes
from Tuscany, but I have
varied it a little so that it
more closely resembles the
much talked-about pâté de
foie gras of goose or duck.
A little of this pâté added
to meaty pasta sauces or to
meat or vegetable stuffings
gives a wonderful flavour.

WOOD PIGEON ON TOAST

3 wood pigeon, ready cleaned, with livers
12 slices of good country white bread
12 salted capers, soaked and drained

Marinade
2 glasses of red wine
4 tbsp olive oil
a few sage leaves
1 tbsp salted capers, soaked and drained
1 garlic clove
3 anchovy fillets in oil, drained
salt and pepper

Blend all the ingredients for the marinade in a liquidiser and pour into a bowl. Add the pigeons and leave to marinate for a few hours.

Preheat the oven to 220°C/Gas 7.

Remove the birds from the marinade and roast for 30 minutes. Leave to cool and then remove all the flesh and the livers from the birds and discard the bones. Put the marinade in a saucepan, add the meat and livers and cook for 10 minutes, stirring from time to time. Transfer to a liquidiser and blend to a paste, then leave to cool.

Toast the bread, spread with the paste and decorate each piece with a caper.

Makes 12 crostini

" Now famous throughout the world, crostini are a type of canapé and consist of slices of toasted bread, which serve as a base for all sorts of spreads. They are very popular topped with liver, but here is a special Tuscan version made with wood pigeon. "

FOIE GRAS WITH BALSAMIC SAUCE

4 slices of fresh foie gras (goose or duck) without the skin, each 2cm thick and about 50g

Sauce
6 tbsp saba
1 tbsp balsamic vinegar
1 tsp brandy
salt and pepper

First make the sauce. Heat the saba in a pan and add the balsamic vinegar, brandy and some salt and pepper to taste.

Heat a non-stick frying pan until it is very hot, then fry the foie gras slices very briefly, searing each side, but leaving the insides almost pink.

Arrange the foie gras on hot plates and surround with the sauce. Serve immediately, with some freshly toasted country bread.

Serves 4

" This recipe is my contribution to the cooking of neighbouring Lombardy and Emilia-Romagna. It was an incredible success in my Neal Street restaurant, impressing many French customers! Saba is a strong reduction of cooked grape must, which, incidentally, is the first stage of the famous Emilian aceto balsamico; you will find it in good delicatessens. "

INSALATE

INSALATA PRIMAVERILE
SPRINGTIME SALAD

350g mixed spring leaves
a few flower heads and petals (violets,
    primroses, dandelions, borage)
4 large eggs
3 tbsp extra virgin olive oil
1 tbsp wine vinegar
salt and pepper
12 anchovy fillets in oil, drained

Briefly wash the salad leaves and flowers, and drain very well. Hard-boil the eggs, but not too hard, as they are much nicer this way. Shell them, and cut in half.

Mix the oil and vinegar together to make a vinaigrette, adding salt and pepper to taste. Toss the salad leaves with this in a large bowl, and garnish with the egg halves, anchovies and flowers. Eat with good homemade or country bread, preferably wholegrain.

Serves 4

Springtime, when all the tender, new-grown greens such as dandelion, wild garlic and sorrel appear, marks the beginning of the wild leaf season. Later on, in early summer, you can add wild fennel, wild rocket and mint, and decorate this salad with violets or primroses. You could also add some cultivated spring onion for added flavour if you like.

INSALATA VERDE CON FINOCCHIO
GREEN SALAD WITH FENNEL

4 baby gem lettuces
2 fennel bulbs

Dressing
4 tbsp extra virgin olive oil
juice of ½ lemon, plus the finely grated zest,
    or, if you prefer, 3 tbsp balsamic vinegar
salt and pepper

Wash the lettuces and cut in quarters lengthways. Pull the leaves apart, discarding those on the outside if not tender. Put in a bowl. Discard the tougher outer leaves of the fennel, then cut the remaining flesh into very thin slices horizontally. Add to the bowl.

For the dressing, combine the oil, lemon juice and rind (or vinegar), salt and pepper in a bowl and mix well. Pour over the salad, toss and serve.

Serves 4

" My favourite salads are the simplest ones, where the ingredients – and not too many of them – complement each other. The combination here of crisp gem lettuce and tender fennel bulb is extremely refreshing. "

INSALATA DI CASTELFRANCO
RADICCHIO SALAD FROM CASTELFRANCO

2 thick slices of good country white bread
½ garlic clove
3 tbsp olive oil
400g Castelfranco radicchio
60g speck, approx. 2 slices, cut into small strips
60g San Daniele ham
100g Asiago cheese, cut into small strips

Vinaigrette
6 tbsp extra virgin olive oil
juice of 1 lemon
salt and pepper

Make the croutons first. Toast the bread, rub lightly with the garlic, then dice and fry in the olive oil until crisp. Drain.

Clean, wash and drain the radicchio leaves, and cut them into 5cm chunks. Put in a bowl with the speck, ham and cheese. Make a vinaigrette with the oil, lemon juice, salt and pepper. Toss the salad with the vinaigrette and serve with the croutons.

Serves 4

The radicchio cultivated north of Treviso in the county of Castelfranco is totally different from the Treviso radicchio. It is more bushy, like a real salad head, and is a wonderful yellow colour with red speckles. It is very tender and slightly bitter, and is ideal for this salad using local ingredients.

INSALATA DI CICORIA BELGA CON OLIO AL TARTUFO
BELGIAN CHICORY SALAD WITH TRUFFLE OIL

4 heads Belgian chicory
30g summer truffle, thinly sliced (optional)

Dressing
2 tbsp extra virgin olive oil
½ tsp truffle oil
2 tbsp balsamic vinegar
salt and pepper

Trim off and discard the root ends of the chicory. Cut the white leaves into small strips and place in a bowl.

For the dressing, combine the olive oil, truffle oil, vinegar, a little salt and plenty of pepper in a small bowl and mix together well. Pour into the bowl with the chicory and toss together. Serve topped with the summer truffle slices, if using.

Serves 4

" I tend not to use too much truffle oil because it is very intense, preferring to eat the real thing in season, but to counteract the slight bitterness of the chicory, the truffle oil is very good here. This salad can be served as a starter, but also makes a wonderful side dish to roast beef or fillet steak. "

INSALATA DI CARCIOFI
RAW ARTIICHOKE SALAD

8 very small, tender artichokes,
   before any chokes have formed
juice of ¼ lemon
6 tbsp extra virgin olive oil
salt and pepper
85g Parmesan, shaved very thinly

Trim the artichokes of all tough outer leaves. Cut
off and discard the top and bottom, then slice very
thinly and put into a bowl of water with the lemon
juice to prevent discolouration until ready to serve.

Prepare a vinaigrette with the olive oil, remaining
lemon juice, and salt and pepper to taste. Drain the
artichokes and arrange them on the serving plates.
Pour the vinaigrette over the artichokes and sprinkle
the Parmesan shavings on top. Eat with grissini.

Serves 4

Artichokes eaten raw in thin
slices are also part of the
ingredients of a Bagna Cauda
(p10). I particularly like to eat
them this way, but it is only
possible at the beginning of the
season when the artichokes
are small and tender.

INSALATA DI LENTICCHIE
LENTIL SALAD

300g Castelluccio lentils
1 small onion, halved
1 celery stalk, trimmed
1 bay leaf
1 rosemary sprig
4 tbsp extra virgin olive oil
1 tsp dried wild oregano
2 tbsp balsamic vinegar
salt and pepper

Cook the lentils in plenty of water with the onion,
celery, bay leaf and rosemary for 20–30 minutes.
Drain and discard the flavourings. While they are
still warm, dress the lentils with the olive oil, oregano,
vinegar, salt and plenty of black pepper.

Serves 4 as a starter

" I love eating freshly cooked pulses which
are flavoured with olive oil, vinegar and
oregano, and the nuttiness of Castelluccio
lentils is wonderful. This recipe is sheer
simplicity – you just need a nice bruschetta,
a good bottle of wine and your friends to
be able to enjoy it. "

INSALATA DI BARBABIETOLE CON MENTA
BEETROOT SALAD WITH MINT

16 small fresh beetroot
20 mint leaves

Dressing
4 tbsp extra virgin olive oil
1 tbsp white wine vinegar
salt and pepper

Cook the beetroot in plenty of boiling water until the tip of a knife enters the beetroot very easily, about 30 minutes. Drain well.

When cool enough to handle, peel the beetroot and cut into thin slices. Put in a bowl and add the mint.

For the dressing, combine the oil, vinegar, salt and pepper in a small bowl and mix well. Toss together with the beetroot and mint and serve.

Serves 4

" I can't stress enough that you must buy very fresh, small beetroot for this salad – ready-cooked will not do. I usually get mine in season from my garden, and they are a delicacy. The combination of fresh mint and sweet beetroot make an excellent dish that is not only a great starter but also a wonderful accompaniment to roast chicken or grilled fish. "

INSALATA RUSSA
RUSSIAN SALAD

INSALATA DI CAVOLO VERZA
SAVOY CABBAGE SALAD

250g small and tender garden peas
300g waxy new potatoes, finely diced
300g carrots, scrubbed and finely diced
200g celeriac, peeled and finely diced
200g small cauliflower florets
salt and pepper
100g canned tuna in oil, drained and very finely chopped
1 tbsp white wine vinegar

Mayonnaise
2–3 free-range egg yolks
1 tsp mustard
salt and pepper
250ml light Ligurian olive oil
juice of ½ lemon

Make the mayonnaise first. In a ceramic bowl, beat the yolks with the mustard and a pinch of salt and pepper until creamy. Stir continuously, then add a little stream of the olive oil. Beat until amalgamated. Continue adding a little oil at a time, continually beating, until the volume of the egg has expanded and all the oil has been incorporated. Now add the lemon juice and mix well. Cover until needed.

To prepare the salad base, cook all the raw vegetables in slightly salted water until al dente. Drain, cool down and mix in a bowl with the tuna and vinegar, salt and pepper. Fold them gently into the mayonnaise until the mixture binds together (but is not liquid). You can shape it into little moulds and decorate them with a sprinkling of finely chopped parsley.

Serves 6

1 Savoy cabbage
4 large slices of good country bread
1 garlic clove

Dressing
3 tbsp olive oil
1 tbsp white wine vinegar
2 anchovy fillets in oil, drained and very finely chopped
salt and pepper

Remove the outer leaves of the cabbage (these can be used as suggested below) until you are left with just the white centre. Slice this very thinly. Place the cabbage in a salad bowl.

Rub the slices of bread with the garlic clove.

For the dressing, combine the oil, vinegar, anchovies, a little salt and a lot of pepper in a small bowl and mix well. Pour into the bowl with the cabbage and toss. Eat with the garlic bread.

Serves 4

You will have quite a few outer leaves of cabbage left over in this dish. Use them shredded in soups, like minestrone (p87), or fry them with a little onion, some vinegar, juniper berries, salt and pepper, to make a quick sauerkraut – a perfect accompaniment to boiled meats, sausages, chicken or roast pork.

INSALATA DI PATATE TARTUFATE
TRUFFLED POTATO SALAD

800g young yellow, waxy potatoes, washed
salt and pepper
100g pancetta, sliced
30g chives, finely chopped

Vinaigrette
8 tbsp extra virgin olive oil
1 tbsp truffle oil
juice of ½ lemon

Preheat the oven to 200°C/Gas 6.

Boil the potatoes in salted water until tender. Bake
the pancetta in the preheated oven until very crisp
and dry. Cut the potatoes into 1cm slices. Break the
pancetta into little chunks and add to the potatoes.
Make a vinaigrette with the olive oil, truffle oil, lemon
juice, salt and plenty of pepper. Mix this into the
potato, and sprinkle with chives to serve.

Serves 4

Here you have the
chance to use the truffle
oil which a culinary-
minded friend gave you
for Christmas! Truffles
and potatoes go very well
together; they are both
'tubers', although of quite
different kinds, naturally.

INSALATA CAPRICCIOSA
CARROT, CELERIAC AND ARTICHOKE SALAD

300g raw carrots, scraped and cut into fine julienne
    strips, a little longer than a matchstick
300g celeriac, peeled and cut in the same way
6 preserved artichokes, cut into very small strips
juice of 1 lemon
50g canned tuna in oil, drained
200g homemade mayonnaise (p34)
salt and pepper

Assemble all the cut vegetables in a bowl, and sprinkle
with lemon juice. Mash the tuna with a fork, add to
the mayonnaise and mix well. Add the mayonnaise
to the vegetables and mix thoroughly. Season to taste.

Serves 6

" In selected bars in Torino and Piedmont,
there is always a series of tramezzini, very
elegant little sandwiches of white bread with
various fillings. What I remember best is the
tramezzino con capricciosa, a salad of two
raw vegetables and one preserved one,
with a heavenly sauce. "

VERDURE COTTE AL LIMONE E OLIO

SALAD OF COOKED VEGETABLES WITH LEMON AND OIL

2 large carrots, peeled and cut into quarters
2 fennel bulbs, trimmed and sliced
salt and pepper
200g red peppers, de-seeded and cut into eighths
8 asparagus stalks, trimmed
100g green (French) beans, trimmed
2 courgettes, trimmed and cut lengthways into thick strips
good extra virgin olive oil
juice of 1 lemon

Put the carrots and fennel into a large pan of boiling salted water, and cook for 15 minutes. Then add the peppers, asparagus, beans and courgettes and cook for another 10 minutes, until soft. Remove from the heat, drain and leave to cool.

Once cooled, arrange the vegetables on a serving platter, making a display with a nice sense of colour and shape. Drizzle with the olive oil and some drops of lemon juice. Season with a little salt and plenty of black pepper and serve.

Serves 4

" Vegetables, either simply steamed or boiled and dressed just with extra virgin olive oil and lemon juice, are to die for. Try if you can to get hold of Sicilian lemons or those from the Amalfi coast – their perfume and taste are unbeatable. "

" My mother used to make this interesting dish for the sake of economy, but I make it because to me it tastes of summer – one never goes by without me making it a few times at least. She used stale bread, which was baked in the oven to make it more absorbent and edible. "

PANZANELLA
BREAD AND VEGETABLE SALAD

MOZZARELLA CAPRESE
MOZZARELLA, TOMATOES AND BASIL, CAPRI-STYLE

4 large slices of country bread, crusts removed
4 large ripe tomatoes (about 800g)
the tender centre of 1 celery head, plus leaves, coarsely chopped
10 basil leaves, chopped
10 pitted olives, green or black
1 bunch spring onions, chopped
1 yellow pepper, de-seeded and cut into fine strips
1 garlic clove, puréed (optional)
6 tbsp extra virgin olive oil
salt and pepper

Preheat the oven to 160°C/Gas 3, and bake the bread for about 20 minutes, until golden. Break the cooked bread into small pieces about the size of a large sugar lump.

Put the tomatoes into a bowl of water that has just come to the boil, and leave for 30 seconds. Pull off the skin, then chop the flesh coarsely, collecting all the juices. (If your tomatoes are not very juicy, you'll need some help with soaking the bread; try adding some tomato juice from a carton or can.)

Mix the tomato pieces and juices together with all the other ingredients, including the bread. Leave to infuse for a few hours, so that the bread can absorb all the flavours and soften. Stir occasionally. Add salt and pepper to taste and serve cold.

Serves 4

500g buffalo mozzarella, sliced
2 large, ripe tomatoes, sliced
10 basil leaves
4 tbsp extra virgin olive oil
salt and pepper

Arrange the slices of mozzarella on a plate, alternating them with the slices of tomatoes and basil leaves. Pour over the olive oil, then season with salt and pepper.

Serves 4

The best way of serving buffalo mozzarella as a starter is to combine it with ripe tomatoes, good olive oil and fresh basil. This is often called insalata caprese or even tricolore.

INSALATA DI FUNGHI, SPINACI E PROSCIUTTO
MUSHROOM, SPINACH AND PARMA HAM SALAD
Illustrated on previous page

300g Caesar's mushrooms
250g baby spinach leaves
55g Parma ham, sliced 2mm thick, then cut into strips

Vinaigrette
4 tbsp extra virgin olive oil
1 tbsp sweet mustard
2 tbsp balsamic vinegar
salt and pepper

Clean the mushrooms thoroughly, then cut them into 5mm slices. Wash the spinach well and pat dry.

Make a vinaigrette by mixing together the olive oil, mustard, vinegar and some salt and pepper.

Toss the spinach in the vinaigrette first, then divide between four plates. Garnish with the mushroom slices and strips of Parma ham. Serve accompanied by some good toasted bread.

Serves 4

The mushroom used in this Italian recipe, Caesar's mushroom, is undoubtedly one of the prettiest and most delicate mushrooms, and it would be a sin to cook with it. Caesar's mushroom belongs to the nastiest family, the Amanitas, which includes many of the most poisonous mushrooms. But identify it well, or buy it in season from a reliable vendor, and you will enjoy a real delight.

INSALATA DI FUNGHI MISTI
MIXED FUNGHI SALAD

500ml water
250ml strong white wine vinegar
salt and pepper
4 bay leaves
200g judas ears mushrooms, oyster mushrooms, wood blewits and chanterelles
8 tbsp extra virgin olive oil
1 garlic clove, finely chopped
1 chilli, finely chopped
2 tbsp coarsely chopped flat-leaf parsley
lemon wedges, to serve

Bring the water and vinegar to the boil in a stainless-steel pan with 1 tsp salt and the bay leaves. Throw the mushrooms into the boiling liquid and cook for 8–10 minutes. Drain and discard the liquid.

Put the olive oil, garlic and chilli into a large pan and fry very briefly. Add the drained mushrooms and toss in the pan to let them absorb the oil and its flavourings. Season to taste with salt and pepper and add the parsley. Serve with a wedge of lemon.

Serves 4

" Every time I return from a funghi hunt, even if I only have a few varied specimens, then it is time to make this exciting salad. It can be eaten as a starter by itself, or can accompany fish dishes or cold roast meats. It may be eaten hot or cold. "

INSALATA DI BOSCO SILANO
SALAD FROM THE SILA WOODS

10 of the finest fresh ceps, young and solid
5 black summer truffles, about 100g in total, peeled
6 tbsp extra virgin olive oil
juice of 1 lemon
salt and pepper
3 tbsp finely chopped flat-leaf parsley
lemon wedges, to serve

Make sure the ceps are impeccable, with no larvae inside. Clean them and slice them very thinly. Arrange the cep slices on individual serving plates in a flat circle, leaving a space in the middle.

Cut the truffles very thinly, and use these slices to cover the centre of each plate. Mix the olive oil with the lemon juice and brush gently onto each slice. Sprinkle with salt and pepper and finally scatter over the parsley.

Serve the mushroom salad with lemon wedges. Toasted country bread and good wine are ideal accompaniments.

Serves 4

❝ The best porcini and truffles come from Sila, the high plain of Calabria, which resembles Switzerland. As I am passionate about the world of wild fungi, I dedicate this recipe to all the mycophiles of the world. ❞

INSALATA DI BOTTARGA, ARANCE E POMPELMI
SALAD OF BOTTARGA, ORANGE AND GRAPEFRUIT

2 pink grapefruit
4 oranges
1 red onion, cut into thin rings
100g bottarga (salted mullet roe,
    see p184 for details), thinly sliced
4 tbsp extra virgin olive oil
2 tsp white wine vinegar
pepper
fennel fronds, to decorate

Peel the grapefruit and oranges, removing all the white pith, then cut out the segments from between the membranes. Do this over a bowl to catch the juice, then squeeze out any juice from the membranes. Arrange the fruit segments on a plate and scatter over the onion rings and bottarga slices.

Add the oil, vinegar and some black pepper to the grapefruit and orange juice to make a vinaigrette. Mix well and pour over the salad, add the fennel fronds and mix together well. Serve with good country bread.

Serves 4

" This typically refreshing Sicilian recipe probably came about as a way of using the abundant crops of citrus fruit that would have been brought to the island by visiting ships. "

INSALATA ALL'ABRUZZESE
VEGETABLE AND TUNA SALAD

300g young courgettes
200g green (French) beans, trimmed
salt and pepper
200g tomatoes
1 red pepper
1 sweet red onion
150g good canned tuna in oil, drained
8 anchovy fillets in oil, drained
8 basil leaves, torn
1 tsp dried oregano
1–3 red chillies, chopped
6 tbsp extra virgin olive oil
2 tbsp white wine vinegar

Quarter the courgettes lengthways, then cut into chunks. Cook the green beans in boiling salted water until al dente. Drain and cool. Repeat with the courgettes.

Cut the tomatoes into wedges and remove the seeds. Halve, core and de-seed the pepper, then cut into long thin strips. Finely slice the red onion.

Put the courgettes, beans, tomatoes, red pepper and onion into a bowl. Break the tuna into little chunks and add to the salad with the anchovies, herbs, and as much fresh chilli as you can take! Toss everything together, adding the olive oil, followed by the wine vinegar. Season with salt and pepper to taste. Eat the salad at room temperature, with toasted bread.

Serves 4

" The combination of cooked and raw vegetables in this salad makes it a triumph of flavours. Good ingredients here are paramount, so make it in the summer when sweet tomatoes, young courgettes and tender beans are available. "

INSALATA DI FUNGHI E FRUTTI DI MARE
SHELLFISH AND HEN OF THE WOODS SALAD

500g hen of the woods fungus
100ml white wine vinegar
100ml water
salt and pepper
150g raw prawns, not too large
4–8 fresh scallops in their shell
100g cooked crabmeat

Vinaigrette
6 tbsp extra virgin olive oil
1 tbsp each of coarsely chopped coriander,
   parsley and dill
juice of 1 lemon

Clean the mushrooms, separate into lobes, then cook in the vinegar and water with some salt for 2–3 minutes. Drain and cool. Shell the prawns, then cook briefly in some fresh boiling water, about 4–5 minutes. Shell the scallops (or get your fishmonger to do this for you), then cut into slices. Make sure that there are no pieces of shell in the crabmeat.

Prepare the vinaigrette with the olive oil, herbs and lemon juice, and season with salt and pepper. Marinate the scallops in the vinaigrette for 10 minutes.

Mix the fungus with the prawns and crabmeat. Add the scallops with their marinade, and mix. Adjust the seasoning, and serve the salad at room temperature.

Serves 4

"In summer you want to eat just a small amount of delicate food to combat the heat. This salad is perfect for that purpose, accompanied by some toasted bread and shared with a friend or two, perhaps in the garden, with a glass of crisp, chilled white wine. You could also use chicken of the woods or beefsteak fungus instead of the hen of the woods."

INSALATA DI FUNGHI E QUAGLIE
QUAIL AND FUNGI SALAD

4 large quail, prepared for cooking
6 tbsp extra virgin olive oil
salt and pepper
2 thick slices Parma ham, cut into strips
200g oyster mushrooms
300g mixed salad leaves
juice of ½ lemon

Preheat the oven to 200°C/Gas 6.

Brush the quail with some of the olive oil, then season the birds inside and out with salt and pepper. Roast in the preheated oven for 16–18 minutes. Leave to cool a little. Then, while still warm, carve the meat off the bones, legs and thighs.

Pour the rest of the olive oil in to a pan and fry the Parma ham briefly, then add the mushrooms. Stir-fry for 6–7 minutes. Add the quail pieces to warm through.

Arrange the salad leaves on plates. Add the lemon juice to the quail, fungi, ham and oil, then season to taste. Arrange this mixture over the salad. Serve warm, accompanied by grissini, tarallucci (round savoury biscuits), or toasted crostini.

Serves 4

Quail are probably the smallest birds that the British will eat without feeling like 'baby snatchers'. Of course the Italians eat birds that are much smaller, such as sparrows or thrushes, and although I have tasted their forbidden volatili in my youth, I do actually prefer bigger birds such as quail. We shall leave the consumption of songbirds to a few hunters and gourmets in Lombardy and Veneto…

ZUPPE

RIBOLLITA
'RE-BOILED' CABBAGE SOUP

300g cannellini beans, soaked for 12 hours
400g cavolo nero (black cabbage), or outer leaves
   of a Savoy cabbage
2 leeks, trimmed and cut into thin discs
1 large carrot, cubed
2 celery stalks, trimmed and cubed
50ml olive oil, preferably Tuscan, as required
2 large potatoes, peeled and cubed
2 courgettes, trimmed and cubed
400g polpa di pomodoro or chunky passata
300g Swiss chard, green part only, cut into strips
1 small thyme sprig
salt and pepper
6 slices of stale bread, toasted
extra virgin olive oil, to serve

Drain the beans and cook in plenty of water (without salt) for 1 ½ hours until tender. Purée 150g of the cooked cannelini beans in a blender.

Trim the black leafy part of the cavolo nero from the white stalk.

Put the leeks, carrot and celery in a pan with the olive oil, and sweat gently for 10 minutes. Add the potatoes, courgettes, cabbage and tomato pulp and cook for 1 hour. Then add the Swiss chard and thyme, and cook for another 20 minutes. Now add the puréed cannellini beans and the rest of the beans whole, and cook for another 30 minutes.

When everything is soft and cooked, taste the soup and correct the seasoning. To serve, put a slice of toasted bread in each deep soup bowl and pour the soup on top, letting it soak into the bread. Drizzle generously with good extra virgin olive oil, and grate on lots of black pepper.

If you want to reheat the soup from cold, put the whole lot in a pan (apart from the bread, of course), and cook gently for 30 minutes before serving.

Serves 6

" Tuscany seems to be the birthplace of this peasant soup, which is eaten mostly in autumn and winter, though its exact place of origin is disputed between Florence and Siena. The name ribollita or 'reboiled' comes from the fact that the soup tastes best reheated the day after it has been made. **"**

Even in Italy, cavolo nero, or black cabbage, is not known everywhere. By replacing it with the outer leaves of a Savoy cabbage, you can achieve a similar result. The typical dense and unsalted Tuscan bread can be replaced by stale Pugliese bread which has similar characteristics because of its low salt content.

ZUPPA DI CAVOLO ALLA NINA
NINA'S CABBAGE SOUP

800g white cabbage, trimmed and cut into chunks
salt and pepper
250g stale bread, cut into cubes
300g fontina cheese, or an equivalent melting cheese
  (like Taleggio), cut into cubes
1.2 litres hot chicken stock (p314)
85g butter
3 garlic cloves, finely sliced

Preheat the oven to 200°C/Gas 6.

Cook the cabbage in plenty of lightly salted water until soft, then drain well and keep warm. In a large ovenproof pot (possibly terracotta), make layers of cabbage, bread cubes and cheese. Wet with a little ladleful of the stock. Continue making these layers until you have run out of ingredients, and finish with the rest of the stock. Season to taste.

Put the butter in a pan and heat it gently until it becomes foamy. Add the garlic and cook until it just becomes soft. Pour this mixture over the cabbage leaves and bake in the preheated oven for 15 minutes. Before serving, mix the entire dish with a spoon to amalgamate the ingredients.

Serves 4–6

"In almost every one of my books, there is a recipe by Nina Burgai, a good friend of mine, who used to run a little hotel around 6,000 feet up in the Valle d'Aosta. The food she produces is utterly delicious, but it can't be called light, as it is created mostly for energetic skiers in the winter and robust mountaineers in the summer. Very few dishes containing cabbage are refined, but the taste and flavour of this soup more than makes up for its lack of elegance."

PAPPA AL POMODORO
BREAD AND TOMATO SOUP

FRESELLA
BREAD SOUP

150ml extra virgin olive oil, preferably Tuscan
2 garlic cloves, sliced
300g fresella (see below) or dark stale bread
100ml water
6 sage leaves
salt and pepper

Homemade tomato pulp
500g good, ripe tomatoes
1 celery head, tender centre stalks and leaves only
1 onion, chopped
1 small carrot, chopped
3 basil leaves

To make the homemade tomato pulp, put all the ingredients into a pan, cover with water and simmer gently until everything is soft. Blend to a fine purée in a blender.

Put 120ml of the olive oil into an earthenware pot (if possible), add the garlic and sweat for a minute. Add the bread, water, sage leaves and some salt and pepper to taste. Over a low heat, let the bread dissolve; you may need to add a little more water. When the bread is soft, add the tomato pulp and cook slowly for 1 hour. You will end up with a thick mixture which you should serve hot with a little of the remaining olive oil poured on to each plate.

Serves 4

400g fresella (see below)
600g polpa di pomodoro or chunky passata
2 celery stalks, trimmed and cut into small cubes
1 large sweet onion, finely sliced, or 4–6 large
   spring onions, finely chopped
10 pitted black olives, quartered
2 garlic cloves, very finely chopped
2 basil leaves, chopped
6 anchovy fillets in oil, drained and finely mashed
50g Pantelleria salted capers, soaked, drained
   and finely chopped
85g small gherkins preserved in vinegar, sliced
120ml olive oil, preferably Pugliese
salt and pepper

Soften the fresella with a little water and then reduce to coarse crumbs. Place in a bowl, add all the other ingredients except for the olive oil and seasoning. Amalgamate and let the mixture rest for a couple of hours to allow all the flavours to infuse. Add the olive oil and seasoning and eat as a starter on hot summer days.

Alternatively, after softening the fresella you can leave it whole, then top it with the other ingredients and serve with olive oil.

Serves 4

Fresella is a twice-baked, handmade granary bread from Calabria, and it has a wonderful flavour and texture. You can find it in good Italian delicatessens. To 'reconstitute' it, simply dip in cold water or hold it under the cold tap for a few seconds.

" Nothing is ever discarded in an Italian kitchen, with the imagination of the cook always finding a good use for leftovers. What was once the food of the poor – a bread and vegetable soup such as this – is now fashionable due to its simplicity, flavour and healthiness. "

" Autumn and winter offer lots of roots and squash which can be used in soup. This type of pumpkin soup is more likely to be served in the north and especially the northeast of Italy, from where speck (an air-dried, smoked shoulder of pork) originates. "

PASSATO DI ZUCCA
PUMPKIN SOUP

1 onion, finely chopped
6 tbsp olive oil
1 litre chicken or vegetable stock (p314)
600g pumpkin flesh, cut into cubes
200g celeriac, peeled and cut into cubes
salt and pepper
a thick slice of speck or pancetta, about 60g,
    cut into cubes
a few rosemary needles

Fry the onion in 2 tablespoons of the olive oil in a large saucepan until soft, but not browning, about 10 minutes.

Add the stock and, when boiling, the cubes of pumpkin and celeriac, and cook until soft, about 15–20 minutes. Add salt and pepper to taste.

Liquidise in a food processor or blender and return to the pan to reheat gently.

Meanwhile, heat the remaining oil in a frying pan. Add the speck and cook until crisp. Add the rosemary and stir to combine. Set aside.

Pour the warmed soup into serving bowls and top with the speck and rosemary mixture. Serve hot.

Serves 4

CIPOLLATA
UMBRIAN ONION SOUP

1kg onions, finely sliced
60g lardo battuto (lard beaten or chopped finely)
    or very fatty unsmoked bacon, beaten similarly
2 tbsp olive oil, preferably Umbrian
5 basil leaves, torn into pieces
salt and pepper
400g polpa di pomodoro or chunky passata
1 litre water
125g Parmesan, grated
2 eggs, beaten
4 slices country bread, toasted and brushed with
    extra virgin olive oil

Cover the sliced onions with water and leave to soak overnight to sweeten them. Drain well.

Put the tiny pieces of lard or bacon into a big pot with the olive oil and fry until crisp. Add the drained onion, basil, salt and pepper. Cook gently with the lid on until the onions are cooked but not burnt. Now add the tomato pulp and water. Mix well and cook gently for 1½ hours.

Add the Parmesan to the beaten eggs and whisk into the hot soup in a similar way to making stracciatella, the Italian egg and stock soup. Add salt and pepper to taste, and ladle the soup into deep serving bowls with the toasted bread at the bottom.

Serves 6–8

Small onions and shallots, which are fiddly to peel, can be plunged into boiling water for 5 minutes and then refreshed in cold water. This does help the skins come off more easily and is worth it if you are preparing a lot of them.

ZUPPA D'AGLIO SELVATICO
WILD GARLIC SOUP

18 wild garlic leaves
6 large eggs
55g Parmesan, grated
salt and pepper
1.2 litres chicken or vegetable stock (p314)
55g unsalted butter, softened
4 large slices of brown bread, toasted

Cut 12 of the wild garlic leaves into small strips, and finely chop the remainder. Beat the eggs with a whisk in a large bowl, and then add the Parmesan and some salt and pepper to taste.

Bring the stock to a simmer, and when it is boiling, pour a little at a time on to the egg mixture and whisk immediately. This should result in the egg coagulating to form a thick soup. Ladle into hot bowls and sprinkle the strips of garlic leaves on top. Mix the finely chopped garlic leaves with the softened butter and spread on the toast. Serve this with the soup.

Serves 4

" While out walking between March and May you might happen upon wild garlic, with its distinct aroma and wonderful luscious green leaves and pretty white flowers, which can be used in many different ways – as an addition to salads, stews or grilled foods. This particular soup is very easy to make and is a nice way to celebrate springtime. "

MINESTRA DI BORRAGINE
BORAGE STEW

600g borage leaves
200g Neapolitan hot sausage
6 tbsp olive oil
1 garlic clove, sliced
1 small chilli, finely chopped (optional)
10 cherry tomatoes, chopped
400ml chicken or beef stock (p314)
salt
85g pecorino cheese, grated

Clean the borage leaves, then coarsely chop them. Slice the sausage thickly, then fry in the olive oil for a few minutes on each side. Add the garlic and chill, if using, and fry for 30 seconds. Add the tomatoes, stock and borage, bring to the boil, and cook until tender, about 5–6 minutes. Adjust the salt, and serve immediately, sprinkled with the cheese.

Serves 4

CICORIA IN BRODO
WILD DANDELION BROTH

600g wild dandelion leaves
salt and pepper
100g Parma ham, diced
100g pecorino cheese, grated
500ml hot beef stock (p314)

Wash the dandelion leaves, then boil in salted water for 15 minutes to take away the bitterness and to tenderise them a little. Drain well. Add the diced ham, pecorino and dandelion to the hot stock and cook gently for another 15 minutes. Season to taste with salt and pepper. Eat with good country bread or as an accompaniment to other dishes.

Serves 4

" This dish was once an essential part of wedding celebrations in Basilicata. The 'ritual' menu was pasta flavoured with lamb ragù, various boiled meats served with cicoria (dandelion), and the actual lamb from the ragù. The tradition still continues in rural places. "

Dandelion cooked in this way can be replaced by the curly-leaved endive, which is of the same family but looks slightly different and is not too bitter. On the other hand, dandelion grows wild everywhere. Try to make an effort and get some.

ACQUA COTTA
COOKED WATER

1 celery stalk, trimmed and cubed
1 onion, sliced
1 garlic clove, sliced
1 fresh red chilli, chopped
4 tbsp extra virgin olive oil, plus extra for serving
200g polpa di pomodoro or chunky passata
1.5 litres chicken or vegetable stock (p314)
300g fresh ceps, finely sliced
salt and pepper
40g small slices of stale bread, toasted

Put the celery, onion, garlic and chilli in a pan with
the olive oil and fry gently for 5 minutes. Add the polpa
di pomodoro and leave to cook a little, then add the
stock. Cook for 10 minutes, then add the ceps. Cook
for another 10 minutes, then add the salt and pepper to
taste. Serve poured on top of the toasted bread in deep
bowls, with a little extra virgin olive oil to taste on top.

Serves 4

" There are several versions of this curious
Tuscan soup. It used to be a soup of the poor,
made from just boiling water with some
flavourings such as carrot, a little garlic
and some olive oil, which would have been
poured onto a slice of stale toasted bread.
Today this soup is enjoying a revival,
and has obviously become a little more
elaborate, but in principle it is still the same. **"**

PASSATA ESTIVA DI CETRIOLI E POMODORI
RAW CUCUMBER AND TOMATO SUMMER SOUP

1 large cucumber, peeled and cut into chunks
2 tbsp finely chopped dill
3 tbsp double cream
salt and pepper
2 large beef tomatoes
10 basil leaves, plus extra to garnish
1 white onion, roughly chopped

Liquidise the cucumber with the dill in a liquidiser
or food processor. Add the cream and season to taste
with a little salt and pepper. Chill in the fridge.

Put the tomatoes into a bowl of water that has just
come to the boil and leave for 30 seconds. Pull off the
skins. Liquidise the peeled tomatoes with the basil
and onion. Season to taste and chill in the fridge.

To serve, first put the cucumber soup in a deep soup
plate, then carefully add the tomato soup in the centre
and garnish with a few basil leaves.

Serves 4

For extra colour and
texture, try adding a
tablespoon of very finely
chopped mixed tomato
and cucumber to the
centre of each bowl
before serving.

❝ For this soup, the ingredients are raw, and the mixture
of the two soups and two colours is spectacular to look at.
It is a delightfully refreshing dish for a hot summer's day! ❞

" A delicious soup, which makes an elegant starter at a dinner party. Needless to say, you may use cultivated sorrel instead of wild, but it will be much less satisfying! "

CREMA DI ACETOSA CON BRUSCHETTA
CREAM OF WILD SORREL WITH GARLIC CROUTONS

150g wild sorrel
1 small onion, finely chopped
1 celery stalk, finely chopped
1 medium potato, about 200g, peeled and cubed
25g unsalted butter
salt and pepper
55g mascarpone cheese
40g Parmesan, grated

Garlic croûtons
2 slices of good country bread
1 garlic clove
55g unsalted butter

Wash the sorrel, and remove any tough stalks. Coarsely chop the leaves.

Fry the onion, celery and potato in the butter for approximately 5 minutes. Add enough water to cover, about 1 litre, along with some salt, and bring to the boil. After cooking for 8 minutes, add the sorrel and cook for a further 6 minutes. Leave to cool a little, then liquidise in a food processor. It will be thick.

Toast the slices of bread until golden, then rub a little of the garlic on both sides of the toast. Cut into cubes, then fry in the butter until crisp.

Put the liquidised soup into a pan to warm through, then add the mascarpone, stirring well. Season to taste. Serve hot with Parmesan and croûtons sprinkled on top.

Serves 4

ZUPPA DI BIETOLE E POLPETTINE
SWISS CHARD SOUP WITH DUMPLINGS

600g Swiss chard, white part only
4 tbsp olive oil
1 small onion, finely chopped
½ garlic clove, finely chopped
1.5 litres chicken stock (p314)
2 eggs
300g luganega sausage (p203)
85g Parmesan, grated
1 tbsp dried breadcrumbs
1 tbsp finely chopped parsley
salt and pepper
freshly grated nutmeg

Clean the Swiss chard and cut it into 2cm segments. Put the olive oil into a deep pan and gently fry the onion for a few minutes, then add the garlic and fry for a couple more minutes. Pour in the stock, bring to the boil, then add the Swiss chard and cook for 15 minutes.

In a bowl, beat the eggs, then mix in the sausage meat, half the Parmesan, the breadcrumbs, parsley and salt, pepper and nutmeg to taste. While the stock is boiling, make small dumplings the size of half a walnut from the sausage mixture, and add them to the broth. Let this all cook for a further 5 minutes, then remove any froth from the top of the broth. Serve the soup with the remaining Parmesan sprinkled on top.

Serves 4

The dumplings made here can be used in other ways, too. Coat them in breadcrumbs and fry them to eat as little rissoles, or cook them in a good tomato sauce made with oil, garlic, chunky passata and basil and serve with pasta.

FAVATA
BROAD BEAN STEW

85g lard, or 85ml olive oil
200g salt-cured fatty pork belly (lardo) or bacon, cut into cubes
200g hot Italian sausage, cut into rounds
2 onions, finely sliced
400g wild fennel bulbs (or normal fennel bulbs with the addition of fennel seeds), cut into cubes
3 tbsp coarsely chopped parsley
2 tbsp concentrated tomato paste
500g dried broad beans, skinless, soaked in water for 24 hours
dried chilli (optional)
salt and pepper
1.5 litres water
extra virgin olive oil

Put the lard or olive oil into a large pot and slowly fry the bacon and the sausage to brown them. Add the onion and allow to soften. Add the fennel, parsley, tomato paste and a little water and cook for 10–15 minutes. Now, add the beans, a pinch of chilli for heat if you like, some salt and pepper to taste, and the hot water. Leave to simmer gently for 2½ hours, stirring occasionally.

Serve it as a main course, accompanied by some good country bread, with a little stream of extra virgin olive oil and lots of black pepper sprinkled on top.

Serves 6

" The Sardinians love broad beans in any shape or form, especially if they are cooked with lardo and with pork products in general. There is a phrase when something desired never happens: 'The year in which broad beans and lardo will rain from the sky!' This very rich dish is normally eaten in winter, and in some places also on the day before Lent starts. "

ZUPPA DI PISELLI SECCHI
DRIED PEA SOUP

500g green split peas, soaked overnight
100g butter
200g smoked speck or smoked pancetta, cut into cubes
1 leek, trimmed and finely chopped
1 large potato, peeled and finely diced
2 litres water
Parma ham bone, for flavour (optional)
salt and pepper
3 slices of stale bread, diced
2 tbsp finely chopped parsley

Drain and check the peas for impurities. Put half of the butter in a pan and fry the speck and leek until tender. Add the potato, peas, the water and the Parma ham bone, if using. Bring to the boil, reduce the heat and simmer for 1¼ hours, stirring occasionally. Add salt and pepper to taste at this stage, when the soup has some texture. (It would become a cream if you cooked it a little longer.)

Meanwhile, fry the bread cubes in the remaining butter until golden. Serve the soup sprinkled with the croûtons and parsley. A twist or two of black pepper will finish the dish.

Serves 6

"A rare soup in Italy, mostly found in the areas of Germanic influence like the north-east, using dried peas for a change. It is a winter soup which is very comforting and requires only minimal attention."

RISI E BISI
RICE AND PEA SOUP

60g butter
1 small onion, finely sliced
300g frozen garden peas (petit pois)
850ml chicken stock (p314)
salt and pepper
2 tbsp finely chopped parsley
250g vialone nano or Arborio rice
60g Parmesan, grated

Put the butter in a large pan, add the onion and fry until soft. Add the frozen peas and a few spoons of stock and put the lid on, stirring occasionally, until the peas are defrosted. Add salt and pepper to taste, the parsley and the rest of the stock, bring to the boil and cook for 8 minutes. Add the rice and cook for 15 minutes, stirring occasionally.

Taste a grain of rice for the desired tenderness. Remove from the heat and leave to rest for a couple of minutes before serving, sprinkled with Parmesan.

Serves 4

I have seen many atrocities attempting to emulate and reproduce this gentle Venetian soup. It should be brothy, and will be very moist, so that a spoon is needed rather than a fork. Although I am usually averse to frozen food, peas and broad beans are an exception, and frozen should be used here.

PASTA E FAGIOLI
PASTA AND BEAN SOUP

300g fresh borlotti beans, or 200g dried beans
    soaked in cold water overnight and drained
6 tbsp olive oil
1 onion, finely chopped
2 basil leaves
1 rosemary sprig
1 litre chicken or vegetable stock (p314)
1 red chilli, chopped (optional)
1 tbsp concentrated tomato paste
salt and pepper
150g tubetti pasta
4 tbsp extra virgin olive oil

Put the beans into a heatproof earthenware pot or large pan and cover with cold water. Bring to the boil and cook gently, allowing 1 hour if using fresh beans, or 1½–2 hours if using dried. Don't salt the water or the skins will remain tough. When soft, drain and purée half of the beans in a blender or food processor, then mix together with the whole beans.

Heat the olive oil in a saucepan, add the onion and fry until softened. Add the basil, rosemary, stock, chilli, if using, tomato paste, beans, and salt and pepper to taste. Bring to the boil, then add the pasta and cook for 7–8 minutes, or until the pasta is al dente.

Leave to stand for 30 minutes before serving to allow the flavours to mingle. Reheat if you like, but in Italy soups are more often served warm rather than hot, or even cold in summer. Top each portion with a drizzle of extra virgin olive oil to serve.

Serves 6

❝ There exist as many recipes for this pasta and bean soup as there are Italian regions. This one, made with borlotti beans, is typical of the Veneto and the north east of Italy. **❞**

ZUPPA TOSCANA CON FUNGHI
TUSCAN SOUP WITH SAFFRON MILK CAPS

500g saffron milk caps
200g fresh ceps or 40g dried ceps, soaked in warm
    water for 30 minutes
4 garlic cloves
4 tbsp extra virgin olive oil
400g polpa di pomodoro or chunky passata
600ml hot chicken or vegetable stock (p314)
salt and pepper
4 slices of country bread (preferably Tuscan), toasted
6 basil leaves, torn
60g Parmesan or pecorino cheese, grated

Clean the fresh mushrooms thoroughly and slice them finely. Rinse the dried ceps, if using, and save their soaking water.

Chop 3 of the garlic cloves and put in a pan to fry in 2 tablespoons of the olive oil. When they start to colour (but not too much), add the polpa di pomodoro and cook for 10–15 minutes. Add the mushrooms, stock and ceps soaking water and cook until the mushrooms are tender, about 8–10 minutes. Check for salt and pepper.

Rub the remaining garlic clove gently over each slice of toast and brush with olive oil. Add the basil to the soup and cook for 1 minute. Place the toasts in 4 deep plates and cover with the soup, dividing the ingredients evenly. Add the Parmesan and serve.

Serves 4

ZUPPA DI FINFERLI
CHANTERELLE SOUP

250g fresh chanterelles, cleaned
90g butter
60g plain flour
1.5 litres hot chicken stock (p314)
1 small onion, finely chopped
1 garlic clove, finely chopped
salt and pepper
1 tbsp finely chopped flat-leaf parsley
4 tbsp double cream

Chop the fresh chanterelles, keeping a few whole for the garnish.

To make the soup base, melt 50g of the butter in a pan, then add the flour and cook, stirring continuously, until the flour starts to change colour. Gradually add the chicken stock, a little at a time, continuing to stir to avoid lumps.

Melt the remaining butter in another pan and fry the onion and garlic until softened. Add all the chanterelles and fry for 6–7 minutes. Add some salt to taste, and the chopped parsley. Take out the whole chanterelles and set aside. Tip everything else into the soup base liquid and stir well. Taste and adjust the seasoning, then stir in the cream.

Serve in warm bowls, topped with the whole mushrooms and accompanied by lightly toasted country bread.

Serves 4

" As you may know I am passionate about wild mushrooms. This soup, also called Schwammerlsuppe, is from the Alto Adige and it reminds me of Vienna, where I studied for two years and often went picking mushrooms in the local woods. "

MINESTRONE
MINESTRONE

3 tbsp olive oil
1 onion, chopped
1 small garlic clove, chopped
2 rashers streaky bacon, rind removed and finely
    chopped, or 25g Parma ham, finely chopped (optional)
4 celery stalks, diced
1 tomato, peeled, de-seeded and finely chopped
1 large carrot, diced
2 potatoes, peeled and diced
a few basil leaves, or 1 tbsp pesto sauce
900ml chicken stock (p314)
salt and pepper
1 x 375g can borlotti beans, drained
100g dried tubettini
75g Parmesan, grated

Heat the olive oil and fry the onion and the garlic
with the chopped bacon until soft. Add the remaining
vegetables and the basil and toss until combined. Add
the stock and bring to the boil. Cook for 10 minutes.

Add salt and pepper to taste and stir in the borlotti
beans and the pasta. Cook for about 10 minutes,
or until al dente. Serve hot with the Parmesan.

Serves 4

There are many different
varieties of minestrone, each
one varying according to
regional customs. Minestrone
is usually prepared with
leftover fresh vegetables such
as peas, shredded cabbage
and courgettes. I'll allow you
to substitute a stock cube for
homemade stock in this recipe;
but only if you really have to!

MINESTRONE DI FUNGHI
MUSHROOM MINESTRONE
Illustrated overleaf

1kg mixed wild mushrooms
1 onion, finely chopped
200g Parma ham, diced
6 tbsp olive oil
2 garlic cloves, finely chopped
5 fresh bay leaves
1 small rosemary sprig
3 tbsp chopped parsley
500ml vegetable or chicken stock (p314)
300g cooked borlotti beans
salt and pepper
6 slices of good Italian bread,
    toasted for bruschetta (optional)
freshly grated Parmesan (optional)

Clean and prepare the mushrooms as appropriate.
You could use chicken of the woods, wood blewits,
hedgehog fungus, chanterelles or ceps.

Fry the onion and diced ham in the olive oil until the
ham has taken on some colour, then add the garlic
and herbs. Add the cleaned mushrooms and the stock
and cook for 10 minutes. Add the cooked beans. Bring
to the boil again, and cook for 3–4 minutes. Remove
the bay leaves and rosemary, and season the soup.

Put a toasted bruschetta in each soup bowl, if using,
and pour the soup on top. Sprinkle with Parmesan
if liked. *Buon appetito!*

Serves 6

" The famous Italian thick soup, or
minestrone, uses all sorts of mixed
vegetables, so I used mixed mushrooms
instead to give a collection of flavours,
textures and colours – a celebration of
nature. This recipe is useful for when you
come home with only a few specimens
of each mushroom – or you could use
cultivated ones. Some dried mushrooms
can always come to the rescue if need be. "

ZUPPA DI GAMBERETTI E GRANCIPORRO
CRAB AND SHRIMP SOUP

1 x 750g–1kg crab, cooked or uncooked
salt and pepper
150g shrimps, peeled
1 small onion, finely chopped
50ml extra virgin olive oil
1 garlic clove, finely chopped
1 chilli, finely chopped
juice of ½ lemon
juice of 1 lime
fish or vegetable stock (p314), to taste
150ml double cream
4 tbsp chopped coriander leaves

If your crab is uncooked, poach it in abundant boiling salted water for 15–20 minutes. Leave it to rest in the cooking water for 15 minutes (this will ensure tender meat). Set aside to cool.

Crack the claws and extract the crabmeat with the help of a skewer. Then open the main body and extract the brown and coral meat. Mix all the meat together in a bowl. Cook the shrimps in salted water for 6–8 minutes, then peel and chop roughly.

Fry the onion in the olive oil until transparent, then add the garlic and cook until soft. Add the chilli, lemon and lime juices, crabmeat and shrimps. Transfer to a blender and liquidise until smooth. Add stock until you have the consistency you require. Reheat, and season to taste, then add the cream and sprinkle the coriander leaves on top. Serve immediately.

Serves 6

ZUPPA DI PESCE
SIMPLE FISH SOUP

6 tbsp olive oil
1 small onion, finely chopped
2–3 tbsp chunky passata
1kg mussels, cleaned (p173)
1 monkfish, about 300g, cut into medium cubes
1 squid, about 300g, cleaned and cut into rings (p36)
500ml good French soupe de poissons
   (available in most supermarkets or delicatessens)
4 thick slices of country bread, toasted

First of all, heat the olive oil in a large saucepan and fry the onion until softened, about 6–7 minutes. Add the passata, and in this cook the mussels, monkfish and squid rings, for about 10 minutes. Discard any mussels that haven't opened.

Stir in your fish soup and heat through gently for about 5 minutes. Placing a slice of toasted bread at the base of each, pour the soup into bowls and serve.

Serves 4

" Fish soups are very regional, being made differently, often from village to village, all along the coastline of Italy. In the Marche region they are often called brodetto (little broth), in Tuscany cacciucco. The classic Venetian version incorporates various molluscs from the lagoon. "

SMALL TORTELLINI IN BROTH

4–5 tbsp deglazed juices from a pork or beef roast
200g dried breadcrumbs
50g Parmesan, grated, plus extra to sprinkle
2 egg yolks
salt and pepper
freshly grated nutmeg
200g egg pasta dough (p315)
1 litre very good beef stock, or a mixture of beef
    and chicken stock (p314)

Collect the deglazed juices (from the bottom of the dish in which you have roasted some pork or beef). Put the breadcrumbs into a bowl and mix in enough of the meat juices to moisten. Add the Parmesan, egg yolks, and salt, pepper and nutmeg to taste.

Now make the tortellini. Roll out the pasta dough very thinly and cut out little circles. Place a teaspoonful of the filling to one side of each circle, then fold the opposite sides over to make half-moon shapes. Press the edges together to seal well, then curl the two ends round to meet, and pinch together. This isn't difficult, but it is fiddly as the circles are very small. If you lose patience, then make little flat round ravioli.

Bring the stock to the boil in a large pan. Add the tortellini and cook until al dente, about 3–4 minutes. Ladle the soup into warm bowls and sprinkle with Parmesan to serve.

Serves 4

" Every respectable Emilian housewife knows how to turn pasta on her little finger to make tortellini. For this classic regional dish, the filling for the mini tortellini is simply freshly grated Parmesan and special breadcrumbs – flavoured with the deglazed juices from a pork or beef roast. "

EGG BROTH WITH CHICKEN DUMPLINGS

1 litre chicken stock (p314), boiling
2 eggs plus 2 egg yolks, beaten together
20g Parmesan, grated
2 tbsp chopped chervil leaves
salt and pepper

Dumplings
200g minced chicken
2 egg whites, beaten to stiff peaks
30g Parmesan, grated
2 tbsp very finely chopped chives

To make the dumplings, first mix the chicken mince in a bowl with the stiffly beaten egg whites, the Parmesan and chives. Season to taste with salt and abundant pepper. Using two teaspoons, shape the chicken mixture into quenelles or dumplings and plunge into the boiling stock. Cook for 8 minutes before scooping out and setting aside.

In another bowl, mix the beaten eggs and yolks with the Parmesan, chervil and salt and pepper to taste. Carefully pour this mixture into the boiling stock while whisking quickly to obtain a thickish broth. Return the dumplings to the broth and serve immediately.

Serves 4

ZUPPA DI TAGLIONI E POLLO
CHICKEN SOUP WITH TAGLIOLINI

450g chicken bones, with some meat on them
1.5 litres water
1 chicken stock cube
150g dried tagliolini or 250g fresh taglioni (p315)
2 lovage leaves
salt (optional)
75g Parmesan, grated
2 tbsp chopped parsley

Put the chicken bones and the water in a large pan with the stock cube, cover and simmer for 1 hour. (You can do this in advance.) Remove the bones, strain the stock, and cut the meat off the bones and into small slivers. Discard the bones.

Return the stock to a clean pan, bring to the boil and add the pasta, lovage and the chicken slivers. Leave to simmer for 2 minutes, then discard the lovage. Check and continue cooking the pasta until soft, tasting and adding a little salt if necessary.

Serve sprinkled with the grated Parmesan and chopped parsley. Because of the difficulty of eating this dish, the usually forbidden act of using a fork and spoon is allowed!

Serves 4

"As often happens, by experimenting and testing one recipe another comes out as a by-product. The result was so remarkable with this experiment that I had to include it in this book! After I tested a recipe based on chicken breast, I put the rest of the chicken in water to be boiled for the cat. I went to the garden, collected a few leaves of lovage, a herb similar in flavour to celery, and a handful of parsley. I cheated a little by adding a stock cube but the revelation was the lovage, which gave so much flavour to the stock that it had to be discarded after a short part of the cooking time. With the addition of the pieces of boiled chicken, I, not the cat, had a wonderful meal!"

ZUPPA DI CARDO CON POLPETTE
CARDOON SOUP WITH VEAL DUMPLINGS

1 cardoon, about 300–400g, trimmed
1.5 litres chicken stock (p314)

Dumplings
150g veal, finely minced
60g veal sweetbreads, pre-cooked and finely minced
1 egg, beaten
75g Parmesan, grated
1 tbsp very finely chopped parsley
salt and pepper
¼ tsp freshly grated nutmeg
1 tbsp dried breadcrumbs (or as required)

Wash the cardoon and cut into chunks 2–3cm long. Bring the stock to the boil and add the cardoon. Cook for 20 minutes or until tender.

Meanwhile, prepare the dumpling mixture by mixing together the minced veal and sweetbreads, the egg, 25g of the Parmesan, the parsley, salt, pepper, nutmeg and enough breadcrumbs to obtain a consistent paste.

While the cardoon is boiling, shape little dumplings by hand, about half the size of a walnut. Throw these dumplings into the boiling stock, and simmer for 10 minutes. Serve hot and add more grated Parmesan.

Serves 4

" In my family, we traditionally had this soup as soon as the first cardoons were available. Their appearance meant winter had started, and it was time for comforting, warming stews and soups. In Piedmont, cardoon is also used as the main vegetable to accompany bagna cauda, the famous hot anchovy dip (p10). "

ZUPPA DI FICHI D'INDIA E PROSCIUTTO DI PARMA
PRICKLY PEAR AND PARMA HAM SOUP

12 large prickly pears
½ pomegranate
salt and pepper
juice of 1 lime
140g thinly sliced Parma ham, cut into strips
1 tbsp chopped chervil leaves

Peel the prickly pears using a knife and fork. Spear the fruit on the fork, and top and tail with the knife. Make a cut lengthways, not too deeply, then peel back the skin with the blade of the knife. Reduce the flesh to a pulp using a fork.

Carefully scoop the seeds out of the half pomegranate and discard the skin and yellow pulp (which is very bitter). Add the pomegranate seeds, some salt and pepper and the lime juice to the prickly pear pulp, then chill for an hour.

Just before serving, divide the soup between 4 plates. It will be quite thick. Add a couple of pieces of ice to each plate, and then top with the Parma ham slices and chervil leaves.

Serves 4

To make this unusual soup for vegetarians, simply omit the Parma ham and replace with the pulp and seeds of 4 passionfruit.

ZUPPA DI SOFFRITTO
NEAPOLITAN SOFFRITTO SOUP

300g pigs liver
300g pigs heart
300g pigs lung
300g pigs kidneys
100g pork lard
2 tbsp olive oil
400g polpa di pomodoro or chunky passata
100g concentrated tomato paste
2–3 hot red chillies, cut into pieces
salt and pepper
hot water or stock, to serve
bay leaves
slices of country bread, toasted

To make the soffritto, cut all the pig's offal into very small pieces. Melt the lard with the olive oil in a large pan, and fry the meat ingredients to brown a little.

Add the tomato pulp, the concentrated tomato paste, chillies and seasoning, plus some water if necessary – you want it to remain slightly moist, but not too liquid. Cook for 20–30 minutes, stirring occasionally, then set aside to cool. Refrigerate for up to 3 days or freeze in little blocks and defrost as needed.

When the soup is required, take a large spoonful of the cold soffritto per person, dilute with hot water or stock to taste, and add one fresh bay leaf per person. Bring to the boil, lower the heat and simmer for a few minutes. Taste and adjust the seasoning.

Place a hot slice of toast in the bottom of each warm soup plate, pour on the soup and enjoy.

Makes 1 batch (20 portions)

" This cucina povera dish is simply a concentrated ragù of pork offal, prepared in advance, then revived with hot stock and served poured over a slice of toasted bread. My mother used to make a lot of this soffritto and I remember her taking a few spoonfuls to make lunch from a reddish frozen block kept outside on the balcony. "

" When morels are in season in springtime, there is still some feathered game – pheasant, grouse, partridge and pigeon – available. You can also use dried morels if it is not possible to find fresh ones – for example, if you want to make this dish during the autumn game season. "

CONSOMME DI SELVAGGINA E SPUGNOLE
GAME CONSOMME WITH MORELS

200g fresh morels, or 55g dried
1 small pheasant, cleaned
1 bouquet garni (bay, parsley, thyme)
1 celery stalk, trimmed and finely chopped
1 shallot, finely sliced
1 carrot, finely chopped
salt and pepper
chicken stock (p314) or water, to cover
75ml port
50ml crème fraîche
1 tbsp finely chopped chives

Clean the fresh morels carefully, or soak the dried morels in warm water for 20 minutes.

Put the pheasant into a pan with the bouquet garni, celery, shallot, carrot and some salt and pepper. Cover the pheasant with stock or water, put the lid on and simmer for 1 hour. Add the soaked dried morels or the fresh morels, and simmer for a further 30 minutes.

Drain everything through a fine sieve, reserving the morels, and season the consommé to taste. Add the port and warm the consommé through. Add the crème fraîche and chives, and serve immediately with a portion of morels in each bowl.

Serves 4

ZUPPA DI CECI E COSTINE
SOUP OF SPARE RIBS AND CHICKPEAS

4 tbsp extra virgin olive oil, plus extra for drizzling
800g meaty pork spare ribs, separated
2 celery stalks, trimmed and finely chopped
2 garlic cloves, finely chopped
2 medium carrots, finely chopped
10 sun-dried tomatoes, finely chopped
1.5 litres water
3 x 400g cans cooked chickpeas, drained
½ chilli, chopped
4 basil leaves, chopped
salt and pepper

Put the olive oil in a large saucepan and fry the spare ribs, browning each side. Keep in the pan. Add all the chopped fresh vegetables and sun-dried tomatoes and cook for a further 10 minutes.

Add the water and bring to the boil. Simmer over a medium heat for 1 hour, then scoop off and discard the fat from the top of the liquid. Add the drained chickpeas, the chilli and basil and cook until the meat is tender, another 30–40 minutes, adding a little water if the soup looks as though it needs a little extra liquid.

Season with a little salt and pepper and pour into bowls. Drizzle with a little extra virgin olive oil and serve.

Serves 4

This soup, which is very much loved by southern Italian farmers, is not only cheap to produce, but tasty and rewarding. The chickpeas can be from a can or a jar, thus avoiding hours of soaking and cooking. Try to find meaty spare ribs to give this soup plenty of body.

PASTA

SPAGHETTI AGLIO, OLIO E PEPERONCINO
SPAGHETTI WITH GARLIC, OIL AND CHILLI

180g spaghetti
salt
6 tbsp olive oil
2 garlic cloves, finely chopped
1 small red chilli, finely chopped

Cook the pasta in plenty of boiling salted water until nearly done, about 5–6 minutes.

Now start the sauce by heating the olive oil gently in a deep frying pan. Add the garlic and chilli and fry for a few seconds, or until the garlic starts to change colour. Take care not to burn the garlic.

Drain the pasta well and put in the pan with the 'sauce', adding a little salt and perhaps 1–2 tablespoons of the pasta cooking water. Stir a couple of times and serve.

Serves 2

" This is probably one of the most popular recipes for native Italians. They like to eat it at any time, but it's probably the prime dish to be eaten for a midnight feast, when they arrive home late and hungry. It takes only about 6–7 minutes to cook the pasta, while the 'sauce' is ready in less than half that time. You don't even have to grate any Parmesan, as the pasta is better without it. "

SPAGHETTI ALLA CARRETTIERA
CART DRIVER'S SPAGHETTI

25g dried ceps
4 tbsp olive oil
1 garlic clove, crushed
55g pancetta, finely chopped
200g canned tuna in oil, drained and flaked
600g cherry tomatoes, chopped,
    or 500g polpa di pomodoro or chunky passata
salt and pepper
400g spaghetti
pecorino cheese, grated

Soak the ceps in warm water for 20 minutes, then drain and chop, reserving the soaking liquid.

Heat the olive oil in a frying pan, add the garlic and fry gently until soft. Add the pancetta and allow to brown a little. Stir in the ceps and tuna and fry for a few minutes, then add the tomatoes and some salt and pepper. Simmer for 20 minutes, then stir in a few tablespoons of the cep soaking liquid just to flavour the sauce, and cook for about 5 minutes longer.

Meanwhile, cook the spaghetti in a large pan of boiling salted water until al dente. Drain and mix the spaghetti together with the sauce. Season with black pepper and sprinkle with pecorino cheese.

Serves 4

❝ This dish, in which virtually none of the ingredients is fresh, is said to have been made by the cart drivers transporting goods from the provinces to Rome: hungry on the long journey, they would want to make themselves something that would not go off, that was quite undemanding, and that would still be delicious.**❞**

TAGLIOLINI CON TARTUFO NERO
TAGLIOLINI WITH BLACK TRUFFLE

400g fresh taglioni (p315)
salt and pepper
85g butter
55g fresh black truffle, cleaned and finely sliced
a few drops of truffle oil (optional)
55g Parmesan, grated

While the pasta is boiling in plenty of salted water, melt the butter in a pan, then add the sliced truffle with a few drops of truffle oil. (If using Alba truffle, the oil is not necessary.)

Drain the pasta, reserving a few tablespoons of water, and put in the pan with the butter and truffle. Add the Parmesan and some salt and pepper. Mix together well, using a little of the reserved cooking water, and serve immediately with more truffle and/or more Parmesan if you like.

Serves 4

❝ This is a Venetian speciality, and is very easy to make. In the Veneto, people still make the special pasta by hand with the help of a little implement – a torcolo – which has a chamber through which the pasta is pushed. This produces a thick spaghetti with a 4mm diameter and no hole. The alternative is bucatini, which is the same size, but has a little hole inside. ❞

GIANT SPAGHETTI WITH ONION AND ANCHOVY SAUCE

400g bigoli or bucatini
salt and pepper

Sauce
600g onions, finely chopped
6 tbsp olive oil
40g anchovy fillets in oil

For the sauce, fry the onions in a pan with the olive oil until soft, about 6–7 minutes, then add the anchovies, which will dissolve in the heat. Stir them in very briefly.

Cook the pasta in plenty of boiling salted water until al dente, probably about 8–9 minutes. Drain and mix into the sauce. Season with a little salt and plenty of pepper. Mix well and serve hot.

Serves 4

If you are feeling greedy and want to give this sauce a little more substance, try adding 150g tuna flakes in oil, drained, once you have fried the onions until soft.

TAGLIONI WITH GARLIC AND ANCHOVY SAUCE

2 whole bulbs of garlic, peeled and broken into cloves
300ml milk
3 firm and fleshy yellow and red peppers
16 anchovy fillets in oil
100g butter, roughly chopped
450g fresh taglioni, bought or homemade (p315)
salt

Cook the garlic gently in the milk for approximately half an hour until softened.

Meanwhile, put the peppers under a hot grill until the skins are blackened. Allow to cool slightly, then peel the skin away from the peppers; halve, discarding the inner seeds, and finely slice the flesh. Keep the pepper slices warm.

When the garlic is soft, take the pan off the heat. Add the anchovies and stir with a spoon until dissolved. Pass the milk, garlic and anchovies through a metal sieve into a pan. Heat gently, then add the butter. Do not cook the sauce, you just want to heat it enough to melt the butter. Take the sauce off the heat.

Meanwhile, cook the pasta in boiling salted water for 3–5 minutes or until al dente. Drain and toss with the sauce. Serve the slices of pepper on top of the pasta.

Serves 4

" I discovered that by making a bagna cauda (p10) in a milder form, you can create a valuable sauce for pasta and other ingredients. Here it blends perfectly with the contrasting smoky sweetness of the charcoal-flavoured peppers. "

SPAGHETTINI AL POMODORO E BASILICO

THIN SPAGHETTI WITH TOMATO AND BASIL

200g spaghettini
salt and pepper
extra virgin olive oil

Sauce
2 garlic cloves, sliced
4 tbsp olive oil
200g pomodorini (cherry tomatoes), chopped
10 basil leaves, shredded

For the sauce, fry the garlic in the oil until soft but not brown, about 2 minutes. Add the tomatoes and basil and cook for a few more minutes. Season if needed.

Cook the pasta in plenty of boiling salted water in a large saucepan until al dente, about 5–6 minutes, before draining. Add to the sauce, mix well and serve drizzled with a little extra virgin olive oil.

Serves 2

This simple tomato sauce is made with pomodorini (cherry tomatoes), though it works with very ripe chopped ordinary tomatoes or canned chopped tomatoes as well. I deliberately don't add any Parmesan to this dish because I like the pure taste and simplicity of the tomatoes; should you desire it, grate a little over the top before serving.

PENNE CON PINOLI E MELANZANE

PENNE WITH PINE NUTS AND AUBERGINE

400g aubergine, trimmed and cut into small cubes
salt
90ml extra virgin olive oil
1 garlic clove, finely chopped
3 tbsp concentrated tomato paste
25g pine nuts
10 large salted capers, soaked, drained and chopped
1 small chilli, finely chopped
20 pitted black olives
400g penne
60g mature pecorino cheese, grated

Leave the aubergine cubes in lightly salted water for 1 hour, then drain, squeeze out the water and pat dry on kitchen paper. Fry them in the oil with the garlic until brown. Add the tomato paste, pine nuts, capers, chilli and olives and fry gently for 10 minutes. Add a little water if the mixture is too dry.

Cook the pasta in boiling salted water until al dente, then drain and mix well with the sauce. Serve with the pecorino cheese.

Serves 4

MANILLI DE SETA
SILK HANDKERCHIEF PASTA SHEETS WITH PESTO

350g very thin fresh pasta sheets (p315),
   1mm thick and 15–20cm long
salt
a little olive oil (optional)

Pesto
80g basil leaves
2 garlic cloves
30g pine nuts
60g Parmesan, grated
10g coarse sea salt
100ml olive oil

To make the pesto, pound the basil, garlic, pine nuts, Parmesan and salt together, using a pestle and mortar, to a smooth paste. Slowly add the olive oil, stirring all the time.

Add the pasta sheets, one by one, to a large pan of boiling salted water, with a little olive oil to avoid sticking if you like, and cook until al dente. Being so fresh and thin, the pasta cooks quickly, within 2–3 minutes.

Scoop the pasta sheets out of the boiling water, drain well and divide between warm plates. Gently mix each pile of pasta with a quarter of the pesto and serve at once.

Serves 4

" Before I knew of this recipe, I made stracci, which is pasta torn from a big sheet of dough, to go with pesto. Here the pieces are larger, like a handkerchief, and thin and silky. The pasta must be made at home and rolled with a pasta machine to make the thinnest sheets possible, to be cut into 15–20cm lengths. The sauce is the classic Genovese pesto. "

RIGATONI ALLA GIARDINIERA CON POLPETTINE DI SPINACI

PASTA WITH COURGETTE SAUCE AND SPINACH BALLS

1 recipe spinach balls (p15)
salt and pepper
400g rigatoni

Sauce
2 garlic cloves, finely chopped
1 chilli, finely chopped
8 tbsp olive oil
2 courgettes, trimmed and finely grated
60g Parmesan, grated
salt and pepper

Prepare the spinach balls in advance and keep warm in a very low oven.

In a saucepan of boiling salted water, cook the pasta until al dente, about 8–10 minutes. When ready, drain, reserving a few tablespoons of the pasta cooking water.

Meanwhile, make the sauce. Fry the garlic and chilli in the olive oil for about a minute – don't let the garlic brown – then add the courgettes, and cook for about 3–4 minutes, until the courgettes have started to soften.

Add the Parmesan to the sauce, season to taste and mix well, then toss thoroughly with the drained pasta and reserved cooking water. Serve hot with the warmed spinach balls on top.

Serves 4

" This is a recipe I created for Carluccio's Caffés. It is still on the menu, and every time someone orders it, some money goes to charity. It has proved so popular that Carluccio's was able to collect £700,000 in just two years! "

MALLOREDDUS
LITTLE BULLS

2 garlic cloves, finely chopped
6 tbsp olive oil
1–2 red chillies, chopped (optional, but recommended)
500g cherry tomatoes, halved
100g polpa di pomodoro or chunky passata
5 basil leaves, torn, plus extra to garnish
salt and pepper
300g small malloreddus pasta (or other saffron pasta)
100g pecorino cheese, grated

Put the garlic in a pan with the olive oil, and chilli if using, and fry for a few minutes. Add the fresh tomatoes and tomato pulp. Stir briefly to amalgamate, bring to a simmer and cook gently for 15–20 minutes. Add the basil and season with salt and pepper to taste.

Meanwhile, cook the pasta in a large pan of boiling salted water until al dente. Drain and toss with the sauce. Serve generously covered with grated pecorino and scattered with a few basil leaves ... delicious.

Serves 4

" Don't worry, this is the name of a specific pasta shape, and has nothing to do with the real animal. Malloreddus come in many different sizes, and I have chosen to use a minimal one here. It is also called gnocchetti sardi and is often flavoured with saffron, which is cultivated in Sardinia. "

PASTA AND PEAS

100g pancetta, finely diced
2 large white onions, or 2 bunches spring onions,
   chopped
1 garlic clove, crushed
1 celery stalk, trimmed and diced,
   plus a few chopped leaves
6 tbsp olive oil
700g small and tender, fresh garden peas
   (podded weight)
salt and pepper
400g spaghetti, broken into 5cm pieces
1 tbsp coarsely chopped parsley

Put the pancetta, onion, garlic, celery and olive oil
in a pan, and fry for 5 minutes. Add the peas and
cook gently until the peas are soft. Season to taste.

Cook the pasta separately in boiling salted water until
al dente. Drain the pasta and add to the peas. Leave for
2 minutes so that the flavours combine and then serve,
sprinkled with parsley. If you have used frozen peas,
it takes a little longer, and should the dish be too dry,
add a little of the pasta boiling water.

Serves 4–6

66 This is one of the very traditional dishes
of the so-called alla Napoletana. Neapolitan
cuisine has been exported all over the
world, thanks to emigrants and Neapolitan
chefs living abroad. The cooking principles
are very basic – very simple – with the
quality of the ingredients contributing to the
flavour and taste. This dish has to be cooked
with spaghetti or vermicelli, 'little worms', as
the Neapolitans call it. 99

WIDE PASTA RIBBONS WITH SPRINGTIME SAUCE

salt
350g pappardelle
Parmesan, grated (optional)

Sauce
8 small artichokes
300g asparagus
300g white young onions, finely sliced
300g broad beans, podded
200g garden peas, podded
6 tbsp olive oil
100ml water
salt and pepper
3 tbsp coarsely chopped parsley

To make the sauce, first prepare the artichokes by
removing the tough outer leaves and trimming the
base of the stems. With a sharp knife, trim the tips
of the leaves, leaving only the tender parts. Cut into
quarters and remove any choke.

Put all the vegetables into a large saucepan with the
olive oil and water. Cook gently for 20 minutes then,
when you are sure everything is cooked, add some
salt and pepper and the parsley. Mix well.

In a saucepan of boiling salted water, cook the pasta
until al dente, about 7–8 minutes. Drain and mix with
the sauce. Sprinkle with Parmesan cheese, if you like,
and serve.

Serves 4–6

" Frittedda, in the Sicilian dialect, means a stew of asparagus, young onions, small broad beans, peas and artichokes – all of which are in season between March and April. It makes an excellent sauce for the largest size of pasta ribbon, pappardelle, but is often eaten with bread. "

ORECCHIETTE CON BROCCOLI
ORECCHIETTE WITH BROCCOLI

500g purple-sprouting broccoli
  or trimmed cime di rape (rape tops)
salt
90ml extra virgin olive oil
2 garlic cloves, finely chopped
1 small chilli, finely chopped
500g orecchiette pasta
pecorino cheese, grated (optional)

Cook the broccoli in lightly salted boiling water until tender, then drain. Put the oil in a pan over a low heat, then add the garlic and chilli and cook gently for a few minutes until softened. Add the broccoli florets and mix well. Season with salt to taste.

Cook the pasta in boiling salted water for 14–18 minutes, until al dente, then drain. Mix with the broccoli sauce and serve, accompanied by pecorino cheese if you like.

Serves 4

" In Puglia, broccoli and orecchiette are almost synonymous. The combination of pasta and the very strong flavours of local broccoli, tomatoes, olive oil and some chilli makes it a really wonderful dish. "

TAGLIATELLE CON CAVOLO E CIPOLLA
CABBAGE AND ONION PASTA

salt and pepper
250g large dried egg tagliatelle, broken into small pieces

Sauce
8 tbsp olive oil or 60g lard
200g white onion, finely chopped
600g white cabbage, cut into small chunks
150ml water
50g caster sugar
a few drops of white wine vinegar

To make the sauce, heat the olive oil or lard in a large saucepan and add the onion. Cook gently until soft, about 6–7 minutes. Add the cabbage and water, put the lid on and cook gently for a further 20–30 minutes, until the cabbage is soft.

Take the lid off the pan, and add the sugar. Cook gently until it has melted, stirring constantly. The cabbage will caramelise and begin to brown. Add a little salt and the vinegar. The mixture should be dry.

In a saucepan of boiling salted water, cook the pasta until al dente, probably about 10 minutes, but follow the instructions on the packet. Drain well.

Mix the pasta and sauce together and serve with plenty of black pepper.

Serves 4

PIZZOCCHERI DELLA VALTELLINA
BUCKWHEAT PASTA WITH CABBAGE, BEANS AND CHEESE

200g potato, peeled and diced
150g green (French) beans, trimmed and halved
300g Savoy cabbage or spinach, shredded
salt and pepper
300g pizzoccheri pasta
150g Bitto or Asiago cheese, cut into small cubes
100g unsalted butter
3 garlic cloves, finely sliced
60g Parmesan, grated

Preheat the oven to 200°C/Gas 6. Cook the potato, beans and cabbage together in boiling salted water until tender, about 15 minutes. Meanwhile, cook the pizzoccheri in a separate pan of boiling salted water until al dente. Drain the vegetables and pasta.

Layer the pasta and vegetables in a shallow ovenproof dish, starting with the pizzoccheri, and interspersing the vegetables with the diced cheese. Melt the butter with the garlic in a small pan until it foams, then pour over the top of the layers. Scatter the grated Parmesan and black pepper on top, and bake for 15 minutes. Mix everything together – it's a messy dish – and serve!

Serves 4–6

" Pizzoccheri is a type of short, wide tagliatelle made from a mixture of buckwheat flour and wheat flour. It originates from Teglio in the Valtellina, the valley north of Milan where the famous bresaola (air-dried beef) comes from. The use of grano saraceno (buckwheat) was widespread in ancient times, as it was a grain that could grow almost anywhere. This rustic, rich pasta bake is a favourite in Lombardy. "

VINCISGRASSI
'LITTLE LASAGNE'

1 recipe egg pasta dough (p315)
120g butter
50g plain flour
500ml milk
salt and pepper
500g fresh ceps, cleaned and sliced
2 tbsp olive oil
1 garlic clove, finely chopped
2 tbsp chopped flat-leaf parsley
200g Parmesan, grated

Preheat the oven to 200°C/Gas 6. Cut the pasta into 15cm square sheets for lasagne.

Melt half the butter in a saucepan, stir in the flour and cook for 1 minute, then add the milk gradually, stirring all the time, to make a smooth sauce. Season with salt and pepper to taste.

To cook the fresh ceps, heat the remaining butter and the olive oil in a sauté pan, add the ceps with the garlic and parsley, and sauté until the ceps have softened and the juices have evaporated. Season with salt and pepper to taste.

Cook the pasta sheets in boiling salted water until al dente, about 4 minutes, then drain well.

Layer the vincisgrassi in 6 small individual baking dishes. Start with a thin layer of béchamel, cover with a layer of lasagne sheets, then spoon half the mushrooms over. Add another layer of béchamel and scatter plenty of Parmesan over. Repeat these layers, finishing with béchamel and cheese. Bake for 15 minutes until golden and bubbling, then serve.

Serves 6

The best time to cook this vegetarian version of the rich, offal-based vincisgrassi is in autumn, when fresh ceps are available. At other times, use oyster or shiitake mushrooms, plus 20g soaked dried ceps.

TIMBALLO DI PENNE CON MELANZANE E MOZZARELLA
TIMBALLO DI PENNE WITH AUBERGINES AND SMOKED MOZZARELLA

450g dried penne lisce (smooth penne)
salt and pepper
40g butter, cut into pieces, plus extra for greasing
200g green (French) beans, fresh or frozen
2 tbsp olive oil
450g carrots, cut into large matchsticks
2 large aubergines, peeled and chopped into 1cm strips
1 small garlic clove, finely chopped
freshly grated nutmeg
600g smoked mozzarella cheese, cut into strips
400g ricotta cheese
150g Parmesan, grated
8 eggs, lightly beaten

Preheat the oven to 200°C/Gas 6.

Cook the pasta in boiling salted water for 5–6 minutes, or until al dente, and drain. Mix the pasta with the butter, and set aside.

Boil the beans until tender. Drain and set aside.

Heat the oil and fry the carrots until lightly browned on all sides. Add the aubergines and the garlic, and fry until golden. Add a pinch of nutmeg, and salt and pepper.

Lightly butter a 20 x 25cm baking dish with sides 7.5cm deep. Cover the bottom with a third of the cooked pasta. Put one-third of the beans, carrots, aubergines, mozzarella cheese, and ricotta cheese over the pasta, and sprinkle with the Parmesan. Repeat this sequence twice more, finishing with the Parmesan. Pour on the beaten eggs, which will bind the pasta together. Bake for 30 minutes.

Serves 6–8

" In Italy the combination of pasta and vegetables has always been made interesting, with no one missing, or even thinking it should contain meat. This is a good example. Again, it's a recipe worth cooking for several people. Serve with a salad and a good Soave wine. "

PASTA IMBOTTITA CON VEGETALI AL FORNO
RICH OVEN-BAKED VEGETABLE PASTA

600g large rigatoni
600g melting cheese, like fontina, Bel Paese,
    Taleggio, cut into little chunks
200g Parmesan, grated

Tomato sauce
2 large onions, finely chopped
100ml olive oil
1.5kg polpa di pomodoro or chunky passata
10 basil leaves, shredded
salt

Filling
2 aubergines, cut in 8mm thick slices lengthways
2 courgettes, cut in 8mm thick slices lengthways
plain flour, for dusting
6 eggs
olive oil, for shallow-frying
1 recipe spinach balls (p15)
8 baby courgettes, trimmed
2 fennel bulbs, trimmed

Make the tomato sauce first by frying the onions in the olive oil until soft, about 5–6 minutes. Add the tomato pulp and basil and cook gently for 20–30 minutes. Season with salt and set aside.

For the filling, dust the aubergine and courgette slices with flour. Beat 4 of the eggs together, and dip the vegetable slices into this. Pour enough olive oil into a large frying pan to cover the base generously and heat gently. Shallow-fry the vegetable slices a few at a time until golden, about 3–4 minutes on each side. Set both vegetables and oil aside. If you haven't cooked them in advance, the spinach balls can also be cooked in this oil.

Meanwhile, boil the courgettes and fennel in lightly salted water until al dente, about 6–7 minutes. Drain well and cut the fennel into slices.

Now cook the pasta in plenty of boiling salted water until al dente, about 5–6 minutes. Drain and mix with a little of the sauce. Preheat the oven to 200°C/Gas 6.

In a baking tray or dish, then assemble all the ingredients. First put a layer of pasta on the base on which you distribute slices of aubergine and courgette, slices of fennel, the whole baby courgettes and a few spinach balls. Sprinkle over some of the cheese chunks, some of the tomato sauce and some of the Parmesan. Build a few layers according to the size of the baking tray, and finish on top with tomato sauce, a few chunks of cheese, a few spinach balls and the remaining Parmesan.

Bake for 30–40 minutes in the preheated oven. Let it rest for 10–15 minutes before serving, cut in squares. Wonderful…

Serves 8–10

" A while back I had the enviable task of cooking a famous timbale for a documentary about the Sicilian Tomasi di Lampedusa (author of the famous book *Il Gattopardo*). The historical recipe turned out to be a triumph. I have adapted it here to make it a bit less elaborate, though it still needs a bit of work and should probably be made for celebrations and special occasions. To make life simpler you can assemble it the day before serving and bake it when required. **"**

" It is around the 15th October that, seemingly out of nowhere, the honey fungus suddenly appears in the woods. I am always very excited at the sight of a colony, still with closed caps, very tightly packed in bunches at the foot of the trees, or sometimes just shooting out of the grass. When raw they have a strange smell, but once cooked they are fantastic. "

SPAGHETTI CON FAMIGLIOLE
SPAGHETTI WITH HONEY FUNGUS

800g honey fungus mushrooms
salt and pepper
500g medium spaghetti
8 tbsp olive oil
2 garlic cloves, sliced
1 red chilli, sliced
2 tbsp coarsely chopped parsley
60g Parmesan, coarsely grated

Clean the honey fungus, and remove the toughest part of its stem. Boil for 3–4 minutes in slightly salted water, then drain well.

Cook the pasta in plenty of salted water for 6–7 minutes until al dente.

Meanwhile, heat the oil in a large pan over a medium heat and add the garlic and chilli. Before the garlic browns, add the mushrooms and parsley. Cook for a few minutes only.

Drain the pasta well, and mix it with the mushroom sauce. Add the Parmesan, season and enjoy!

Serves 4

RAVIOLO APERTO CON FUNGHI
OPEN RAVIOLO WITH MUSHROOMS

600g mixed wild mushrooms, cleaned
60g butter
1 garlic clove, finely chopped
1 tbsp concentrated tomato paste
1 tbsp chopped flat-leaf parsley
salt and pepper
1 small glass of white wine
8 sheets of egg pasta dough, 15cm square (p315)
55g Parmesan, grated (optional)

Cut the mushrooms in half if large; otherwise leave them whole. Heat the butter in a pan, add the garlic and fry gently until softened but not browned. Add the mushrooms and stir-fry for about 5 minutes, then add the tomato paste, parsley and some salt and pepper. Pour in the wine, bring to the boil and let it bubble for a few minutes.

Cook the sheets of pasta in boiling salted water until al dente, then drain. Carefully lay 4 sheets of pasta on 4 hot serving plates. Divide the mushroom mixture between them, reserving some of the sauce. Top the mushrooms with the remaining sheets of pasta and brush the top with the remaining sauce. Sprinkle with the Parmesan if you like and serve immediately.

Serves 4

" This is a modern pasta dish found in very good restaurants. The filling can vary from fish and meat to vegetables and, in this case, mushrooms. "

AGNOLOTTI IN TOVAGLIOLO
RAVIOLI WITHOUT SAUCE

1 recipe egg pasta dough (p315)
2 litres vegetable stock (p314)
a little oil

Filling
2 tbsp olive oil
100g diced veal
100g diced pork
100g diced rabbit
80g finely diced mixed celery, carrot and onion
30g spinach or Swiss chard
2 tbsp fresh ricotta cheese
1 egg
20g Parmesan, grated
freshly grated nutmeg
salt and pepper

To make the filling, heat the olive oil in a large pan, add the diced meats and vegetables (but not the spinach or chard) and fry, stirring, until the meats are evenly browned. Lower the heat and continue to cook, stirring occasionally, until the meat is almost cooked, about 45 minutes.

Meanwhile, cook the spinach or chard in a little water until tender, then drain and squeeze out the excess liquid. Mince or finely chop and add to the meat. Continue to stir over the heat until the mixture is quite dry. Leave to cool, then mince, using a mincer or food processor. Add the ricotta, egg, Parmesan and nutmeg. Mix well and season with salt and pepper to taste.

Roll out the pasta into two long, thin sheets, about 1.5mm thick. Using a serrated pasta wheel, cut into 5cm wide strips. Place small balls of filling (the size of a hazelnut) at 2cm intervals along the centre of each strip. Brush the edges with a little water, then bring the long edges over the filling and press them together to seal. With the join uppermost, pinch into little pockets between the filling and cut with a serrated wheel to make agnolotti.

Bring the stock to the boil in a large pan. Plunge the pasta into the hot stock, along with a few drops of oil to avoid sticking. Cook for 6–7 minutes, until a little more than al dente, then drain. Serve immediately, without sauce.

Serves 4

" I encountered this curious way of eating ravioli – or agnolotti as the Piedmontese call them – during one of my visits to Cocconato in the province of Asti. Those made by Fabrizio at the Trattoria del Ponte are served in an immaculate white napkin – the filling is so tasty that they don't need a sauce. Originally made from leftover roast meats, the filling is now made from small cuts of tender pork, rabbit and veal – oven-roasted and then minced. Delicious! "

TORTELLI DI ZUCCA
PUMPKIN RAVIOLI

1.3kg pumpkin
2 or 3 eggs, beaten, depending on pumpkin
160g Parmesan, grated
100g dried breadcrumbs
4 amaretti biscuits, crumbled
salt and pepper
freshly grated nutmeg
1 recipe egg pasta dough (p315)
plain flour, for dusting
60g butter, melted

It would be best to steam the pumpkin until soft, depending on its thickness. You could also put in a pan with very little water. My mother used to bake it in the oven. The object is to have the pumpkin cooked but not very wet. Remove the skin from the flesh, put the flesh into a cloth and squeeze out as much liquid as you can. Reduce the fleshy pulp to a mash with a fork, and add the eggs, 100g of the Parmesan, breadcrumbs, amaretti biscuits and salt, pepper and nutmeg to taste. Amalgamate all this to obtain quite a consistent and solid paste.

Roll the pasta dough out into long sheets and spread on a work surface sprinked with flour. Put teaspoons of the mixture on one of a pair of pasta sheets at 2–3cm intervals. Lay another pasta sheet on top to cover the filling and press down all around to stick the pasta together. Cut the ravioli into squares with a serrated pasta wheel and set aside.

Plunge the ravioli into lightly salted boiling water and cook for 4–5 minutes. Scoop them out and place in a warm dish. Cover with the butter and the remaining Parmesan, and serve.

Serves 6–8

" For some reason, ravioli are called tortelli in Emilia-Romagna and parts of lower Lombardy. The most famous are those of Cremona, and there are many variations of fillings. Here, though, is the most classic recipe. It is a typical Christmas dish, but people love it throughout the whole winter when the wonderfully thick-fleshed, orange-red pumpkin, which can also be bought in pieces, is available. "

CULURZONES
SARDINIAN RAVIOLI

300g Italian '00' flour, plus extra for dusting
1 egg yolk
120ml water
salt
50g butter
8–10 sage leaves, shredded
10 saffron strands, steeped in 1 tbsp warm water
pecorino cheese or Parmesan, grated

Filling

800g potatoes, peeled, boiled and drained
200g fresh pecorino cheese
50g mature pecorino cheese
120g Parmesan, grated
3 tbsp olive oil
3 tbsp chopped mint leaves
pepper

For the filling, mash the potatoes smoothly in a bowl. Crumble in the fresh pecorino and grate in the mature pecorino. Add the Parmesan, olive oil, mint and pepper to taste. (No salt because of the cheese.) Mix thoroughly and set aside.

To make the pasta dough, mix the flour, egg yolk and water together to obtain a smooth dough. Cover and set aside to rest for 20–30 minutes.

Roll out the pasta on a floured surface to a 2mm thickness and cut out 10cm rounds. Re-roll the pasta trimmings and cut out more rounds. Fill and shape the ravioli one by one. Place a small ball of the filling (the size of a small cherry) in the middle of a pasta round. Starting at the front edge, lift this onto the filling, covering half of it. With the other hand, now lift the lower left side of the pasta over the filling, then the lower right. Repeat folding in left and right again. You should obtain a sort of plaited ravioli, and then you just squeeze the top together to seal. Repeat with the rest of the dough and filling.

When you are ready to cook, bring a large pan of salted water to the boil. Add the culurzones and cook for 6–8 minutes.

In the meantime, heat the butter, sage and saffron in a pan until the butter is melted. Drain the pasta and toss with the flavoured butter. Serve sprinkled with pecorino or Parmesan.

Serves 4

You can make these, and indeed any ravioli, in advance. Freeze them (to prevent the filling seeping out) and cook from frozen, allowing 10–12 minutes.

❝ Culurzones or culingiones are best described as a sort of plaited ravioli, and they are stuffed with various different fillings in Sardinia. I like this version with potatoes, mint and plenty of cheese. Spinach, eggs and pecorino is another popular filling, and sometimes the culurzones are served with a meat or tomato ragù. ❞

TAGLIATELLE AL RAGU DI CONIGLIO
TAGLIATELLE WITH RABBIT SAUCE

20g dried ceps
1 large onion, finely sliced
60g Parma ham fat, in little cubes
40g butter
500g boneless rabbit, minced
200ml dry white wine
3 tbsp concentrated tomato paste
salt and pepper
600g egg tagliatelle (p315)
60g Parmesan, grated

Soak the dried ceps in hot water for 20 minutes. Drain the ceps, reserving the liquid, then chop and set aside.

Put the onion in a pan with the Parma ham fat and butter. Brown a little, then add the rabbit meat and fry, stirring, for 6–8 minutes. Add the wine and let bubble to evaporate the alcohol, then add the tomato paste diluted with a little water. Add the ceps to the pan with the reserved liquid (leaving the sediment behind). Now cook very slowly and gently for 2 hours. Season with salt and pepper to taste at the end of cooking.

Cook the pasta in plenty of boiling salted water until al dente, then drain well. Dress with the ragù and serve sprinkled with Parmesan. Delightful.

Serves 4

It is customary to have a ragù bolognese with tagliatelle, and in Emilia-Romagna rabbit often features in the ragù. Farmed rabbit is very good, but the sauce tastes even better with a wild one.

TAGLIATELLE AI FEGATINI
TAGLIATELLE WITH CHICKEN LIVERS

300g chicken livers
6 tbsp olive oil
1 large onion, very finely sliced
4 bay leaves
freshly grated nutmeg
2 tbsp dry Sherry
2 tbsp concentrated tomato paste
2 tbsp stock or water
salt and pepper
450g fresh tagliatelle (p315)
75g Parmesan, grated

Cut the chicken livers into small slivers. Heat the olive oil and fry the onion very gently for 5 minutes. Add the chicken livers and bay leaves, and fry gently for another 6 minutes over a low heat.

Add a pinch of nutmeg and the Sherry, and let the alcohol evaporate for 1–2 minutes. Stir in the tomato paste, and enough stock or water to bring the sauce to a smooth consistency. Add salt and pepper to taste.

Meanwhile, cook the pasta for 3–5 minutes, or until al dente. Drain and toss well in the sauce. Serve sprinkled with Parmesan.

Serves 4

" Chicken livers are very much part of many Italian sauces, and in this dish they predominate. Extremely easy to prepare, this is a particularly tasty recipe. "

PICI AL RAGU DI MAIALE
TUSCAN PASTA WITH PORK SAUCE

6 tbsp olive oil
1 small onion, finely chopped
1 celery stalk, trimmed and finely diced
1 carrot, finely diced
400g pork mince (not too fatty)
100ml dry red wine
500g polpa di pomodoro or chunky passata
5–6 bay leaves
salt and pepper
400g pici (or the largest spaghetti as possible)
80g pecorino cheese or Parmesan, grated

To make the ragù, heat the olive oil in a pan, add the onion, celery and carrot, and fry gently until soft. Add the meat and stir to brown a little, then add the wine and let the alcohol evaporate. Stir in the tomato pulp and add the bay leaves and some seasoning. Cook very slowly for 2 hours.

Plunge the pasta into plenty of boiling salted water and cook until al dente, about 15–17 minutes. Toss with the sauce and serve with pecorino cheese.

Serves 6

" Pici is possibly the only original Tuscan handmade pasta. It is made by pulling on a piece of dough made of durum wheat flour and water (usually no egg) until you have a lengthy string the size of a bucatino without the holes. It's similar to the Venetian bigolo, so quite substantial. In Tuscany, it is regularly eaten with a ragù of wild boar, hare, rabbit or pork. "

GNOCCHETTI SARDI AL RAGU DI AGNELLO
SARDINIAN PASTA WITH LAMB SAUCE

400g gnocchetti sardi
salt and pepper
80g aged pecorino cheese, grated

Sauce
5 tbsp olive oil
1 large onion, finely chopped
600g lamb on the bone, or slices of
    the lower part of the leg (ossobuco)
100ml dry white wine
polpa di pomodoro or chunky passata
    to cover the meat
2–3 bay leaves
a few rosemary needles

For the sauce, heat the olive oil in a pan, add the onion and fry gently to soften, about 6–7 minutes, then add the meat and stir to brown on all sides. Add the wine and heat to allow the alcohol to evaporate for a few minutes. Add the tomato pulp and herbs, cover and stew slowly on top of the stove for 2–3 hours. Check from time to time, and add a little water if the sauce seems too thick.

Remove the meat from the juices and discard the bones. Cut or flake the meat into smaller pieces and return to the sauce. Season with salt and pepper to taste, and if extra moisture is still needed, add 2–3 tablespoons of pasta cooking water.

Cook the pasta in plenty of boiling salted water until al dente, about 8–9 minutes. Drain and put in a large bowl with half of the sauce. Mix well, divide between the plates and top with a little more sauce and the pecorino.

Serves 4–6

❝ The Sardinians, during their centuries of isolation due to so many invasions, lived mainly inland. As a result, they acquired more of a taste for meat and game. Many different types of pasta and breads are also unique to the island. Gnocchetti sardi, or malloreddus as it is also called, is a delightful pasta, ideally cooked with tomato-based, meaty sauces. You can buy it in packets in good delicatessens. ❞

RIGATONI WITH RICH BOLOGNESE

20g dried ceps (optional)
150g sweetbreads, cleaned
6 tbsp olive oil
I onion, finely chopped
200g chicken livers, cut into small pieces
200g chicken breast or veal, coarsely minced
100g lean Parma ham, thickly sliced and cut into strips
200g fresh ceps, finely sliced, or 200g button
    mushrooms, finely sliced
150ml dry Marsala wine
1.4kg polpa di pomodoro or chunky passata
salt and pepper
450g dried rigatoni
butter, for greasing
150g Parmesan, grated

White sauce
1 litre milk
50g butter
2 tbsp plain flour
salt
freshly grated nutmeg

Preheat the oven to 220°C/Gas 7.

If using dried ceps, soak them in warm water for 20 minutes. Drain and squeeze the ceps dry, then roughly chop them.

Put the sweetbreads in boiling water and blanch for 10 minutes. Strain and remove the skin and nerves. Slice the sweetbreads.

To make the meat sauce: heat the olive oil in a large, heavy-based pan and fry the onion for 1 minute. Add the chicken livers, minced chicken or veal, Parma ham, and fry for another few minutes. Add the sweetbreads and continue to fry. Then add the fresh and dried ceps with the Marsala wine. Simmer gently for about 2 minutes, then stir in the tomato pulp. Cover and simmer the sauce very gently for 2 hours, stirring from time to time. Taste and add salt and pepper.

To make the white sauce: bring the milk to the boil in a saucepan. In a separate pan melt the butter and stir in the flour. Cook the butter and flour for 1 minute over a medium heat and gradually stir in the milk until the sauce has thickened. Add salt and nutmeg to taste and set aside.

Cook the pasta for just 4 minutes, and drain. Toss in a little of the white sauce to prevent the pasta shapes from sticking together.

Lightly grease a 20 x 25cm baking dish with sides about 7.5cm deep. Put a layer of pasta in the dish, then add one-third of the meat sauce, followed by one-third of the white sauce. Sprinkle with Parmesan. Repeat this sequence twice more, finishing with Parmesan. Bake for 40 minutes.

Serves 5–6

66 'Bologna la Ricca' they say in Italy, referring to the rich city. In Bologna the food is usually rich, too, and this dish is a fine example of the local cuisine. 99

To make life easier, you can prepare this dish a day in advance, let it set for 24 hours and bake it at the last minute, leaving you time for your guests.

ZITI AL FORNO ALLA NAPOLETANA
ZITI NEAPOLITAN-STYLE

300g minced beef
1 garlic clove, finely chopped
1 tbsp chopped parsley
25g Parmesan, grated
2 eggs, lightly beaten
40g fresh breadcrumbs, soaked in a little milk
   for 5 minutes, then squeezed dry
salt and pepper
oil, for frying
450g dried ziti
butter, for greasing
100g spicy Neapolitan salami, sliced
350g Fontina cheese or good mozzarella cheese
75g Parmesan, grated
4 eggs, lightly beaten

Sauce

4 tbsp olive oil
1 onion, chopped
100g chicken livers, chopped
800g polpa di pomodoro or chunky passata
5 basil leaves

Preheat the oven to 200°C/Gas 6.

To make the meatballs, mix together the minced beef, garlic, parsley, Parmesan, eggs and breadcrumbs in a bowl. Add salt and pepper and mix thoroughly. Use your hands to shape the mix into walnut-sized meatballs.

Heat a little oil in a frying pan and fry the meatballs in batches for about 3 minutes until browned on all sides. Remove and drain on kitchen paper.

To make the sauce, heat the olive oil in a clean pan and fry the onion until nearly transparent. Add the chicken livers and cook for another 3 minutes. Stir in the tomatoes, cover and simmer for 20 minutes over a low heat. Add the basil, salt and pepper and simmer for another 10 minutes.

Meanwhile, cook the pasta in salted boiling water for 5–7 minutes, or until al dente, and drain. Toss with some of the sauce so that the pasta is coated.

Lightly butter a 20 x 25cm baking dish with sides 7.5cm deep. Spread a layer of sauce over the bottom, then add a layer of pasta. Arrange some salami, some of the meatballs and slices of Fontina or mozzarella cheese on top. Cover with some more sauce and a sprinkling of Parmesan. Repeat this sequence until all the ingredients are used. When you reach the final layer of Fontina or mozzarella cheese, pour on the beaten eggs which will bind the pasta together. Finish with a layer of sauce and Parmesan.

Bake for 25 minutes. When cooked, let the dish stand for 5 minutes before dividing it into portions with a knife and serving.

Serves 8

" Ziti, zita or zite is a sort of long tubular noodle for everyday eating, served with just a tomato sauce and perhaps some small cubes of mozzarella cheese. But it is also something we use for a grand occasion. Then we create a dish like this one here, which is very rich and you really only need a little square to be satisfied. This is how my mother taught me to cook it … **"**

BUCATINI ALLA CARBONARA
BUCATINI WITH BACON, CHEESE AND EGGS

400g dried bucatini
salt and pepper
50g butter or 6 tbsp olive oil
100g pancetta or bacon, rind removed
    and cut into small strips
4 egg yolks
1 tbsp milk
40g mature pecorino cheese, grated

Cook the pasta in plenty of salted boiling water for 7–8 minutes or until al dente, and drain.

Meanwhile, heat the butter and or olive oil and fry the pancetta or bacon until lightly browned, and set aside. Lightly beat the egg yolks and milk in a bowl and add the pecorino cheese. Pour the egg mixture into the bacon and add the pasta. Warm through, if necessary, but do not scramble the egg. Toss well, adding plenty of pepper.

Serves 4

" I don't believe this sauce needs any introduction. It is well known in Britain, although it is not always made as it should be! The eggs must be just cooked but not as solid as scrambled egg; it is this that gives the character to the sauce. In some places double cream is added, too, but I think it then becomes too rich, although I leave these things up to you … "

Bucatini, also known as perciatelli, are like spaghetti but with a hollow centre. In the Lazio region, surrounding Rome, buccatini is used more often than spaghetti with this sauce. Pancetta helps produce the authentic flavour but you can substitute green or smoked bacon for it, although the result is a little different.

BUCATINI ALL'AMATRICIANA
AMATRICE-STYLE BUCATINI

3 tbsp olive oil
150g pancetta or bacon, rind removed and cut into strips
1 small onion, finely chopped
1 small chilli, finely chopped
450g polpa di pomodoro or chunky passata
375g dried bucatini
salt
50g Parmesan, grated

Heat the oil and fry the pancetta or bacon, the onion and the chilli for 3–4 minutes until slightly brown. Add the tomatoes, cover and cook gently for 10–15 minutes.

Meanwhile, cook the pasta in plenty of boiling salted water for 7–8 minutes or until al dente, and drain. Toss in the sauce, and serve sprinkled with Parmesan.

Serves 4

LINGUINE VONGOLE E COZZE
LINGUINE WITH CLAMS AND MUSSELS
Illustrated overleaf

400g linguine
salt and pepper
bunch of flat-leaf parsley, finely chopped
extra virgin olive oil

Sauce
1kg mussels, cleaned (p173)
1kg small clams, cleaned (p173)
6 tbsp olive oil
100ml dry white wine
2 garlic cloves, finely diced
1 small red chilli, chopped (optional)

For the sauce, put the mussels and clams in a large saucepan with the olive oil, wine, garlic and chilli, if using. Bring to the boil with the lid on and cook for a further 10 minutes before removing from the heat. Discard any mussels that haven't opened. Remove the meat from the shells (reserving a few for garnish) and keep to one side. Discard the empty shells.

At the base of the pan will be the sauce made of oil, wine, juices from the shells, garlic and chilli. Keep this warm.

In a separate pan, cook the pasta in plenty of boiling salted water until al dente, about 6–7 minutes. Drain and add to the sauce. Add salt, lots of pepper and the parsley, along with the shellfish flesh.

Divide between 4 plates, adding a few drops of extra virgin olive oil and the few remaining shell-on fish. Serve immediately.

Serves 4

" You will find this dish in all the coastal towns and villages, most famously in the laguna of Venice and on the Amalfi coast. It is the seafood pasta 'par excellence'. There exist two versions of the sauce: in rosso (with tomatoes) or in bianco (without tomatoes). I prefer the second, featured here, as you can appreciate the taste of the seafood much more easily. "

LINGUINE ALLA MOLLICA
LINGUINE WITH ANCHOVIES, CAPERS, OLIVES AND BREADCRUMBS

300g linguine
salt and pepper
12 tbsp olive oil
60g pitted black olives, chopped
2 small red chillies, finely chopped
1 tbsp salted capers, soaked and drained
6 anchovy fillets in oil, drained
60g fresh breadcrumbs

Add the linguine to a large pan of boiling salted water and boil until al dente.

Meanwhile, heat half of the olive oil in a pan, add the olives, chillies, capers and anchovies, and heat, stirring to dissolve the anchovies. Drain the pasta as soon as it is ready and toss into this sauce.

At the same time, heat the rest of the olive oil in a large non-stick pan. Add the breadcrumbs and fry until slightly brown.

Now mix the dressed pasta into the breadcrumbs. Fry for a few minutes until a crust forms underneath. Invert onto a warm plate, so the crusted side is on top. Cut into portions with a knife and serve.

Serves 4

TAGLIATELLE CON FINOCCHIO E GAMBERONI
PASTA WITH FENNEL AND PRAWNS

50g butter
4 tbsp olive oil
2 garlic cloves, finely chopped
2 fennel bulbs, trimmed and finely sliced
200ml water
50ml white wine
juice of ½ lemon
2 sprigs dill, plus 2 tbsp chopped dill
   or fennel fronds to garnish
400g fresh prawns
380g tagliatelle
salt and pepper
extra virgin olive oil

Heat the butter and olive oil in a pan, add the garlic and cook for a minute until soft. Add the fennel and water, stir and cover with a lid. Cook for 15 minutes, until the fennel is soft and translucent.

Remove the lid, add the wine, lemon juice, dill sprigs and prawns. Cook over a gentle heat until the prawns are cooked through and the liquid has reduced by half.

Meanwhile, add the tagliatelle to a pan of boiling salted water. Cook until al dente. Drain and add to the pan with the prawns, stirring to combine. Season to taste.

Divide between the plates, adding a few drops of extra virgin olive oil and the chopped dill. Serve immediately.

Serves 4–6

" The Italian composer, Ruggero Leoncavallo, who wrote *I Pagliacci* among other operas, was very partial to this dish. It is traditionally eaten on Christmas Eve in Calabria. "

"The Italians traditionally only use cheese with seafood when baking or grilling it — with lobster or crab, say, cooked under the grill. Otherwise they believe the cheese spoils the fresh flavour of the sea, and does not complement it at all."

" I chose the black capelli d'angelo pasta for this. Made with the addition of cuttlefish ink to give it its colour, and obtainable from the best Italian food shops, it combines with the very tender scallops to produce a wonderful marriage of taste, colour and texture. It is also an extremely quick recipe, taking just minutes to prepare. "

CAPELLI D'ANGELO NERI CON CAPESANTE
BLACK ANGEL'S HAIR WITH SCALLOPS

8 large fresh scallops, about 50g each, or
    16 small fresh scallops, about 25g each, cleaned
6 tbsp extra virgin olive oil
1 garlic clove, finely chopped
1 small chilli, finely chopped
150ml dry, white wine
2 tbsp finely chopped parsley
salt
375g black capelli d'angelo

Detach the coral and cut the white meat into 4 slices, or use the small scallops whole. Heat the oil and gently fry the garlic, chilli and white meat, with the corals, for 1 minute. Add the wine, parsley and salt to taste.

Cook the pasta in salted boiling water for 2–3 minutes, or until al dente, then drain. Add to the scallop mixture, mix well and serve.

Serves 4

LINGUINE CON ARAGOSTA
LINGUINE WITH LOBSTER

salt and pepper
1 live lobster, about 1.25kg, or 2 live lobsters,
    about 600g each
90ml extra virgin olive oil
½ garlic clove, finely chopped
1 glass of white wine
700g tomatoes, peeled, de-seeded and chopped
400g linguine
1 tbsp coarsely chopped flat-leaf parsley

Bring a large pan of lightly salted water to the boil. Put the lobster in, cover and simmer for 15–25 minutes, depending on size. Remove the lobster and leave to cool, then cut it in half lengthways and remove the 2 gills (near the head), the dark vein running down the tail and the small stomach sac in the head. Do not discard the green, creamy liver in the head. Take out the tail meat, then crack open the claws and remove the meat. Cut it into small chunks.

Heat the olive oil in a pan and briefly fry the garlic without letting it brown. Add the wine and bubble for a few minutes to allow the alcohol to evaporate, then stir in the tomatoes and simmer for 10 minutes. Add the lobster meat, plus the liver and the shells, and heat through gently.

Cook the linguine in the water in which the lobster was boiled, then drain. Season the sauce with salt and a generous amount of pepper. Remove and discard the shells and mix the sauce with the linguine. Serve sprinkled with parsley.

Serves 4

" You will find this 'posh' pasta dish in most of the coastal regions, cooked in many different ways. This is the simplest. "

RISOTTO, GNOCCHI & POLENTA

RISOTTO ALLA MILANESE
RISOTTO WITH SAFFRON

2.5 litres chicken or vegetable stock (p314)
2g saffron strands
100g unsalted butter
1 large onion, finely chopped
100ml dry white wine
500g arborio rice
salt and pepper
60g Parmesan, grated

Bring the stock to the boil in a large pan and keep it at a low simmer.

In a dry frying pan, toast the saffron strands for a few seconds, being careful not to burn them.

Melt 50g of the butter in a large saucepan over a low heat and fry the onion until soft, about 10 minutes. Add the wine and let it evaporate, about 2–3 minutes.

Add the rice and stir to coat with the butter for a minute, then start to add the hot stock, ladle by ladle. Avoid drowning the rice in stock and wait until each ladleful is absorbed before you add the next. After 10 minutes cooking and stirring, add the saffron and season with salt and pepper. Continue to cook and add stock in the same way until the rice is al dente, another 8–10 minutes, then add the rest of the butter and half the Parmesan.

Stir well and serve, sprinkling the remaining Parmesan on top.

Serves 4

This is a classic dish symbolising its region – in this case Lombardy, the region most associated with rice. Saffron is always included and sometimes bone marrow. If you omit the saffron, you will be left with the most basic of risottos.

RISOTTO DI ZUCCA
PUMPKIN RISOTTO

2 tbsp olive oil
90g butter
4 rosemary sprigs, 2 finely chopped
1 garlic clove
600g pumpkin flesh, chopped into very small chunks
1 small onion, finely chopped
30g carnaroli rice
1 litre hot chicken stock (p314)
50g Parmesan, grated
salt and pepper

In a pan, heat the olive oil and a third of the butter, then add the 2 whole sprigs of rosemary, the garlic clove and pumpkin. The pumpkin will automatically exude some liquid so no water needs to be added. Cook for about 20 minutes, or until the pumpkin softens and dissolves. Remove the rosemary sprigs and garlic clove.

In another large pan, heat half the remaining butter and fry the onion gently until soft, then add the rice and fry equally gently, stirring continuously, for a few minutes. Add a little of the chicken stock and then the pumpkin mixture. Add more stock gradually until it is all used up and has been absorbed by the rice, stirring from time to time to avoid it sticking to the pan. Take off the heat and beat in the remaining butter and the Parmesan, season and sprinkle with the chopped rosemary.

If you have a spare pumpkin, seed it, warm it inside with hot water then drain; fill it with the risotto, and serve.

Serves 4

"Pumpkin risotto is one of those comforting dishes which can please anybody. This specific recipe comes from the kitchen of the Hotel Cipriani in Venice. The chef, Renato Piccolotto, showed me his little secrets which I will now pass to you. It is a wonderful dish."

RISOTTO CON RADICCHIO
RADICCHIO RISOTTO

2 small heads of radicchio from Treviso (long, not round)
6 tbsp olive oil
1 garlic clove, finely chopped
1 small onion, finely sliced
300g luganega sausage meat (p203), in small chunks
400g vialone nano or arborio rice
2 litres hot chicken or beef stock (p314)
salt and pepper
50g butter
50g Parmesan, grated

Clean and finely chop the radicchio leaves, and dice the stems. Put in a large pan with the oil, garlic, onion and sausage meat, and leave to brown for a few minutes. Then add the rice and mix well to coat each grain with fat. Now add the hot stock, ladle by ladle, stirring continuously. Wait until each ladleful has been fully absorbed before you add the next. After 15–20 minutes the rice should be cooked al dente. Remove from the heat, adjust the seasoning, and add a little more stock if required. Add the butter in chunks, along with the Parmesan, and mix well before serving.

Serves 4

" This is a very simple risotto from the Treviso area, where the best radicchio is found. Treviso radicchio is very special because it has a nutty taste, which is not so bitter. In Treviso they eat radicchio in every possible form; there is even a radicchio jam and tart! **"**

RISOTTO PRIMAVERA
SPRING VEGETABLE RISOTTO

1 onion, finely chopped
4 carrots, finely diced
2 celery stalks, trimmed and finely diced
50g fresh peas, podded
100g green (French) beans, trimmed and cut into pieces
2 artichoke hearts, finely diced
12 asparagus tips
50g hop shoots (optional)
2 litres boiling chicken or vegetable stock (p314)
100g butter
400g risotto rice
salt and pepper
60g Parmesan, grated

Have all the vegetables ready. Bring the stock to the boil in a pan and keep it at a low simmer.

Melt 50g of the butter in a large pan and fry the onion until soft. Add the carrots and celery and cook for 5 minutes, then add the peas, green beans and artichokes. Stir over the heat briefly, then add the rice and stir to coat with the butter.

Ladle by ladle, add the boiling stock, allowing each addition to be absorbed before you add the next. After 10 minutes, add the asparagus and the hop shoots, if using. Carry on adding stock and stirring, until the rice is al dente, about 20 minutes. When the rice is cooked, everything else will be.

Remove from the heat and season with salt and pepper to taste. Add the rest of the butter and the Parmesan. Stir briskly and serve warm.

Serves 4

" I had always assumed that Lombardy was the birthplace of risotto, but it is Veneto. There are hundreds of risottos in Venice. This one is made with spring vegetables, as its name suggests, which gives it the flavour of new life. "

RISOTTO DI BRUSCANDOLI
WILD HOP RISOTTO

250g hop tops
1.5 litres chicken stock (p314)
1 small onion, finely chopped
1 garlic clove, finely chopped
75g unsalted butter
375g carnaroli rice
55g Parmesan, grated
salt and pepper

Wash the hop tops, and cut into 5cm pieces.

The most important element in making a risotto is to keep a pot of boiling stock next to the risotto pan. This is necessary because you want to be able to add liquid at the same temperature as the rice to avoid interrupting the cooking. Heat the stock to a simmer.

Start by frying the onion and garlic in 55g of the butter. Add the rice, stirring to coat every grain with the butter. Start to add the hot stock, ladle by ladle, stirring occasionally. After 10 minutes add the hops, which should cook for approximately 8 minutes, or continue until the risotto is creamy and the rice al dente. Remove from the heat, add the rest of the butter and the Parmesan, and adjust the seasoning. Serve immediately.

Serves 4

RISOTTO CON ASPARAGI
ASPARAGUS RISOTTO

900g green asparagus
salt and pepper
1 litre vegetable stock (p314)
1 small onion, finely chopped
85g butter
4 tbsp olive oil
350g carnaroli or vialone nano rice
55g Parmesan, grated

Trim the asparagus and cook it in boiling salted water until tender. Drain, reserving the cooking liquid. Cut the asparagus into 1cm chunks, leaving the tips whole.

Make up the asparagus cooking liquid with stock to 1.75 litres. Fry the onion in the butter and oil. Add the chopped asparagus and rice, stirring to coat with the butter. Start to add the hot stock, ladle by ladle, stirring occasionally. Carry on adding stock and stirring, until the rice is al dente, about 20 minutes. Decorate with the asparagus tips and Parmesan before serving.

Serves 4

RISOTTO CON FUNGHI
RISOTTO WITH MUSHROOMS

2 litres chicken or vegetable stock (p314)
4 tbsp olive oil or 50g unsalted butter
1 onion, very finely chopped
300g firm button mushrooms, finely sliced
50g dried ceps, rehydrated (see below) and chopped
350g carnaroli or arborio rice
60g Parmesan, grated
80g unsalted butter
salt and pepper

Put the stock in a pan, bring to the boil and keep at a low simmer.

Heat the olive oil or butter in a large pan over a low heat, add the onion and fry until soft, about 10 minutes. Add the button mushrooms and the ceps and cook for 5 minutes, until soft and lightly browned.

Add the rice and stir for a minute or two, then add one or two ladles of boiling stock. Stir continuously over the heat, adding stock a ladleful at a time as each addition is absorbed. After 18–20 minutes, check for the required al dente texture – the rice should be tender, but with a firm bite in the centre, and the risotto should be moist.

Remove the pan from the heat, add the Parmesan and butter and stir in well. Season to taste and serve on warm plates. *Buon appetito!*

Serves 4

To rehydrate dried ceps, soak them in water to cover for about 20 minutes. Pick the mushrooms out of the water and put into a sieve over a bowl. Then very carefully strain the water, preferably through muslin. This will remove any dust that may have come off the mushrooms. The liquid will taste intensely mushroomy, and can be used in addition to the stock to add extra mushroom flavour to this risotto.

" Perhaps alongside risotto with truffles, risotto with ceps is the best-known
of Italian rice dishes. Italians eat this only in season when the porcino (cep) is
around, but this recipe I have devised will enable you to enjoy a mushroom risotto
throughout the year. Should you manage to find some fresh ceps, however,
I urge you to try them, the taste is sensational! **"**

BOMBA DI RISO CON TARTUFO
RICE BOMB WITH TRUFFLE

20g dried ceps
2 large pigeons or 6 large quail, cleaned
plain flour, for dusting
150g butter
50ml olive oil
1 onion, finely chopped
2 tbsp finely chopped parsley
a few sage leaves
1 small rosemary sprig
salt and pepper
freshly grated nutmeg
a few juniper berries
100ml chicken or beef stock (p314)
2 tbsp saba (p45)
1 tsp truffle oil
dried breadcrumbs, to dust
20g fresh truffle, finely sliced
50g Parmesan, grated

Rice
800g carnaroli rice
100g butter
150g Parmesan, grated
2–3 tbsp milk
6 eggs, beaten
½ tsp freshly grated nutmeg

Soak the dried ceps in hot water for 20 minutes. Drain, reserving the liquid, and finely chop the mushrooms.

Dust the pigeons with flour. Heat 50g of the butter and the olive oil in a large pan and brown the pigeons on each side. Add the onion, parsley, sage and rosemary and cook until the onion has softened. Add some salt, pepper and nutmeg, the juniper berries, chopped ceps and enough stock just to cover. Cover and cook gently for about 20 minutes until the meat is cooked, adding some strained cep liquid if necessary. Set aside to cool.

Bone the birds and put the meat back into the pan, discarding the rosemary and sage leaves. Warm through and add the saba and a few drops of truffle oil. Cook to let the flavours develop and reduce the sauce slightly, until it becomes quite dense, about 10 minutes.

Cook the rice in plenty of salted water. Meanwhile, preheat the oven to 200°C/Gas 6. When the rice is cooked, drain thoroughly and mix in the butter and Parmesan while still warm. Add the milk, beaten eggs and nutmeg, and mix together well.

Grease a 25cm ovenproof pudding basin with 20g of the butter and dust all around with breadcrumbs. Put two-thirds of the rice into the bowl, and press onto the base and against the sides, leaving a large well in the centre. Pour the pigeon mixture into this well, add the sliced truffle, then cover with the rest of the rice. Sprinkle with more breadcrumbs and dot with the remaining butter and Parmesan. Bake in the oven for 20 minutes.

Leave to rest for 10 minutes before serving. With a knife, loosen the sides, turn upside down onto a large serving plate and remove the bowl. In my opinion, a green salad dressed with balsamic vinegar complements this dish magnificently.

Serves 6–8

" This is a speciality of Piacenza, and one of the few rice dishes in Emilia, where pasta is so popular. You can find similar dishes elsewhere, notably the sartù of Naples. It is an ideal dish for grand occasions – quite rich and time-consuming, but well worth the effort. "

VELLUTATA DI FUNGHI CARDONCELLI

MUSHROOMS WITH CANNELLINI BEAN PUREE AND RICE

200g dried cannellini beans, soaked in
   cold water overnight
8 tbsp olive oil
2 garlic cloves, chopped
1 thick slice of Parma ham (with fat)
   or pancetta, about 100g
1 onion, finely sliced
200g cardoncelli (or oyster mushrooms),
   cleaned and sliced if large
200g risotto rice
salt and pepper
80g mature pecorino cheese, grated

Drain the soaked beans. Heat half the olive oil in a pan and fry the garlic with the ham or pancetta for a few minutes. Add the cannellini beans and enough water to cover generously, then cook for a few hours until soft.

Remove the ham or pancetta from the beans. Purée the cannellini beans with some of the cooking liquor in a blender or food processor to a pulp. Transfer to a bowl. Chop the ham and stir into the bean purée; keep warm.

Heat the remaining olive oil in another pan and gently fry the onion until soft. Add the mushrooms and fry gently for 5–10 minutes until softened.

At the same time, cook the rice in salted water until al dente. Now combine the three mixtures – the bean purée, the mushrooms and the rice. You should have a very tasty soupy rice, almost like a wet risotto. Check the seasoning and scatter plenty of pecorino over. Humble and delicious.

Serves 4

" A curious recipe from Basilicata, where all the ingredients are produced locally, except the rice. Cardoncelli belong to the same family as oyster mushrooms. They grow wild in the south of Italy, but they are also cultivated. **"**

" This risotto, with its base of poached, boned red mullet and lemon sole, has a lovely, creamy texture. It is quite a work-intensive recipe but it is really worth it! I have chosen to use vialone nano rice for this dish. It is short-grained and very absorbent, which makes the risotto much tastier. "

RISOTTO ALLA MARINARA
SEAFOOD RISOTTO

1 large onion, finely sliced
6 tbsp olive oil
20 mussels, cleaned (p173)
150ml white wine
100g scampi or large prawns, shelled
100g baby octopus or squid
170g cooked shrimps, shelled
500g vialone nano rice
extra virgin olive oil
juice of 1 lemon

Fish stock
1.5 litres water
1 small onion
1 carrot
a few celery leaves
a few parsley leaves
2 red mullet, about 150g each
1 lemon sole, about 300g

Bring the water for the stock to the boil with the onion, carrot, celery and parsley leaves and boil for 15 minutes. Add the red mullet and sole and poach gently for a further 10 minutes. Remove the fish from the stock and fillet, discarding the bones, heads and skin. Set the fish flesh aside. Remove the flavourings from the fish stock and keep at a simmer.

Fry the onion in a large pan in the olive oil until soft, about 5 minutes. Add the mussels and the wine, cover and steam for a few minutes until the mussels open. Remove the mussels from the pan, discarding any that remain closed. Working quickly, extract the mussel meat from the shells. Reserve the meat and a few shells for decoration, discarding the rest.

To the same pan add the scampi or prawns, octopus or squid, shrimps and the reserved fish flesh and mussel meat. Add the rice, stirring so that it is coated with the oil. Add the simmering stock, ladle by ladle, as it is absorbed by the rice. The rice should be cooked in about 20–25 minutes.

Serve with a little extra virgin olive oil and a few drops of lemon juice.

Serves 4–6

RISOTTO CON GAMBERI E ACETOSA
WILD SORREL AND PRAWN RISOTTO

150g wild sorrel leaves
1.5 litres chicken or vegetable stock (p314)
3 tbsp extra virgin olive oil
55g unsalted butter
1 small onion, finely chopped
375g carnaroli rice
200g cooked peeled prawns
55g Parmesan, grated
salt and pepper

Wash the sorrel well, then remove any tough stalks. Chop the leaves roughly.

Keep the stock on the boil next to the risotto pan. Add the oil, 40g of the butter and the onion to the risotto pan, and fry until the onion becomes transparent. Add the rice and stir to coat every grain with the fat. Ladle by ladle, add the hot stock to the rice, stirring until the rice has absorbed all of the liquid.

After approximately 10 minutes, add most of the sorrel and cook for 8 minutes, by which time the risotto will have turned slightly green. Next add the prawns, the rest of the butter and the Parmesan, stirring to form a creamy consistency. Season to taste, scatter with the remaining sorrel and serve immediately.

Serves 4

Sorrel is interesting to cook because of its distinctive sour taste. As well as making this wonderful risotto it is also very good made into a soup (p81), fritters, or added to an omelette.

RISOTTO ALL'ISOLANA
RISOTTO ISOLA-STYLE

l litre chicken stock (p314)
300g luganega sausage (p203)
1 onion, finely chopped
85g unsalted butter
400g vialone nano or arborio rice
1 tsp ground cinnamon
salt and pepper
60g Parmesan, grated

Put the stock in a pan, bring to the boil, reduce the heat and keep at a low simmer.

Take the sausage meat out of its skin and crumble it. Gently fry the meat and onion in 55g of the butter until the onion is translucent and the meat slightly browned.

Add the rice and stir to coat every grain with the fat. Add one or two ladles of boiling stock. Stir continuously over the heat, adding stock a ladleful at a time as each addition is absorbed. Carry on adding stock and stirring, until the rice is al dente, about 20 minutes.

Remove from the heat, add the cinnamon, seasoning and the rest of the butter and stir to mix well. Serve topped with the Parmesan.

Serves 4

RISOTTO ALLA SARDA
SARDINIAN RISOTTO

800ml beef stock (p314)
6 tbsp olive oil
1 small onion, finely chopped
150g lean minced pork
150g lean minced veal
300g risotto rice
3 tbsp dry red wine
200g polpa di pomodoro or chunky passata
pinch of saffron strands
salt and pepper
40g butter
60g mature pecorino cheese, grated

Put the stock in a pan on the stove and bring to a simmer; keep it at simmering point. Heat the olive oil in a flameproof casserole or heavy-based pan, add the onion and fry until soft. Add the minced pork and veal, and fry, stirring from time to time, until the meat is browned and cooked.

Add the rice and stir for a minute or two, then add the wine and let the alcohol evaporate. Add the tomato pulp, saffron and a ladleful of the stock. Stir continuously over the heat, adding stock a ladleful at a time as each addition is absorbed. After 15 minutes, check for the required texture: the rice should be tender, but with a firm bite in the centre, and the risotto should be moist. Taste for seasoning.

When ready take off the heat, mix in the butter and serve, sprinkled with pecorino.

Serves 4

" Isola, south of Verona, is the area from which this remarkable risotto comes. The use of cinnamon reflects the influence of nearby Venice, which imported spices from the East during the Middle Ages. "

ARANCINI DI RISO
LITTLE RICE BALLS

400g leftover risotto of any kind
4 eggs, beaten
salt and pepper
freshly grated nutmeg
50g Parmesan, grated
100g dried white breadcrumbs
vegetable oil, for shallow- or deep-frying

Put the leftover risotto in a bowl, and add half of the beaten egg, some salt, pepper, a pinch of nutmeg and Parmesan. Mix well with wet hands, then shape into apricot-sized balls.

Place the remaining beaten egg on one plate and the breadcrumbs on another. Roll the rice balls first in the egg, then in the breadcrumbs, then shallow- or deep-fry in hot oil on all sides until golden, about 5 minutes or so. Drain on kitchen paper, and serve warm or cold.

Makes 24 rice balls

" This is a Sicilian speciality, which is offered in bars and cafés as a small meal or snack. The rice is usually cooked specifically, though this version of mine can be made with leftover risotto. Made in smaller sizes, as here, they are ideal for party finger food. **"**

POLENTA SULLA SPIANATORA
POLENTA ON THE TABLE
Illustrated on previous page

1.2kg pork (not too lean)
10 tbsp olive oil
4 garlic cloves, finely chopped
100ml white wine
2 tbsp concentrated tomato paste
1kg firm and fleshy red and yellow peppers
2 red chillies, or more
20g salt
6 tbsp white wine vinegar
3.5 litres water
600g polenta flour (or quick polenta)
Parmesan or pecorino cheese, grated

First, prepare the ragù. Cut the pork into walnut-sized pieces. Heat half the olive oil in a pan and fry the meat until browned on all sides. Add the garlic and cook gently for 10–15 minutes, stirring from time to time. Mix the white wine with the tomato paste, add to the pan and cook for a further 20 minutes.

Meanwhile, halve, core and de-seed the peppers, then cut into strips. Heat the remaining olive oil in a frying pan and fry the peppers quite briskly until soft, letting only the edges caramelise. Add the chillies (as much as you can take), a little salt and the wine vinegar, and sauté for a minute or two. Add the peppers to the meat, and taste for salt and chilli. Cook for a further 30 minutes, or until the meat is tender.

Meanwhile, make the polenta. Bring the water to the boil in a large pan with 20g salt. Pour in the polenta and cook, stirring, until thickened and smooth, about 30–40 minutes (or just 5–6 minutes if you've cheated and used quick polenta).

Pour the polenta onto the spianatora (see below), then spoon the pork ragù into the middle. Sit everyone around, armed with a fork and a big appetite! Serve the Parmesan or pecorino cheese in a separate bowl.

Serves 6–8

Here steaming polenta is poured onto the middle of the spianatora (special round wooden table), a ragù goes into the middle and everyone tucks in.If you don't have a spianatora, you could always large wooden board instead.

POLENTA CONCIA CON RAGU DI POLLO E SALSICCIA
POLENTA WITH CHICKEN AND SAUSAGE STEW

1.5 litres water
salt and pepper
300g quick polenta
150g fontina cheese, cut into cubes
150g unsalted butter
150g Parmesan, grated
1 large onion, finely chopped
8 tbsp olive oil
400g chicken meat, cut into in chunks
200g luganega sausage (p203),
    skinned and in little chunks
100ml dry white wine
800g polpa di pomodoro or chunky passata

Bring the water to the boil and add 15g salt. Pour the polenta in slowly and cook, stirring, until thickened and smooth, about 5–6 minutes. Add the fontina cubes, butter and Parmesan and stir to combine.

In another pan, fry the onion in the olive oil until soft, about 5 minutes, then add the chicken and sausage pieces. Allow to brown slightly, then add the wine and some salt and pepper. Cook for 5 minutes then add the tomatoes and cook until everything is tender, about 20 minutes.

Spoon the polenta and ragù onto individual serving plates, and enjoy!

Serves 4

" I have very fond memories of Nina Burgai of the Aosta Valley, who used to have a hotel above Champorcher that could only be reached by a funicular railway as it was 2,000 metres high. Whenever you went there she would be making a rich yet delicious polenta. This is the recipe she taught me. "

POLENTA SVELTA CON GAMBERETTI
QUICK POLENTA WITH SHRIMPS

1 litre water
5g salt
200g quick polenta
120g Parmesan, grated
150g unsalted butter
300g pink shrimps, shelled
juice of 2 lemons

In a saucepan, bring the water to the boil with the salt and add the polenta slowly, stirring well, so that you don't produce lumps. After 5 minutes add the Parmesan and 100g of the butter, and mix well.

In another pan, gently fry the shrimps in the remaining butter for 5 minutes, before adding the lemon juice.

Pour the polenta onto plates, spooning the shrimp sauce over the top.

Serves 4

" This delightful, simple dish comes from Venice, where the little pink shrimps of the lagoon taste very nice indeed. "

POLENTA CONCIA AL FORNO
BAKED POLENTA

2 litres water
25g salt
1kg stone-ground polenta flour
200g butter
250g fontina or Toma cheese, cubed
250g Gorgonzola cheese, cubed
200g Parmesan, grated

Put the water and salt in a heavy pan and bring to the boil. While stirring with a long wooden spoon, drizzle the flour in a little at a time. Reduce the heat and cook, stirring, for 40 minutes or so, until you see the polenta coming away from the sides of the pan. When the polenta is ready, add the butter and stir in well.

Preheat the oven to 220°C/Gas 7.

Spread a layer of the polenta out in a high-sided baking tray and make the top smooth. Sprinkle some of the three cheeses on top. Repeat the layers one more time, and finish by adding just the Parmesan on top. Put into the preheated oven for 15 minutes, then eat as an accompaniment to stewed meat dishes, especially ragùs of game. The leftovers, when cold, can be cut into slices and either fried in butter or grilled.

Serves 8–10

❝ This should be tasted by all those who say they do not like polenta. I agree that every single morsel of this dish is a meal in itself, but knowing this, you can regulate your intake of less calorific food, You don't need to eat it every day, but when you do eat it, your body will be completely satisfied! ❞

CESTELLI DI POLENTA CON SPINACI E GORGONZOLA
POLENTA BASKETS WITH SPINACH AND GORGONZOLA

900ml water
salt and pepper
400g stone-ground polenta flour
85g Parmesan, grated
85g butter, plus extra for greasing
250g spinach, cooked, drained and squeezed dry
85g mascarpone cheese
freshly grated nutmeg
125g Gorgonzola or Dolcelatte cheese, cubed
4 tbsp milk

Preheat the oven to 180°C/Gas 4. Bring the water to the boil and add 10g salt. Pour the polenta in slowly and cook, stirring, until thickened and smooth, about 40 minutes. Add half the Parmesan and half the butter. Pour into a container which is at least 30 x 15cm and in which the polenta can stand 5cm high. Let it cool and solidify, then turn out the set polenta upside-down on to a work surface. Using a pastry cutter, cut out of this eight circles 7cm in diameter all the way through to the bottom of the polenta. Cut out of each of these circles, using a 4cm cutter, a well in the middle 5cm deep, but not right through this time. Remove the cutter. Cut in with a knife at an angle to take a wedge out. Scrape the rest out with a spoon. You should end up with small containers with sides and a well in the middle (the baskets). Place these on a lightly buttered tray.

Chop the cooked spinach finely and mix with the mascarpone, a pinch of nutmeg and a little salt and pepper in a bowl. Add the Gorgonzola, remaining Parmesan and the milk, and mix further to obtain a mixture which you put into the little polenta baskets.

Add little flakes of butter on top and bake in the preheated oven for 15 minutes. Serve immediately.

Makes 8 baskets

Polenta, when stiffly cooked, can be the base or 'carrier' for lots of other ingredients. This is a particularly nice idea for a starter, popular in some Piedmontese restaurants. A little skill is required to make the baskets, but I'm sure you will manage! Of course, it is up to you to find suitable fillings, should you want to experiment a little with other ingredients.

CROSTE DI POLENTA CON CICORIA
POLENTA CRUST WITH BRAISED CHICORY

6 tbsp olive oil
½ small red chilli, chopped
1 tbsp salted capers, soaked and drained and chopped
2 garlic cloves, chopped
600g Belgian chicory, cut into quarters lengthways
300ml water
1 chicken stock cube

Polenta
200g quick polenta
salt and pepper
2 tbsp olive oil, plus extra for frying
150ml boiling water

Put the polenta in a bowl, add a pinch of salt and pepper and olive oil and mix well. Pour in the boiling water and stir to make a dough. Divide the dough into 6 pieces and shape into hamburger-sized cakes.

Pour a little olive oil into a large frying pan and heat gently. Add the cakes and shallow-fry for 8 minutes on one side, until a thick crust has formed. Pour in a little more oil, turn the cakes over and repeat.

Meanwhile, put the olive oil, chilli, capers and garlic in a pan and cook gently, covered, for about 3 minutes. Add the chicory and water, and crumble in the stock cube. Reduce the heat and cook, covered, until the chicory has released a lot of its juices and is tender, about 15–20 minutes.

Arrange the polenta and the chicory on plates and spoon over a little of the chicory cooking juices to finish.

Serves 6

" My granny used to make a large maize cake to be put in the oven when she was making bread. The resulting crunchy polenta pieces, which we ate with braised chicory, were stunning, and inspired this recipe. "

The polenta cakes are equally good eaten cold, when they become even crunchier and more biscuit-like in texture. Try serving these with some cold Zucchini e Fagiolini alla Menta (p20) for a perfect picnic lunch.

GNOCCHI DI ZUCCA
PUMPKIN GNOCCHI

1kg orange-red pumpkin
1 egg
salt and pepper
150g plain flour, plus extra for dusting
200g Parmesan, grated
freshly grated nutmeg
60g butter, melted

Preheat the oven to 200°C/Gas 6.

So that the pumpkin doesn't become too wet, it is necessary to bake it for a little while in the oven, or you could steam it until soft. The pulp should be quite dry but still soft. Cut the flesh off the skin and pass the flesh through a mouli.

In a bowl, beat the egg, add salt and pepper to taste, and mix with the puréed pumpkin, flour, 150g of the Parmesan and a pinch of nutmeg. This should result in a soft and workable dough. To make the gnocchi, take a little dough at a time and roll it on a floured work surface with the palms of your hands until you have a long baton about 2cm thick. Cut this into 3cm long sections and sprinkle with extra flour so that they don't stick together. Make the little dumplings one by one: run each one down the tines of a fork, using gently pressure, to obtain a patterned shape.

The cooking is very simple. Place the gnocchi in abundant boiling salted water until you see them rising from the bottom of the pan and floating. At this stage they are cooked. Scoop them out with a slotted spoon and gently put them in a pan with the melted butter, turning to coat them well. Sprinkle with the remaining Parmesan and serve (you could fry some sage leaves in the butter first if you like).

Serves 4

GNOCCHI CON TROMBETTE E POLLO DEL BOSCO
GNOCCHI WITH HORN OF PLENTY AND CHICKEN OF THE WOODS

500g cooked and mashed floury potatoes
200g plain flour, plus extra to dust
1 egg, beaten
salt and pepper

Sauce
300g horn of plenty mushrooms, cleaned weight
200g chicken of the woods mushrooms, cleaned weight
    (or use fresh open cap or brown cap mushrooms)
20g dried ceps
4 tbsp olive oil
55g butter
1 onion, finely chopped
150ml dry white wine
3 tbsp finely chopped parsley
60g Parmesan, grated

Make the gnocchi by mixing together the potatoes, flour and egg, adding more flour if the dough is too wet. Season lightly.

Keeping your hands well floured, roll the dough with your hands into a soft sausage, about 2cm in diameter. Cut into chunks about 2.5cm long. Press each chunk against the tines of the fork to mark and shape the gnocchi. Leave to rest on a clean cloth.

For the sauce, clean and cut the fresh mushrooms into thin strips. Soak the dried ceps for 20 minutes in warm water. Drain well, then chop them very finely, reserving their soaking water.

Heat the oil and butter together in a pan and fry the onion in the mixture until soft, then add all the mushrooms. Cook very slowly for 15 minutes to reduce them. Add some of the cep soaking water and the wine and cook for a further 5–10 minutes. Add the parsley, some salt and lots of pepper.

Plunge the gnocchi all together into abundant, slightly salted boiling water. When they float to the surface, scoop them out with a slotted spoon, and add to the sauce. Mix well, divide between warm plates and sprinkle with Parmesan.

Serves 6

" Many types of dumplings exist in the world, but none equals the very simple Italian version, which is typically made with flour and potatoes. Their lightness, when freshly made, is the major characteristic, but when gnocchi are combined with an appropriate sauce they become irresistible. They are good simply with butter and Parmesan, excellent with tomato, pesto, a bolognese or even a Gorgonzola sauce and wonderful combined like this with mushrooms.**"**

" In a way this simple, yet delicious dish can
be seen to represent the colours of the Italian
flag – green, red and white. "

GNOCCHI VERDI AL POMODORO E MOZZARELLA
GREEN GNOCCHI WITH TOMATO AND MOZZARELLA

500g floury potatoes, peeled and quartered
salt and pepper
110g plain flour, plus extra to dust
200g spinach, cooked, drained, squeezed dry
    and very finely chopped
1 egg
40g Parmesan, grated
150g buffalo mozzarella, cut into small cubes

Sauce
1 garlic clove, finely chopped
6 tbsp olive oil
500g polpa di pomodoro or chunky passata
6 basil leaves, plus extra to serve

Cook the potatoes in slightly salted water. When soft, drain them thoroughly. Put them back into the empty pan and stir over a gentle heat for a few seconds to get rid of any lingering moisture. Mash them finely and mix gently with the flour on a work surface, together with the spinach and egg, to make a soft dough. Season lightly with salt and pepper.

Keeping your hands well floured, take part of the dough and roll it with your hands into a soft sausage, about 2cm in diameter. Cut into chunks about 2.5cm long. With the help of a fork and more flour, press each chunk against the tines of the fork with a downwards movement, to mark and shape the gnocchi. Leave to rest on a clean cloth.

Make the simple tomato sauce by frying the garlic in the olive oil for a few minutes, until soft. Add the tomatoes, basil and some salt and pepper, and cook for 20 minutes.

Plunge the gnocchi all together into abundant, slightly salted boiling water. They will be cooked when they float to the surface. Scoop them out with a slotted spoon, and add to the sauce. Sprinkle with Parmesan and some pepper, and mix well.

Divide the gnocchi between 4 plates, sprinkling over the mozzarella and some more basil leaves to finish.

Serves 4

GNOCCHI ALLA BAVA
GNOCCHI PIEDMONTESE-STYLE

300g Italian '00' flour
300g buckwheat flour
2 eggs
3 tbsp milk
salt and pepper
150g fontina cheese, thinly sliced
150g fresh Toma cheese, thinly sliced
55g Parmesan, grated
60g butter

Preheat the oven to 200°C/Gas 6.

Put the flours into a bowl, then mix in the eggs and enough milk to obtain a firm dough. Roll small portions of the dough at a time into a cigar shape. Cut into small chunks about 3cm long and run them lightly over the tines of a fork to leave an indent, rolling them off the fork on to a clean cloth. Cover and leave to rest for 30 minutes.

Bring to the boil a large pan of lightly salted water and cook the gnocchi in it for a minute or two. They are ready when they swim to the surface. Scoop them out with a slotted spoon and arrange them in layers in an ovenproof dish with the fontina, Toma and a little of the Parmesan. Sprinkle the remaining Parmesan over the top, dot with the butter and bake in the oven for 10 minutes. Serve immediately.

Serves 6

" There are many variations on this dish, most of them from Piedmont. Alla bava means that when you lift the gnocchi from the plate with a fork they should form strings of melting cheese. Most gnocchi are made from ingredients such as potatoes and semolina; unusually these are made from two types of flour. **"**

GNOCCHI FRITTI DI SEDANO RAPA
FRIED CELERIAC DUMPLINGS

500g celeriac (cleaned weight), cut into chunks
200g potatoes, peeled and cut into chunks
salt and pepper
2 eggs, beaten
freshly grated nutmeg
1 tbsp very finely chopped parsley
200g ricotta cheese
100g plain white flour, plus extra to dust
100g butter
3 tbsp olive oil
1 recipe basic tomato sauce (p315)
50g Parmesan, grated

Boil the celeriac and potatoes in plenty of salted water until tender. Drain and put back in the same pan over the heat to remove all the moisture completely. Mash and put in a bowl. Add the beaten eggs, salt, pepper, a pinch of nutmeg, parsley, ricotta and flour. Mix everything until you achieve a smooth mixture.

Heat the butter and olive oil in a large pan.

Take a teaspoon of the mixture at a time and toss in flour to dust (the mixture is very soft) before shaping into irregular round or oval shapes. Fry in the hot butter and oil on both sides until golden. Keep warm until you have finished the mixture.

Serve on hot plates with a little of the tomato sauce, sprinkled with Parmesan and more pepper.

Serves 4

" Most of my recipes come together when I have an idea, and go into the kitchen and try it. Some, like this one, are first 'mentally cooked' and then put down on paper, including all ingredients. When I test the recipe I can see how far I was from obtaining a positive dish. In this case I had the right ingredients and the method was also as I would have expected; I just had to make a few measurements. "

GNOCCHI DI ORTICA CON SALSA AL DOLCELATTE
NETTLE GNOCCHI WITH DOLCELATTE SAUCE

200g nettle leaves
700g floury potatoes, peeled and cubed
salt and pepper
200g plain flour, plus extra for dusting
1 large egg
55g Parmesan, grated

Sauce
100g Dolcelatte cheese, cut into small cubes
100ml milk
55g unsalted butter

Cook the nettles in boiling water for 10 minutes, then drain and squeeze out all the residual liquid. Cook the potatoes in boiling salted water until tender, then drain and mash to a purée while still warm.

Put the potatoes on a clean work surface and mix in the flour. Liquidise the nettles with the egg, and season to taste. Add this to the potato mixture, and knead to a soft dough. On a well-floured surface, take sections of dough at a time and roll them out with the palm of your hand to form a sausage 2cm in diameter. Cut into chunks of about 3cm in length, and dust with a little flour. Take a piece at a time and roll each down over the prongs to form a pattern that resembles little ridged shells. Leave to rest on a clean cloth.

Next, combine the Dolcelatte and milk and process together. Melt the butter in a large pan, then add the milk and cheese mixture and allow to melt over a low heat. Bring a large pot of salted water to the boil, then add the gnocchi. When they rise to the surface after a few seconds, they are ready. Drain them and add to the sauce immediately. Sprinkle with Parmesan and pepper.

Serves 4

" Gnocchi are one of the most satisfying dishes of Italian cuisine. The name, which translates to 'dumplings' in English (and is very difficult for foreigners to pronounce!), is probably derived from the Germanic food culture – from the Knödeln and Nockerln of Germany and Austria. Including nettles in the mix not only gives a nice colour, but also a nutty taste. "

GNOCCHI ALLA ROMANA
ROMAN SEMOLINA DUMPLINGS

1 litre milk
salt and pepper
freshly grated nutmeg
300g semolina flour
100g Parmesan, grated
150g butter, softened, plus extra for greasing
3 egg yolks
olive oil, for oiling

Bring the milk to the boil in a large saucepan with a pinch of salt and a pinch of nutmeg added. Add the semolina slowly, whisking constantly to prevent lumps from forming. Cook for 6–7 minutes, then leave to cool slightly. Preheat the oven to 200°C/Gas 6.

Fold half the Parmesan, 50g of the butter and the egg yolks into the warm semolina, until evenly combined. Spread on an oiled cool marble or metal surface and flatten with a spatula to a 2cm thickness. Leave to cool and set, then cut out rounds using a 3–4cm cutter.

Butter an ovenproof dish and lay the semolina rounds, overlapping, in the dish. Dot with the rest of the butter and sprinkle with the remaining Parmesan. Bake for about 15–20 minutes until browned on top.

Serve sprinkled liberally with coarsely ground black pepper and accompanied by a Basic Tomato Sauce (p315), if you like.

Serves 6–8

" Italians would eat this dish as a first course, but you could also serve it as a side dish to roast meat or a stew. Romans say this recipe was originally made with potatoes and flour rather than semolina, which is how normal gnocchi are made. They also claim that it was a man with poor teeth that developed the recipe. My teeth are OK, but I still like it! **"**

GNOCCHI DI RICOTTA CON SUGO DI PORCINI
RICOTTA DUMPLINGS WITH PORCINI SAUCE

400g fresh ricotta
180g plain flour
4 tbsp dry breadcrumbs, plus
   extra if needed
salt and pepper
freshly grated nutmeg

Sauce
20g dried porcini mushrooms
70g butter
1 garlic clove, crushed
200g fresh porcini mushrooms, finely sliced
1 tbsp torn parsley leaves
2 tbsp dry white wine

To make the dumplings, mix the ricotta, flour and breadcrumbs together, seasoning with salt, pepper and nutmeg to taste. To check that the mixture will stick together (there is no egg here), take a little pellet of the mixture and drop it into boiling salted water. If it falls apart, you need to add some more breadcrumbs to the mixture. When the consistency is right, roll into sausages, 2cm in diameter, and cut into 2–3cm lengths. Press the gnocchi gently on the tines of a fork to give them a rippled effect, rolling them off on to a clean tea towel. Cover and rest for 30 minutes.

Meanwhile for the sauce, soak the porcini in hot water for 20 minutes. Drain and chop the soaked porcini, reserving the liquid. Melt the butter in a pan, add the garlic and fry until softened but not coloured. Immediately add the sliced fresh and dried porcini and sauté for 5–8 minutes. Season with salt and pepper, and add the parsley, wine and porcini liquid (leaving any sediment behind). Bring to the boil and reduce slightly.

Bring a very large pan of salted water to the boil, add the gnocchi and cook for a minute or two, scooping them out with a slotted spoon when they come to the surface. Add them to the porcini sauce and toss to mix. Serve hot, sprinkled with grated Parmesan.

Serves 4

PESCE E FRUTTI DI MARE

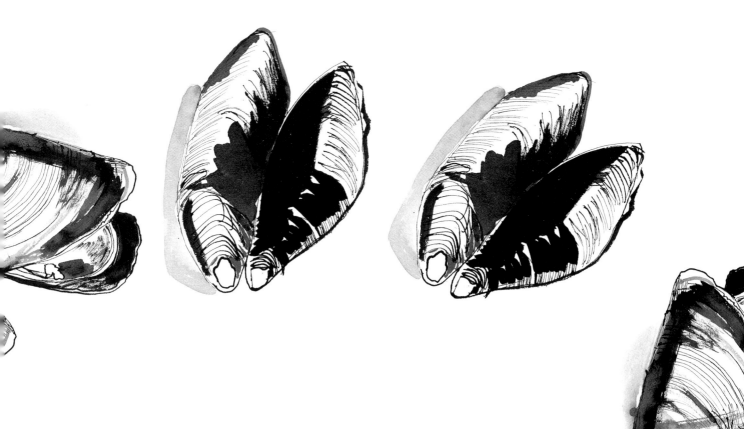

GAMBERONI CON AGLIO, OLIO E PEPERONCINO
SAUTEED GIANT PRAWNS WITH GARLIC, OIL AND CHILLI

16 fresh giant prawns
100ml olive oil
juice of 1 lemon
3 garlic cloves, sliced
1 red chilli, finely chopped

Peel only the body off the prawns, leaving the heads intact (they are full of juice).

Heat the olive oil in a large frying pan until it just starts to sizzle. Add the prawns and, over a high heat, cook them on both sides until they change colour, head included. This should take about 3 minutes. Sprinkle with lemon juice, and add the garlic and chilli.

Serve the prawns on a portion of the sauce in individual bowls. To eat, remove the heads from the prawns and squeeze all the wonderful juices into the sauce.

Serves 4

Extremely simple but very impressive, this dish follows my cooking motto, MOF, MOF (Minimum of Fuss, Maximum of Flavour). However, you do need the freshest prawns you can lay your hands on. The wonderful Imperial Sicilian prawns are best for this recipe, so talk to your fishmonger and see whether he can get hold of some for you.

GAMBERETTI DI MICHELE
MICHELE'S PINK SHRIMPS

500g very fresh pink shrimps
juice of 2 lemons (Sicilian if possible)
80ml olive oil
2 garlic cloves, halved
small bunch of flat-leaf parsley
salt and pepper
50ml brandy

Put the shrimps in an aluminium tray, add the lemon juice, olive oil, garlic, parsley and some salt and pepper. Give it a mix, then add the brandy. Seal the tray with aluminium foil and place on a hot (preferably charcoal) grill. Leave to cook for 20 minutes.

These shrimps are wonderful eaten with your fingers!

Serves 4

" This interesting dish of small prawns is named after a man I met in Palermo, while I was filming a series for BBC TV, who produced it for me on the roadside charcoal grill he was tending. To make it, you will need a rectangular aluminium tray, plus aluminium foil to cover. "

GAMBERI IN SALSA
CRAYFISH IN GREEN SAUCE

4–6 crayfish or scampi per person (depending on size)
salt
1 lemon, cut into wedges

Sauce
3 tbsp chopped mint
4 tbsp chopped flat-leaf parsley
finely grated zest and juice of ½ lemon
½ garlic clove, crushed
1 tbsp white wine vinegar
6 tbsp extra virgin olive oil

To make the sauce, put the herbs, lemon zest and juice, garlic and wine vinegar in a mortar and pound together with the pestle, gradually adding the olive oil to make a textured sauce. (You could use a blender here, but I prefer the sauce with a little texture.)

Cook the crayfish or scampi in lightly salted boiling water for 8 minutes. Drain and shell them, keeping the head and tail attached to the meat.

Serve the freshly boiled scampi or crayfish on a portion of the sauce, with lemon wedges.

Serves 4

To celebrate the very good fish from the lakes and rivers of Umbria, especially the Nera River, here is a traditional recipe, which uses the local crayfish. In Sweden and other parts of the world, including Britain, there are impressive-looking crayfish with very sweet flesh, but I find they are often not meaty enough. I suggest you use scampi instead, which have a different taste but at least they have some meat to eat. This is a wonderful summer starter.

COZZE DEL PESCATORE
FISHERMEN'S MUSSELS

1.5kg mussels
6 tbsp extra virgin olive oil
1 large garlic clove, finely chopped
½ tsp cayenne pepper or chilli pepper
2 tbsp finely chopped flat-leaf parsley
100ml dry white wine
salt

Clean the mussels well (see below). Heat the olive oil in a large lidded pan, and briefly fry the garlic and cayenne or chilli pepper. Add the parsley, wine and mussels then cover with the lid. While holding the lid, shake the pan to allow the mussels to open properly.

After 5 minutes cooking time, make sure that every mussel is open. (Discard any that are still shut.) Season to taste. Transfer to a serving bowl, pouring over the sauce, and serve with crusty country bread.

Serves 4

To clean mussels or clams, scrub them well with water to get rid of sand and barnacles. Pull and cut away any stringy beards. Discard any that do not close when tapped, as they are probably dead. Wash again.

OSTRICHE CON ZABAGLIONE E TARTUFO BIANCO
OYSTERS WITH ZABAGLIONE AND WHITE TRUFFLE

Illustrated on previous page

1 Alba truffle, about 55g
16 fresh oysters, just opened
20g butter
6 egg yolks
150ml dry white wine
juice of ½ lemon
truffle oil
salt and pepper

Clean the truffle very carefully and at the last moment slice it very thinly with a mandoline. Arrange the oysters so that the oyster is displayed in the deeper part of the shell and place 4 to a plate.

Preferably in a zabaglione pan (a copper bowl) over a pan of boiling water, melt the butter, then add the egg yolks, wine, lemon juice, truffle oil and some salt and pepper, and start to whisk. (You could use a double saucepan instead.) Whisk continuously until the mixture becomes semi-stiff.

Spoon this sauce over the oysters, then add a few thin slices of truffle.

Serves 4

CAPESANTE AL BURRO E LIMONE
SCALLOPS WITH BUTTER AND LEMON

12 large scallops, with the corals attached
flour, for dusting
55g butter
juice of ½ lemon
2 tbsp fish stock (p314)
1 tbsp finely chopped flat-leaf parsley
salt and pepper

Dust the scallops with flour. Heat the butter in a pan, add the scallops and fry for 2 minutes on each side. Remove from the pan and set aside.

Add the lemon juice and stock to the pan, stirring to scrape up the sediment from the bottom. If necessary add a little more stock. Stir in the parsley and some salt and pepper. Return the scallops to the pan, heat through briefly and serve.

Serves 4

" Although it's very simple to prepare, this will impress any gourmet, not least because it uses that exclusive fungus, the white truffle. In Italy, the collection of truffles is limited to specially licensed 'trifolau'. With the help of their trained dogs, they rummage through the Alba hills in the middle of the night (so as not to be seen) to get the most expensive food in the world. You could use black truffle here, which would reduce the cost of the dish, though it would also reduce its effect. "

Scallops are one of the most delicate of shellfish. They should be cooked briefly, either by frying or poaching.

POLPI AFFOGATI
STEWED OCTOPUS

8 tbsp olive oil
8 baby octopus, about 120–150g each, cleaned
2 garlic cloves, finely chopped
1 red chilli, finely chopped
500g polpa di pomodoro or chunky passata
bunch of flat-leaf parsley, coarsely chopped
salt and pepper

Heat the olive oil in an earthenware pot or casserole (one with a tight-fitting lid). Add the octopus and fry, stirring, for a minute or so. Add the garlic and chilli and fry for a few seconds, then add the tomato pulp.

Cover with a tight-fitting lid and simmer very gently for 20–30 minutes. The octopus will be cooked by now. Open the lid, scatter in the chopped parsley and season with salt and pepper to taste. Serve with toasted country bread.

Serves 4

For this excellent dish, octopus is cooked in its own juices with tomatoes. You need young octopus, weighing no more than 150g, and they must also be verace (the right kind) identified by the double row of suckers on the tentacles. For me, these are one of the best fish to eat!

SEPPIETTE O CALAMARI RIPIENI DI GRANCHIO
LITTLE CUTTLEFISH OR SQUID STUFFED WITH CRAB

1 cooked medium crab, cleaned
16 small cuttlefish or squid, cleaned but kept whole
5 tbsp olive oil
1 onion, finely chopped
1 tbsp plain flour
4 tbsp milk
2 egg yolks
50g butter
salt and pepper
4 tbsp dry white wine
1 tbsp finely chopped flat-leaf parsley

Remove the meat from the crab and set aside. Rinse the cuttlefish or squid pouches and set aside with the tentacles.

Heat the olive oil in a pan and fry the onion until soft, then stir in the flour. Add the milk and cuttlefish or squid and cook gently, allowing 10–12 minutes for small, 12–18 for larger ones.

Remove the cuttlefish or squid from the sauce. Chop the tentacles very finely and put them into a bowl with the crabmeat, egg yolks and butter. Mix well, seasoning with salt and pepper to taste. Use to stuff the cuttlefish or squid cavities.

Put the stuffed fish back in the sauce. Add the wine and a little water to obtain a thick sauce, and cook slowly for another 10 minutes. Adjust the seasoning and sprinkle with chopped parsley. Serve with polenta.

Serves 4

" The Friulian cuisine is largely based on meat, game, beans and pork, but it is different on the coast, where fish is predominant. This tasty recipe from Grado is eaten locally with fried or grilled polenta. "

CALAMARETTI IN UMIDO
SMALL BRAISED SQUID

1 bread roll, made into breadcrumbs
a little milk, to cover
600g small squid, cleaned
1 garlic clove, very finely chopped
3 tbsp very finely chopped flat-leaf parsley
salt and pepper
4 tbsp extra virgin olive oil
2 large ripe tomatoes, peeled, de-seeded and chopped

Soak the breadcrumbs in a little milk to cover, then squeeze out the excess liquid. Cut off the tentacles from the squid. Chop the tentacles and mix them with the breadcrumbs, garlic, parsley and some salt and pepper. Stuff this mixture into the cavities of the squid, filling them about three-quarters full.

Heat the olive oil in a large pan and briefly fry the squid until they become slightly pinkish in colour. Add the chopped tomatoes and cook for about 15 minutes, until you obtain a lovely sauce.

Serves 4

CALAMARI RIPIENI DI GAMBERI
SQUID STUFFED WITH PRAWNS

8 medium squid (about 800g cleaned weight)
16 small raw prawns, or 8 larger ones, peeled
4 tbsp olive oil
4 tbsp fresh breadcrumbs
2 tbsp finely chopped parsley
1 garlic clove, finely chopped
2 eggs, beaten
salt and pepper
juice of 1 lemon
100ml dry white wine

Unless they are already prepared, clean the squid, cutting off the heads and beak. Leave the pouches whole, and keep the little bunches of tentacles together; discard the heads. Remove the transparent quill from each body pouch, then rinse.

Chop the tentacles finely, and chop the prawns roughly if they are large. Sauté them together in 1 tbsp of the olive oil for 1½ minutes.

For the stuffing, mix the breadcrumbs with the parsley, garlic and eggs, then add the sautéed prawn mixture. Season with salt and pepper and add the lemon juice. Stuff each squid pouch with a little of the mixture and secure the opening with a wooden cocktail stick.

Put the stuffed squid in a pan with the remaining olive oil. Cook over a low heat for 10 minutes, then turn them. Increase the heat a little and pour in the wine. Cook until this has reduced down, then the squid will be ready. Serve with spinach and some good country bread.

Serves 4–6

" This recipe comes from Giulianova in Abbruzi, where it is served in many of the restaurants. I've heard that the idea came from some fisherman who had seen a voracious squid with a whole prawn in its stomach! The rest is easy to imagine. "

" In Italy, dishes that contain seafood and other ingredients
are often cooked together to produce an interesting contrast.
This recipe is a perfect combination of ingredients from the
sea and earth. It would be fantastic eaten with an aperitif, but
also as a light first course accompanied by a green salad. "

FRITTO DI MARE E MONTI
FRIED SEAFOOD AND MUSHROOMS

BRODETTO ALL'ANCONETANA
FISH STEW ANCONA-STYLE
Illustrated overleaf

100g St George's mushrooms
150g fresh ceps
100g raw shrimps
100g raw small prawns
100g whitebait
100g squid or small octopus
salt and pepper
2 eggs, beaten
olive oil, for deep-frying
100g dried breadcrumbs
plain flour, for dusting
2 lemons, quartered

Clean the mushrooms and cut the larger ones in halves or quarters. Prepare all the seafood, cleaning and shelling as appropriate.

Season the beaten eggs, and heat the olive oil in a pan to 180–190°C, until a cube of bread dropped in it browns in 30 seconds.

Dip the mushrooms first in the eggs, then roll in the breadcrumbs. Fry in the hot oil until golden, then remove, drain on kitchen paper, and keep warm. Then dip the fish in the flour and fry in the hot oil until golden.

Serve immediately with the mushrooms and lemon.

Serves 4

1.2kg mixed fresh fish, cleaned
500g mixed fresh shellfish (clams, mussels, opened scallops, prawns)
5 tbsp olive oil
1 large onion, finely sliced
3 garlic cloves, finely chopped
3 tbsp concentrated tomato paste, or 4–5 fresh tomatoes, chopped
a pinch of dried chilli
salt and pepper
3 tbsp coarsely chopped parsley
2 tbsp white wine vinegar
4–6 slices of good country bread, toasted
extra virgin olive oil, for drizzling

Fillet the fish and cut into bite-sized pieces, or leave them whole if small. Scrub the shellfish and clean as appropriate.

Heat the olive oil in a large pan, add the onion and garlic, and fry gently to soften. Add the tomato paste diluted with a little water, or the fresh tomatoes, and a pinch of chilli. Bring to a simmer and cook for 10 minutes, stirring occasionally. Season the sauce with salt and pepper to taste.

Start to add the large pieces of fish to the sauce first, followed by the shellfish and then by the small fish. Cook gently for 5–8 minutes, or until the fish is cooked and the mussels and clams have opened, then add the parsley and wine vinegar. Toss gently to mix.

Serve with toasted bread, which you either put at the bottom of the plate or offer separately. I always add a little stream of extra virgin olive oil on top for flavour.

Serves 4–6

" No other region produces as many different brodetti (somewhere between a fish soup and stew) as the Marche. This is hardly surprising, as many fishing ports along the region's long eastern coastline have excellent fresh fish from the Adriatic every day – often more than a dozen varieties. "

BUTTARICA E UOVA
SALTED MULLET ROE AND SCRAMBLED EGGS

12 eggs
2 tbsp finely chopped parsley
1 tbsp mascarpone or thick double cream
salt and pepper
2 tbsp olive oil
100g mullet bottarga, cut in thin slices

Beat the eggs in a bowl and fold in the parsley and mascarpone or cream. Season with pepper and just a little salt (as the bottarga will be salty).

Heat the olive oil in a pan over a low heat and pour in the egg mixture. Stir constantly until the mixture starts to thicken, then remove from the heat and stir a little bit more until the eggs are softly scrambled and creamy.

Divide the scrambled eggs between warm plates and sprinkle with slices of bottarga. Eat with bread.

Serves 4

Both mullet and tuna roe are cured in salt and air-dried to make bottarga, an expensive speciality in Sicilia and Calabria, as well as Sardinia. The eggs of mullet are more delicate than those of tuna and usually the bottarga is sliced on to food as it is here or grated over pasta.

HERING NACH HAUSFRAUENART
SALT HERRING WITH SOURED CREAM, ONION AND APPLES

8–12 small potatoes, peeled
salt
1 crisp, green dessert apple
fillets of 4 schmaltz herring, not too salty
1 onion, thinly sliced
8 tbsp soured cream

Cook the potatoes in boiling salted water until just tender, then drain. Thinly slice the apple.

Arrange the herring fillets on serving plates along with the apple and onion slices. Add the warm potatoes and drizzle the soured cream on top. Serve with a good glass of schnapps.

Serves 4

" In my limited time in Austria, I learned to appreciate various aspects of Germanic culture. Among other things, I become more punctual and more precise – as an Italian I needed to! Regarding food, I appreciated everything that tasted good. This recipe reminds me of Hamburg, but herrings are popular in Trentino and prepared similarly. "

UCCELLETTI DI MARE ALLO SPIEDO
SEAFOOD ON A SKEWER

800g mixed fresh firm seafood (such as octopus,
   squid, large prawns, cuttlefish, shelled scallops)
150g fresh white breadcrumbs
3 tbsp finely chopped parsley
salt and pepper
olive oil
lemon juice

Pre-soak some wooden kebab skewers in water for around 30 minutes (to prevent them scorching during cooking). Clean the fish as necessary, peeling the prawns but leaving the tail shells intact. Cut the other seafood into chunks, roughly the size of an apricot. Thread these alternately onto double skewers to hold securely.

Mix the breadcrumbs with the parsley, and season with some salt and pepper. Brush the fish with olive oil, then dust with the savoury breadcrumbs on all sides.

Grill or barbecue the kebabs for 3–4 minutes, turning to colour on all sides, and basting with lemon juice and olive oil as they cook. Serve immediately.

Serves 4–6

❝ The literal translation of uccelletti is 'sparrows' but don't be alarmed. There are no birds here, just the very freshest morsels of seafood to grill at home, or on the barbecue. From Marche down towards the south, you will come across fresh breadcrumbs mixed with very finely chopped parsley, sprinkled on to foods for added flavour. ❞

INSALATA DI GIANCHETTI
NEWBORN FISH SALAD

300g gianchetti (newborn fish)
salt and pepper
juice of ½ lemon
3 tbsp olive oil
1 tbsp finely chopped chives
1 lemon, cut into wedges

Wash and drain the gianchetti. Plunge into a pot of slightly salted boiling water for 1 minute or less and drain well.

While still warm, mix with the lemon juice and olive oil. Season with salt and pepper to taste, and add the chives. Serve with lemon wedges and accompany with toasted country bread.

Serves 6

PESCE IN SAOR
SWEET-AND-SOUR FISH

800g fresh sardines, scaled and cleaned
flour, for dusting
olive oil, for shallow-frying
500g onions, sliced
50g pine nuts
50g sultanas
50g caster sugar
50ml white wine vinegar
pepper

Dust the cleaned fish with flour, then shallow-fry in olive oil until crisp and brown on both sides. Drain well on kitchen paper, then arrange the sardines in a single layer in a shallow dish.

Gently fry the onions in the same pan, adding a little more oil if necessary, until soft, then add the pine nuts, sultanas and sugar. Stir well, then add the wine vinegar and allow to evaporate a little.

Pour the sweet-and-sour mixture over the fish and leave to cool, then refrigerate for at least 24 hours. Eat cold, sprinkled with pepper.

Serves 6

Venetians adore fish, and this special way of cooking – frying and then marinating – is also applied inland to freshwater fish. It is a good way to preserve a bumper crop of fish, and a lovely antipasto dish. Prepare a day in advance to allow time for the marinade to flavour the fish.

SARDINE ALLA GRIGLIA CON SALMORIGLIO
GRILLED FRESH SARDINES WITH GREEN SALSA

16 large fresh sardines, scaled and cleaned
salt
1 lemon, cut into quarters

Salmoriglio
150ml extra virgin olive oil
juice of 2 lemons, finely grated rind of 1
1 small chilli, finely chopped
1 garlic clove, very finely chopped
4 tbsp finely chopped parsley

Preheat the barbecue or charcoal grill to hot.

Mix the salmoriglio ingredients together in a small bowl.

Put the sardines directly onto a hot charcoal grill. Sprinkle them with salt, brush with a little of the salmoriglio and cook for 5 minutes per side. Serve the sardines either hot or cold, with the lemon quarters and the remainder of the salmoriglio.

Serves 4

" These little fish, which, like mackerel, contain oils that are beneficial to our health, are popular throughout the Mediterranean. This quick, tasty dish can also be eaten in smaller portions as a wonderful antipasto. **"**

ORATA ALL'ACQUA PAZZA
POACHED SEA BREAM

2 sea bream, about 600g each, cleaned
bunch of flat-leaf parsley
bunch of chervil
16 lemon slices
500ml water
200ml olive oil
50g salt
black peppercorns

Put the fish in a shallow pan large enough to take both with not much space around them. Divide the herbs and lemon slices between the fish, pushing them into the cavities. Pour in the water and olive oil, which should cover the fish. Add the salt and a few peppercorns.

Put the pan on the stove and bring to the boil quickly. Reduce the heat and simmer slowly for 15–18 minutes. Serve with boiled Savoy cabbage.

Serves 4

" In a few restaurants offering southern Italian food, you may find this curious recipe. I have called it alla aqua pazza, which translates literally as cooked in 'mad water', though it is often found as all'acqua di mare, as it is usually cooked in seawater. As unpolluted seawater may be difficult to come by, here I have simply added salt to ordinary water to re-create the effect. "

CHENELLE DI LUCCIO CON SPUGNOLE
QUENELLES OF PIKE WITH MOREL SAUCE

400g fillet of pike, cleaned and completely boned
3 large egg whites
1g saffron strands, or the equivalent of saffron powder
salt and pepper
400ml double cream
chervil sprigs, to garnish

Sauce
2 small onions, very finely sliced
100g unsalted butter
55g dried morels, soaked in warm water for 2 hours
   (reserve the water)
2 tbsp balsamic vinegar
4 tbsp dry Sherry
6 tbsp double cream

Put the fish fillets, egg whites, saffron and seasoning in a blender and process until completely smooth. Don't overbeat, though: the mixture must be cold. Put into an iced bowl (or a bowl sitting in a heap of ice cubes). In a separate bowl, whip the cream to soft peaks. Gently fold the cream into the fish mixture Leave to chill in the fridge for a few hours.

To make the sauce, fry the onions in the butter until transparent. Add the pre-soaked morels and cook for 10–15 minutes, then add the balsamic vinegar, Sherry, cream and some salt and pepper. Cook gently for a further 10 minutes. You may need to thin the sauce at this stage: add a little of the morel soaking water to the pan.

In a wide shallow pan bring some salted water to the boil, then turn down to a simmer. With 2 dessertspoons shape the pike mixture into quenelles, and then lower them into the simmering water. Be very careful not to increase the temperature of the water at all. After 8–10 minutes of gentle simmering, remove the quenelles with a slotted spoon and drain well.

Place the quenelles in hot bowls on top of the warm morel sauce. Garnish with the chervil sprigs and serve immediately. This dish can be accompanied by boiled rice and a Florence fennel salad.

Serves 4

LUCCIO IN SALSA VERDE
PIKE WITH GREEN SAUCE

4 pike steaks, about 200g each
olive oil
2 garlic cloves, very finely chopped
3 tbsp very finely chopped parsley
salt and pepper
1 lemon, cut into quarters

Trim the pike steaks. Pour enough olive oil to cover the steaks into a shallow pan just big enough to hold them. Bring the oil up to a simmering point, then add the garlic and parsley. Make sure that the oil is not too hot, then add the pike steaks. Cook over a low heat for 15 minutes, or until you see little white balls forming in the oil. This is the fish protein coagulating. The oil should not bubble at all.

Drain the fish, season to taste, and serve with a spoonful of the 'green' oil, the lemon quarters and some boiled potatoes.

Serves 4

The idea for this recipe comes from the Basque region of Spain, where I enjoyed merluza in salsa verde or cod in green sauce. To cook, you will need to use a good amount of olive oil; this imparts flavour as well as cooking the fish.

TROTA AL TARTUFO NERO
TROUT WITH BLACK TRUFFLE

85g black truffle
4 brown trout
plain flour, for dusting
1 garlic clove
60g butter
1 tsp truffle oil (optional)
4 tbsp dry white wine
salt and pepper

Clean the truffle well, and then cut into small cubes. Clean, scale and gut the trout, then dust with flour. Rub a large frying pan with the garlic, then discard.

Melt the butter in the pan and fry the trout until slightly brown, about 4–5 minutes on each side. Add the truffle oil, if using, the cubed truffle and the wine, and deglaze the pan by boiling for a minute or two, stirring to release any stuck-on juices. Season to taste.

Serve the fish with freshly boiled waxy potatoes and some of the sauce.

Serves 4

TROTA AL CARTOCCIO
TROUT BAKED IN FOIL

4 rainbow trout, about 250g each
32 thin slices of lemon
salt and pepper
small bunch of chervil, divided into 4
bunch of parsley, divided into 4
100g unsalted butter

Preheat the oven to 200°C/Gas 6. Have ready 4 pieces of foil large enough to wrap the fish fairly loosely.

Clean the trout and remove the scales and all the innards (or get your fishmonger to do this). Wash the trout, and dry them. Cut off the fins. Make 4 incisions in one side of each fish with a knife.

Arrange the 4 pieces of foil on your work surface, and on each, place 4 slices of lemon. In the cavity of each fish, put some salt and pepper, a quarter of the herbs and 15g butter, cut into small pieces. Close the trout and place each one on top of the lemon slices on the foil, cut-side up. Divide the remaining butter, in pieces, between the fish, rubbing into the cuts. Season each fish with salt and pepper, then add another 4 lemon slices to the top of each. Close the foil around each fish to produce a bag.

Bake in the oven for 20 minutes. The fish are delicious served with a simple boiled potato salad.

Serves 4

“ Umbria is the main black truffle region in Italy. The local Urbani brothers have the monopoly of 80 per cent of the world truffle market. When I was in Norcia, part of Umbria, I was invited to join a truffle hunt and to eat a local trout caught in the river Nera. The trout was served with a summer truffle, with some truffle oil added for extra flavour. But if you cook with the black winter truffle, you won't need extra flavouring. ”

This cooking method, designed to keep in all the juices and aromas, has been in use since Roman times. Then, they would cook foods enclosed in terracotta, while now we wrap in foil and oven bake to achieve the same result. So long as the little packages are well sealed, you could also try cooking this on a charcoal grill.

BACCALA MANTECATO
DRIED COD VICENZA STYLE

1 baccalà (dried cod), about 1kg
1½ tsp freshly grated nutmeg
salt and pepper
300ml extra virgin olive oil
1 tbsp very finely chopped parsley

Polenta
300g quick polenta
salt
1.5 litres water
50g butter
50g Parmesan, grated

Beat the dried cod vigorously with a mallet to break up the fibres, then cover and soak in cold water for 48 hours.

Drain the fish and put into a pan. Add water to cover, bring to the boil and cook for 10 minutes. Drain, then remove the skin and reserve. Take off all the bones and fins. Break the flesh into flakes with a fork, then put into a steamer with the skin and steam for 1½ hours.

Push the gelatinous skin through a sieve into a bowl. Flake the fish and add to the bowl. Add the nutmeg, salt and pepper, and start to beat with a wooden spoon. Continue to beat, adding a little stream of olive oil from time to time, as if making mayonnaise. As you beat, the mixture will swell and become whitish in colour.

Meanwhile, make the polenta (get a helper to do this if possible, while you beat the baccalà!). Put the polenta, pinch of salt and water in a pan and heat, stirring, until thickened and cooked (following the packet instructions). Stir in the butter and Parmesan.

When all the oil is incorporated into the baccalà, return to the pan and heat through, stirring, for a couple of minutes, then add the parsley. Eat with the polenta.

Serves 6

" This dish is typical of Vicenza, but you will find it all over Veneto. I still find it interesting that with all the abundance of fresh fish from lakes, rivers and sea, preserved cod from Norway is considered a delicacy in many parts of Italy. "

BISATO SUL'ARA
EEL BAKED WITH BAY LEAVES

20–30 bay leaves
8 large chunks of fresh eel, about 110g each, cleaned
salt and pepper
1 lemon, cut into wedges

Preheat the oven to 200°C/Gas 6.

Lay the bay leaves over the bottom of a shallow baking dish, then place the chunks of eel on top.

Bake in the oven for 30–35 minutes, or until the eel is tender. The fat in the eels and the bay leaves will be enough to flavour the dish.

Season the eels with salt and pepper to taste and serve, with lemon wedges.

Serves 4

" This typical Venetian recipe is traditionally eaten on Christmas Eve. It originates from the Comacchio Valley, south of Chioggia, where the eels are wonderful and fat. This recipe calls for chunks from a large eel and bay leaves only. Oven baking does the rest, as it regulates the amount of fat and cooks the eels perfectly. I suggest you accompany the dish with a beetroot salad. "

TRIGLIE CON CANTARELLI
RED MULLET WITH CHANTERELLES

250g chanterelles
4 red mullet fillets, about 400g
6 tbsp olive oil
juice of 1 lime
salt and pepper
1 shallot, very finely chopped
1 tbsp brandy
4 tbsp double cream
1 tbsp finely chopped parsley

Clean and trim the mushrooms. Marinate the fish fillets in 2 tablespoons of the olive oil with the lime juice and some salt and pepper for 2 hours.

In a pan, heat the rest of the oil and fry the shallot gently to soften. Add the mushrooms and fry gently for 5 minutes. Add the brandy and, when the alcohol has evaporated, the cream, salt, pepper and parsley.

In a non-stick pan, fry the fish fillets skin-side down until the skin is crisp and the flesh is cooked. This should take about 5–8 minutes. Add any remaining marinade to the pan, and heat gently.

Serve the fish immediately on hot plates with the mushrooms at the side. Eat with good country bread.

Serves 4

TRIGLIE AL POMODORO
RED MULLET WITH TOMATOES

4 red mullet, about 300g each, gutted, trimmed
  and scaled
6 tbsp olive oil
2 shallots, finely chopped
1 garlic clove, finely chopped
700g polpa di pomodoro or chunky passata
6 basil leaves
salt and pepper
1 lemon, cut into quarters

In a frying pan large enough to hold all 4 fish, heat the olive oil. Add the shallots and garlic, and sauté gently until cooked but not coloured, about 5 minutes. Add the tomato pulp, basil and some salt and pepper to taste, then bring to the boil.

Reduce the heat to medium, add the fish and cook for about 6 minutes on each side.

Serve the fish whole on individual plates with the lemon quarters and topped with some of the intensely flavoured sauce. Good country bread is all that you need by way of accompaniment.

Serves 4

❝ For me, there is nothing more delicious than freshly caught red mullet fried in olive oil until crisp. For you, however, the easier option might be to find a fishmonger who has already filleted some fish for you. Here I have combined the red mullet with lovely little chanterelles. ❞

This delicate, simple dish also lends itself very well to being served with pasta. Simply bone and fillet the fish before cooking as above and serving with linguine.

CIPOLLOTTI E TONNO
TUNA AND ONIONS

8–10 salad or large spring onions,
  halved and soaked in water for 1 hour
300g canned tuna in oil, drained
6 tbsp extra virgin olive oil
10 salted capers, soaked, drained and chopped
juice of 1 lemon
salt and pepper
2 tbsp chopped celery leaves

Slice the onions very finely. In a bowl, break the tuna into smaller chunks and mix with the onions. Mix together the oil, capers, lemon juice, salt and plenty of pepper. Decorate with the celery leaves and eat as an antipasto with some good country bread.

This dish looks very simple, and indeed it is , but it is definitely very good. To make it you need large spring or salad onions with the fresh green stalk still attached at the top. The celery leaves can be taken from the centre of the celery, but in Italy they have a small celery which is grown especially for its leaves, which are more intense in flavour.

PESCE SPADA MUDDICA
GRILLED BREADED SWORDFISH

4 swordfish (or tuna) steaks, about 150g each
150g fresh white breadcrumbs, finely processed
2 tbsp extra virgin olive oil
1 garlic clove, puréed
1 tbsp very finely chopped parsley
salt and pepper

Preheat the grill to medium-hot, and have the fish at room temperature.

Place the breadcrumbs, olive oil, garlic and parsley in a bowl and season to taste with salt and pepper. Mix the ingredients with your fingers to obtain almost moist but loose breadcrumbs. Coat the fish steaks with the breadcrumb mixture on both sides.

Put the coated steaks under the preheated grill and cook for 5 minutes on each side. Serve with a rocket and chicory salad.

Serves 4

" Muddica is a sort of magic ingredient for Sicilians. Basically, it is fresh, flavoured breadcrumbs, which are used in a variety of ways – to stuff sardines, to coat a slice of fish to be grilled, as here, or even as a cheap, delicious alternative to sprinkling Parmesan on pasta. "

PESCE SPADA ALLA GHIOTTA
BRAISED SWORDFISH

8 thin slices fresh swordfish, about 60g each
4 tbsp olive oil
1 onion, finely chopped
500g polpa di pomodoro or chunky passata
salt and pepper

The stuffing

5 tbsp fresh breadcrumbs
30g salted capers, soaked, drained and chopped
50g pitted black olives, chopped
2 tbsp olive oil
4 tbsp orange juice

To make the stuffing, mix all the ingredients together and season with pepper to taste.

Lay the slices of swordfish on a surface and divide the stuffing mixture between them. Roll up tightly to enclose the filling and secure with wooden cocktail sticks.

Heat 3 tbsp of the olive oil in a large frying pan, add the swordfish rolls and fry gently, turning carefully, until brown on all sides. Remove from the pan, and set aside. Add a little more olive oil to the pan and fry the onion until soft. Add the tomato pulp and cook gently for 20 minutes. Season with salt and pepper to taste.

Place the fish rolls in the sauce, and heat gently for 5 minutes to let the flavours mingle. Serve the braised swordfish rolls at once. Green beans are a suitable accompaniment.

Serves 4

" Calabria is the place in Italy to eat swordfish, and in Bagnara this recipe is common in both family homes and restaurants. In Calabria and Sicily, a ghiotta means 'extremely desirable to eat'. The fish is cooked in a rich tomato sauce, which you will find not only here, but also in Messina, on the other side of the 'pond'. The best part to use for this dish is the ventresca, the belly of this big fish. "

SOGLIOLA CON GAMBESECCHE
DOVER SOLE WITH FAIRY-RING CHAMPIGNONS

4 medium Dover sole
plain flour, for dusting
55g butter
parsley leaves (optional)

Sauce
400g fairy-ring champignons
1 shallot, very finely chopped
40g butter
75ml dry white wine
juice of 1 lemon
2 tbsp finely chopped parsley
2 tbsp dill leaves (optional)
salt and pepper

Clean and skin the fish (or ask the fishmonger to do this for you), then dust with flour. Fry the sole on each side in the butter until crisp. You may have to use 2 large frying pans because Dover sole are normally quite sizeable. While you are preparing the sauce, keep the soles warm in a low oven.

Clean the mushrooms well. Fry the shallot in the butter until soft. Add the mushrooms and stir-fry for a few minutes. Add the wine and lemon juice, and stir for another minute. Add the herbs and finally some salt and pepper. Mix well and set aside.

Fillet the sole carefully by making an incision in the middle of the spine lengthways. Then cut off and discard the edges, fins, tail and head. Carefully lift one of the upper fillets, starting from the centre. If the sole is well cooked, this should come off the bone easily. Do the same with the other. When both upper fillets are off, remove the main bone leaving the lower part of the sole intact. Repeat with all 4 fish. To serve, put the lower fillet on a hot plate, arrange some of the mushroom mixture lengthways along this, and put the 2 upper fillets on top. Decorate with a little parsley, if using, and serve accompanied by plain boiled potatoes.

Serves 4

❝ The Dover sole is to me the height of marine deliciousness. Whichever way you cook it, it is always wonderful, but combined with the delicate fairy-ring champignon, it becomes a dish worthy of serving at the most demanding table. To retain every morsel of full flavour I prefer to cook the fish on the bone, then fillet it before serving. ❞

CARNE

" This simple recipe honours the fishermen of the little island of Burano, in the lagoon of Venice. Their houses, like this dish, are painted in wild colours – supposedly because when they have been drinking they are more likely to recognise the colour than the house number! "

POLLO ALLA BURANEA
CHICKEN BURANO-STYLE

PETTI DI POLLO ALLA PIZZAIOLA
BREAST OF CHICKEN IN PIZZAIOLA SAUCE

1 chicken, about 1.5kg
100g luganega sausage
50g lard (or pork fat), cut into small pieces
2 tbsp olive oil
1 onion, finely chopped
2 celery stalks, diced
2 carrots, diced
1 garlic clove, sliced
1 small rosemary sprig
finely grated zest and juice of 1 lemon
20 large pitted green olives
50ml dry white wine
100ml chicken stock (p314)
salt and pepper
2 tbsp grappa

Cut the chicken into 12 meaty chunks. Remove the skin from the sausage and pinch the sausage meat into pieces. Melt the lard with the olive oil in a casserole dish. Add the chicken, sausage, vegetables, garlic, rosemary and lemon zest, and fry, stirring, for a few minutes until the chicken is lightly coloured.

Add the olives, wine, stock and some salt and pepper. Cover and cook very gently on the hob for 1 hour, or until the chicken is tender. Add more stock or water during cooking if needed.

Just before serving, add the lemon juice and grappa. Accompany with boiled potatoes.

Serves 6

Luganega sausage is a long, thin fresh pork sausage made with relatively coarsely minced pork. Such sausages are very common in Italy, especially in the northern regions.

4 skinless boneless chicken breasts
4 tbsp extra virgin olive oil
2 garlic cloves, finely chopped
1 tbsp salted capers, soaked and drained
1 tsp chopped flat-leaf parsley
2 anchovy fillets in oil, drained and chopped
500g polpa di pomodoro or chunky passata
1 tbsp roughly chopped oregano leaves
salt and pepper

Fry the chicken breasts in the olive oil for about 8–10 minutes on each side, until brown and cooked through. Add the garlic, capers, parsley and anchovies to the pan and fry briefly, then stir in the tomatoes, oregano and salt and pepper. Simmer for 5 minutes and then serve.

Serves 4

" Pizzaiola sauce originally came from Naples and contains more or less the same ingredients as pizza topping, hence the name. **"**

CHICKEN ESCALOPES WITH SHAGGY INK CAPS

400g young shaggy ink cap mushrooms
4 skinless, boneless chicken breasts
plain flour, for dusting
85g butter
4 tbsp olive oil
75ml medium Sherry
4 tbsp roughly chopped dill leaves
juice of ½ lemon
salt and pepper

Clean and trim the mushrooms.

Cut the chicken breasts into 4 pieces each, and beat them out between pieces of cling film until thin. Dust the pieces with flour and fry on each side in a pan in the hot butter and oil until brown. Remove the chicken and set aside.

In the same pan, fry the mushrooms for a few minutes. Add the Sherry and fry for a few minutes to evaporate the alcohol. Add the chicken again, along with any juices that have collected on the plate, and cook for a little longer to let the flavours amalgamate and the chicken finish cooking. Add the dill, lemon juice and salt and pepper to taste.

Serves 4

" These mushrooms appeared on my lawn just in time for this book! You shouldn't use or drink alcohol when cooking or eating them as they may cause a reaction, so I have used a very small amount for flavour. The problem disappears in cooking. "

CHICKEN BAKED WITH ROSEMARY AND GARLIC

1 chicken, about 2kg
8 garlic heads, whole
2 rosemary sprigs
6 tbsp olive oil
salt and pepper
150ml dry white wine

Preheat the oven to 200°C/Gas 6. Put the chicken into a casserole dish or baking tray. Add the garlic and rosemary and then pour in the olive oil. Sprinkle with salt and pepper to taste, then mix with your hands to coat everything well with oil.

Put into the preheated oven and bake for 1½ hours. Halfway through this cooking time, pour in the wine and mix well.

Continue to the end of the cooking time, remove from the oven and serve with spinach or a green salad.

Serves 4–6

Needless to say, for this dish I would use one of those chickens which has lived in the courtyard and eaten the odd seed and piece of corn scratched out of the soil – naturally free-range. Italians like this simple dish, which is good hot or cold.

POLLO STUFATO CON BOLETI

CHICKEN CASSEROLE WITH TWO TYPES OF BOLETE

350g mixed fresh ceps and orange birch boletes,
  cleaned weight
600g boneless chicken pieces
plain flour, for dusting
6 tbsp olive oil
1 onion, finely chopped
55g butter
300g polpa di pomodoro or chunky passata
freshly grated nutmeg
1 thyme sprig
2 tbsp chopped parsley
150ml dry white wine
salt and pepper

Clean and slice the mushrooms. Dust the pieces of chicken in flour and fry them in the olive oil until brown all over. Put to one side.

Add the onion and butter to the oil, along with the sliced mushrooms, and fry for a minute or two. Add the tomato pulp, a pinch of nutmeg, thyme and parsley and cook for a further 2 minutes. Add the wine, salt and pepper.

Return the chicken to the pan, along with any juices, and cook together for a further 15 minutes. Serve with rice.

Serves 4

" Chicken may be the most popular meat in the world, but very often it lacks flavour because it has been battery-raised. For this recipe you have to find the most wonderful chicken, organic and, if possible, reared outdoors. The two boletes provide an irresistible combination; bear in mind, though, that while the orange birch bolete always blackens when cooked, the cep remains immaculately white. The less flavoursome alternative would be to use cultivated mushrooms. "

FAGIANO DEL BRACCONIERE
POACHER'S PHEASANT

a brace of large pheasants, prepared for cooking
6 tbsp extra virgin olive oil
1 large onion, finely sliced
100g speck, cut into small strips
3 cloves
10 juniper berries, crushed
400g mixed wild mushrooms (you could also
    add some reconstituted dried ceps)
4 tbsp concentrated tomato paste
100ml red wine
100ml chicken stock (p314)
salt and pepper

Preheat the oven to 200°C/Gas 6.

Brown the pheasants on all sides in the olive oil in a large cast-iron casserole. Quarter the birds, and cut the leg and thigh pieces in half.

Fry the onion and speck for a few minutes in the same oil, then add the cloves, juniper berries, mushrooms and tomato paste. Stir-fry for a few minutes, then add the wine.

Return the pheasant pieces to the dish, pour over the stock and season to taste with salt and pepper. Cover and braise for 1 hour in the preheated oven, then check for tenderness and seasoning. Serve with boiled rice or polenta.

Serves 4

If you are having difficulty finding the requisite quantity of wild mushrooms you could always add some rehydrated dried ceps instead.

FAGIANO TARTUFATO
TRUFFLED PHEASANT

2 cock pheasants, boned, leaving the legs and wings
80g black truffle
200g Parma ham (on the fatty side), finely chopped
1 tbsp coarsely chopped flat-leaf parsley
salt and pepper
8 slices pancetta (or streaky bacon)
olive oil, to brush
50g butter
150ml double cream
3 tbsp brandy
truffle oil (optional)

Preheat the oven to 200°C/Gas 6. Have the boned pheasants ready. For the stuffing, grate 30g of the truffle and mix with the Parma ham, parsley and some salt and pepper. Put the pheasants flat on their backs, spread the stuffing on top and roll to enclose. Wrap 4 pancetta slices around each bird and tie with kitchen string, to form sausage shapes.

Brush the birds with olive oil. Heat a frying pan, then add the birds and brown for 2 minutes on each side. Take out the pheasants, wrap in foil and bake in the oven for 20 minutes. Put the frying pan to one side.

Slice the remaining truffle, then cut into tiny strips. Put into the frying pan with the butter, cream, brandy and a few drops of truffle oil, if using. Add salt and plenty of pepper, heat gently and allow to reduce a little.

Take the pheasants out of the foil. Cut into slices, discarding the string, and arrange on warm plates. Pour the truffle sauce over the meat and serve. Braised Savoy cabbage and buttered turnips would go very well here. *Buon Natale!*

Serves 4–6

" This is something the Tuscans eat during the hunting season, and it would make a wonderful festive dish. Considering it is finished with a little cream, it may be one of those dishes returned to Italy from France. Ask your butcher to bone the pheasants … he will be delighted! "

" Sardinians are fine hunters and birds of all kinds and sizes are traditionally cooked either at home in the oven or outdoors on a spit. Quail is now a protected bird, so you will need to use farmed quail for this very easy recipe. "

QUAGLIE ARROSTO
ROASTED QUAIL

8 quail, cleaned and oven-ready
flour, for dusting
50g butter
50ml olive oil
1 large onion, finely chopped
100ml dry Vernaccia or other dry white wine
100ml chicken stock (p314)
1 rosemary sprig
6 sage leaves
salt and pepper
freshly grated nutmeg

Preheat the oven to 190°C/Gas 5. Dust the quail with flour. Heat the butter and olive oil in a heavy-based pan and brown the quail for about 30 seconds on each side. Transfer to a roasting pan. Add the onion to the frying pan and fry, stirring, over a medium heat until softened, then add to the quail.

Pour the wine and stock over the quail and add the rosemary, sage, and some salt and pepper. Cook in the preheated oven for 20 minutes, then transfer the quail to a warm dish and set aside.

Discard the herbs and pass the cooking liquor through a sieve into a pan. Reheat, add a little nutmeg and check the seasoning. Pour over the quail and serve.

Sardinians would eat just bread with this, but you may prefer to serve it with a green salad or some peas and broad beans tossed in butter with a little grated pecorino cheese.

Serves 4

QUAGLIE ALLO SPIEDO
QUAIL ON A SKEWER

8 meaty quail
10 pieces of country white bread,
    about 4cm square and 1cm thick
10 thin slices of pancetta,
    the same shape as the bread squares

Basting liquid
4 tbsp olive oil
juice of 1 lemon
1 tbsp finely chopped flat-leaf parsley
2 tbsp dry marsala
1 tsp honey
1 garlic clove, very finely chopped
salt and pepper

Preheat the oven to 250°C/Gas 9. Clean the quail and remove and discard the livers if necessary. Roast the birds for 15 minutes. Remove from the oven and thread them on 2 long skewers, alternating them with the bread and pancetta.

Mix together all the ingredients for the basting liquid, adding lots of salt and pepper. Cook the quail over a wood-fired or charcoal grill for 10–15 minutes, basting their breasts regularly with the liquid and turning the skewers often to prevent the quail burning. When they are golden brown, serve with the bread croûtes, which will have collected some of the juices from the birds, and with polenta.

Serves 4

This Tuscan dish used to be made with a variety of birds. Nowadays the hunting of many birds is restricted, but good-quality raised quail make a fine substitute.

ANATRA ARROSTO CON GRASSO DI PROSCIUTTO
ROAST DUCK WITH PARMA HAM FAT

200g Parma ham fat (from a friendly grocer)
  or pork lard, finely minced or chopped
10g black peppercorns, crushed
1 garlic clove, puréed
freshly grated nutmeg
ground cinnamon
1 tbsp each of finely chopped rosemary needles
  and sage leaves
1 duck, about 2kg
4 tbsp olive oil
salt

Preheat the oven to 200°C/Gas 6.

Mix the ham fat or lard with the peppercorns, garlic, a pinch of nutmeg, a pinch of cinnamon, rosemary and sage until you have a solid paste.

In a roasting tin, coat the duck with the olive oil, and sprinkle a little salt inside and outside. Spread the fatty paste onto the duck breasts, then cover the roasting tin with foil. Roast the duck in the preheated oven for an hour. Remove the foil and return to the oven for a further 30 minutes, basting with the copious fat.

Serve the duck meat with pieces of the delicious skin.

Serves 4–6

" Where else would a dish like this be cooked if not in the 'fatherland' of poetry and pigs? Emilia Romagna, of course. **"**

Parma ham fat may be difficult to find in this proportion outside of Italy (but get to know your local deli well!). Instead you could use lardo, the Italian lard, which is preserved in pieces and rolled as you would bacon. The rendered pork lard is not the same thing at all, but you could use it as a last resort: it is already a paste, which you can mix with the herbs.

PERNICE ALLA SARDA
PARTRIDGE SARDINIAN-STYLE

1 litre chicken or vegetable stock (p314)
4 partridges, cleaned
8 tbsp extra virgin olive oil
4 tbsp white wine vinegar
3 tbsp coarsely chopped flat-leaf parsley
3 tbsp salted capers, soaked, drained and chopped
a few rosemary sprigs
salt and pepper

Bring the stock to the boil in a large cooking pot, add the partridges and simmer for 25 minutes until tender. Drain and leave to cool, then quarter the birds.

Mix the olive oil, wine vinegar, parsley and capers together in a shallow dish and add the rosemary sprigs. Add the cold partridge pieces and turn to coat with the mixture. Cover and leave to marinate in the fridge for at least 6 hours before eating, turning the birds from time to time.

Season the partridge pieces as you eat them, with your hands naturally. The traditional accompaniment is carta da musica, the thin Sardinian bread, made more crispy in the oven and sprinkled with the oil of the marinade.

Serves 4–6

“ When I was in Sardinia I couldn't believe the luxury of eating partridges this way, cold. They prepare thrushes in a similar way, marinating the birds with myrtle leaves and salt for a few days before eating them. Serve as an antipasto or snack. ”

COLOMBACCIO RIPIENO
STUFFED WOOD PIGEON

4 boned wood pigeon
8 thin slices pancetta
4 tbsp extra virgin olive oil

Stuffing
85g fresh white breadcrumbs
2 eggs, beaten
85g mortadella, cut into little cubes
3 tbsp coarsely chopped flat-leaf parsley
30g Parmesan, freshly grated
salt and pepper

Sauce
50g butter
4 tbsp balsamic vinegar
pepper

Preheat the oven to 180°C/Gas 4.

Combine all the stuffing ingredients, mixing well, then season with salt and pepper. Stuff into the cavities of the birds. Cover the breasts with 2 slices of pancetta per bird and secure with wooden cocktail sticks. Brush the birds with the olive oil, and roast, breast down, in the preheated oven for 15 minutes. Turn over, breasts up, and roast for a further 15 minutes. Baste with the cooking juice.

Make the sauce by melting the butter in a pan. When melted and hot, add the balsamic vinegar and some black pepper. Let it evaporate a little.

Serve the pigeon on hot plates with a little of the sauce, and accompanied by baked potatoes or spinach.

Serves 4

Stuffing boned birds is an unusual way of preparing game. It is easier to bone a chicken or duck, but with a little patience and a sharp knife, you should be able to bone your own birds. However, in case you find yourself totally incapable, then persuade your trusted game dealer or butcher to do it for you.

LEPRE IN SALMI
JUGGED HARE

1 large hare, including the blood, about 3kg
55g plain flour
100g butter
1 onion, very finely chopped
100g pancetta, cut into small pieces
200g calves liver, cut into small strips
3 tbsp brandy
55g bitter chocolate
salt and pepper

Marinade
1 bottle of strong red wine, such as Barolo
1 carrot, finely diced
1 onion, finely chopped
4 celery stalks, finely diced
1 garlic clove, smashed
a few thyme sprigs
a few marjoram sprigs
a few sage leaves
a few bay leaves
10 juniper berries
1 tsp black peppercorns, lightly crushed

Mix together all the marinade ingredients. Cut the hare into large chunks, add to the marinade, then cover and leave in the fridge for 24 hours.

Remove the chunks of hare from the marinade and pat dry, then dust them in some of the flour. Heat the butter in a large cast-iron pan and fry the pieces of meat, a few at a time, until browned all over. Remove from the pan and set aside. Reduce the heat, add the onion and pancetta to the pan and fry until the onion begins to colour. Return the meat to the pan together with the blood, calves liver and the marinade. Cover and cook gently for 2 hours, or until the meat is tender.

Remove the pieces of hare and liver from the pan. Strain the sauce through a fine sieve and discard the solids. Mix together the brandy and just enough of any remaining flour to make a paste. Put the meat and the strained liquid back in the pan and bring to the boil. Whisk in the brandy paste a little at a time to thicken. Let it boil for a minute or two, then add the chocolate, allow it to dissolve and season with salt and pepper to taste.

Serve the hare with polenta and the sauce with pappardelle. Hare cooked like this can be kept for a couple of days.

Serves 6

" A classic of northern cuisine, this is usually served with polenta while the sauce is served separately with pappardelle. "

CONIGLIO AFFOGATO ALLA LIGURE
RABBIT STEW LIGURIAN-STYLE

1 rabbit, about 1.5 kg, cut into chunks
flour, for dusting
125ml Ligurian extra virgin olive oil
1 large onion, thinly sliced
1 garlic clove, coarsely chopped
1 rosemary sprig
a few sage leaves
a small thyme sprig
100g pitted black olives, preferably Taggiasca
2 glasses of dry white wine
8 tbsp polpa di pomodoro or chunky passata
salt and pepper
a little stock, if necessary

Wash and pat dry the chunks of rabbit, them dust them with flour. Heat the olive oil in a large casserole dish and brown the rabbit on all sides. Add the onion, garlic, herbs and olives, reduce the heat and cook until softened.

Stir in the wine and bubble to allow some of the alcohol to evaporate, then add the tomato pulp and some seasoning and cook over a medium heat for 1½ hours, until the rabbit is tender. Add a little stock if the mixture becomes too dry. Adjust the seasoning to taste and then serve. Delicious accompanied with polenta.

Serves 4

“ Rabbit is very much loved all over Italy and, as usual, each region has its own recipes. The Ligurian version sees the use of local herbs and, naturally, lots of olive oil. ”

STUFATO DI CONIGLIO ALLA SENAPE
BRAISED RABBIT WITH MUSTARD

300g brown cap mushrooms
salt and pepper
1 large rabbit, about 675g, boned and cut into chunks
plain flour, for dusting
40g butter
100g streaky bacon (or pancetta)
12 small onions
1 garlic clove, crushed
1 bouquet garni (parsley, thyme, bay leaf)
150ml dry white wine
200ml chicken or beef stock (p314)
2 tbsp Dijon mustard
1 tbsp finely chopped parsley

Clean and trim the mushrooms. If large, quarter them. Season the rabbit chunks and dust with flour.

Melt the butter in a large casserole dish until sizzling, add the rabbit and brown on each side. Add the bacon, cut into strips, the whole onions and the crushed garlic, and cook for 5 minutes. Add the bouquet garni, wine and mushrooms and, after a few minutes, the stock.

Bring to the boil, reduce the heat and cook for a further 20–30 minutes, or until the rabbit is tender. Stir the mustard into the sauce and season. Serve sprinkled with parsley, with either boiled potatoes or bread.

Serves 6

FEGATELLI ALLA CORTONESE CON FUNGHI
PIG'S LIVER CORTONA-STYLE WITH MUSHROOMS

Illustrated on previous page

100g caul fat (ask your butcher)
8 medium slices pig's liver, about 650g in total
salt and pepper
4 tbsp fresh breadcrumbs
1 tbsp fennel seeds
8 short twigs of bay leaves
600g firm, fresh ceps, cleaned
2 garlic cloves, crushed
6 tbsp olive oil
100ml water
chopped nepitella or wild mint, to serve

Preheat the oven to 200°C/Gas 6. Put the caul fat in slightly warm water to become soft, then remove and cut into eight 15cm square pieces.

Season each slice of liver with salt and pepper, then sprinkle with the breadcrumbs and fennel seeds, and roll up. Wrap each roll in a piece of the caul, and secure with a bay twig (or you could use cocktail sticks). Place in a shallow baking tin.

Slice the ceps and put into a pan with the garlic, olive oil and water. Cook over a low heat, stirring occasionally for 30 minutes. Flavour with nepitella or wild mint to taste.

Meanwhile, bake the liver in the oven for 25 minutes. Serve as soon as it is ready, with the ceps.

Serves 8

" Cortona is a lovely medieval town in the south of the province of Arezzo. It is of Etruscan origin, and the Cortonese keep gastronomy on top of the local agenda with plenty of food festivals. For this local dish, slices of pig's liver are wrapped in caul fat and baked with fennel and bay flavours, then served with garlicky mushrooms. "

SALSICCE FATTE A MANO CON LENTICCHIE
UMBRIAN LENTIL AND HOMEMADE SAUSAGE STEW

2 garlic cloves, squashed
50g sun-dried tomatoes, cut into strips
7 tbsp extra virgin olive oil
250g Castelluccio lentils
450ml chicken stock (p314)
2 celery stalks, with leaves, trimmed and chopped
salt and pepper

Sausages
500g minced pork
50ml strong red wine
1 tsp fennel seeds
1 mild chilli, finely chopped
1 tsp chopped rosemary

For the lentils, fry the garlic and sun-dried tomatoes in 6 tbsp of the olive oil for a few minutes in a large pan. When the garlic starts to turn pale golden, add the lentils, stock and celery, and cook for 30 minutes, or until the lentils are soft. Cover and keep warm over a low heat.

Meanwhile, in a medium-sized bowl, mix the sausage ingredients together well and season with salt and pepper. Take a handful of mince and roll it into a sausage shape, 8cm long and 3cm in diameter. Wrap tightly in a piece of foil, closing by turning the ends as you would a sweet.

Bring a large pan of water to the boil. Poach the sausages in the boiling water until they pop up to the surface, about 2–3 minutes. Leave to cool a little, then take off the foil. This poaching should ensure that the sausages hold together.

Moisten the sausages with the remaining olive oil, then fry or grill until golden on all sides, about 5 minutes.

Add the sausages to the warm lentils, and allow to cook gently together for 5 minutes. Eat with bread or, if you like, with a few boiled potatoes.

Serves 4

" This dish is truly wonderful when using the fresh sausages made by the local Norcian master butchers, who are known as norcini. As they may be difficult to find, I suggest making the sausages from scratch instead – it's not too complicated, and it is well worth it. You can get hold of Castelluccio lentils, the Italian puy lentils, in a good delicatessen. "

CASSOEULA ALLA MILANESE
PORK STEW

2 pig's trotters, cut into pieces and pre-cooked
800g meaty spare ribs
4 tbsp olive oil
1 large onion, sliced
400g carrots, peeled and cut into chunks
400g celeriac, peeled and cubed
200g pork skin without fat, cut into squares
salt and pepper
200g small pure pork sausages
1.5kg Savoy cabbage, cored and divided into leaves
3 tbsp concentrated tomato paste
a few celery leaves

Put the pig's trotters and spare ribs in a pan with water to cover, bring to the boil and boil for 20 minutes to render some of the fat. Drain and put into a large casserole dish. Add the olive oil, onion, carrots and celeriac.

Season the porkskin squares with pepper, roll up and tie with string. Add the pork skin rolls to the casserole with the sausages. Cover with water, season with salt and pepper and cook gently for 2 hours. Meanwhile, blanch the cabbage leaves in boiling salted water for a few minutes and drain.

Skim off the fat from the surface of the stew. Dilute the tomato paste with a little water and stir into the stew with the cabbage and celery leaves. Cook for a further 20 minutes. Serve with country bread or polenta, or with baked potatoes.

Serves 4–6

" You won't find cazzoeula (or casserole) in a posh Milanese restaurant, but rather in a good family-run trattoria or – better still – a Lombardian home. On a winter's evening, when it's already dark and foggy in Milan (it usually is), this is the ideal comforting dish to lift your spirits after a hard day's work. There are many local versions of this dish, but I have chosen the one from Milan. "

SPARE RIBS AND CABBAGE

1kg meaty pork spare ribs, cut into 5cm chunks
40g butter
2 garlic cloves, crushed
salt and pepper
freshly grated nutmeg
150–300ml chicken or vegetable stock
800g Savoy cabbage, cut into julienne strips

Put the spare ribs, butter, garlic, seasoning and a pinch of nutmeg into a pot with a lid (preferably terracotta). Brown the ribs well, but make sure that they don't stick, by stirring frequently. Add 100ml of the stock and leave to cook for 25 minutes, covered, on a medium heat.

Add the cabbage and more stock if required. Put the lid on and cook for 1½ hours on a medium heat until the meat starts to come off the bone. Adjust the seasoning and serve.

Serves 4–6

STUFFED PIG'S TROTTERS

2 pig's trotters, about 800g each, fresh or pre-cooked
200g dried cannellini beans,
    soaked in cold water overnight
8 tbsp olive oil
1 carrot, diced
1 celery stalk, trimmed and diced
2 garlic cloves, diced
1 tomato, diced
250g Castelluccio lentils
2 tbsp tomato purée
500ml chicken or vegetable stock (p314)
salt and pepper
1 small, tender rosemary sprig, leaves only
600g spinach, washed
75g butter

If using fresh trotters, cook in boiling water to cover for 3 hours. If using the pre-cooked variety, boil for about 20 minutes only. Drain the beans and cook in plenty of water (without salt) for 1½ hours until tender.

Heat 6 tbsp olive oil in a pan and gently fry the carrot, celery, garlic and tomato until soft. Add the lentils, tomato purée and stock. Bring to a simmer and cook until all the stock is absorbed and the lentils are tender, about 20 minutes. Check the seasoning; keep warm.

Drain the cooked beans and dress with the remaining olive oil, the rosemary leaves, and salt and pepper to taste; keep warm. When the trotters are ready, drain and remove the skin. Cook the spinach briefly in the tiniest amount of salted water until just wilted, then drain very well and toss with the butter.

Cut the trotters into thick slices. Put a pile of lentils on each warm serving plate with a spoonful of beans, a mound of spinach and a few trotter slices.

Serves 6

66 This very hearty simple dish comes from Piedmont, where it is eaten during the winter months. Savoy cabbage is used for its taste and for its wonderful leaves. 99

This celebration dish is eaten, with variations, all over Italy. You can prepare it in advance and just warm it up for the big occasion. Serve it with cren (horseradish) or mostarda di Cremona (the crystallised fruit relish), and mashed potato if you like.

“ This rather elaborate preparation, also called Schlachter Platte mit Knödeln, is a great winter dish for ravenous appetites. Originally from Austria and Germany, the Schlachter Platte is made with fresh black pudding and smoked pork products. It is also eaten in Alsace and the French call it choucroûte garnie, not surprisingly as sauerkraut is the main ingredient. If prepared properly it is a delight, and for me it is a wonderful dish to enjoy in northern Italy. ”

CRAUTI CON SPECK E CANEDERLI
CHOUCROUTE GARNIE

MAIALE E PEPERONI
PORK AND PICKLED PEPPERS

1kg sauerkraut (from a jar)
100ml apple juice
100ml water
1½ tsp caraway seeds
6 black peppercorns
160g smoked pork belly
200g smoked pork cutlets or 4 slices of pork loin
4 Frankfurters
4 little Blutwurst (black pudding), (optional)
olive oil, for frying (optional)

Canederli
350g stale bread, crusts removed, cut into small cubes
200ml milk
4 eggs, beaten
4–6 tbsp plain flour, plus extra for dusting
50g speck, finely cubed (optional)
100g good salami, finely cubed (optional)
1 tbsp finely chopped flat-leaf parsley
1 tbsp finely chopped marjoram
freshly grated nutmeg
salt and pepper

For the canederli, put the bread cubes in a bowl with the milk and eggs and leave to absorb for 1 hour.

Meanwhile, tip the sauerkraut into a pan and add the apple juice, water, the caraway seeds and peppercorns. Cook slowly for 1 hour, adding more water if necessary.

To make the canederli, add a third of the flour to the bread mixture, then the cubed meats and herbs. Mix well, seasoning with nutmeg, salt and pepper to taste. The mix should be firm enough to shape into balls; if not, add more of the flour. Shape into balls, each the size of a tangerine, and dust with flour. Plunge the canederli into a pan of boiling salted water, reduce the heat and simmer for 20 minutes or until they come to the surface.

Meanwhile, steam the smoked pork belly, cutlets and Frankfurter in a steamer until hot and tender, about 15–20 minutes. Fry the black pudding slices in a little olive oil, if using.

Put a portion of the sauerkraut in the middle of each plate. Arrange a slice of pork, a cutlet, a slice of black pudding and a frankfurter on top. Drain the canederli and place two on each plate. Serve with mustard.

Serves 4

40g lard
9 tbsp olive oil
600g diced pork (lean and fat), or fillet, cut into medallions
3 garlic cloves, finely sliced
1 red chilli (optional), finely chopped
salt and pepper
600g fleshy red peppers
4 tbsp white wine vinegar

Melt the lard with 3 tbsp of the olive oil in a pan and fry the pork on all sides until brown. Add the garlic, chilli, if using, and some salt and pepper. Sauté until the pork is cooked, about 20–25 minutes.

Halve, core and de-seed the peppers, then cut into slices. Heat the remaining olive oil in another pan and fry the peppers until soft and caramelised at the edges. Add the wine vinegar and season with salt.

Add the peppers to the meat (or add sliced, pickled peppers at this stage) and toss to mix. Cook, stirring, for a further 5 minutes to let the flavours combine. Serve as a main course with good country bread.

Serves 4

We used to cook this dish regularly in winter. It relies on very meaty peppers called pepacelle, which have been preserved in vinegar during the summer. For this we use a damigiana (demijohn), or a big flask with an opening at the top large enough to take the peppers. Alternatively, you can fry fresh peppers until soft, then add vinegar at the end, as I have done here. The combination of pickled peppers and pork is a truly peasant dish, but it is also one for gourmets.

COSTOLETTE DI MAIALE ALLA MILANESE
MILANESE BREADED PORK CUTLET

4 large pork cutlets, bone in
salt and pepper
2 eggs, beaten
6 tbsp dried white breadcrumbs
olive oil and vegetable oil, for shallow-frying
500g purple sprouting broccoli
2 garlic cloves, sliced
½ chilli, chopped
1 lemon, quartered

Place the cutlets on a piece of cling film or greaseproof paper, and cover with another piece. Beat the fleshy parts with a mallet or something heavy. You want the meat to spread and become a little thinner. Remove the film or paper.

Season the cutlets and dip in the beaten eggs, then coat with breadcrumbs.

Pour enough mixed oil into a large shallow pan to cover the base. Heat it until it starts to bubble, then fry the cutlets on a medium-high heat for at least 5 minutes on each side until golden brown. Set aside and keep warm.

Blanch the broccoli in a pan of boiling water for a few minutes before gently frying in a pan with the sliced garlic, chopped chilli and a little olive oil until softened. Serve with the cutlets and the lemon quarters.

Serves 4

" Meat cooked the Milanese way is almost always breaded and fried. The most typical example is usually made with veal, but the dish is also possible with chicken or pork. For this one here, you need a large pork cutlet with the bone, the flesh beaten quite thinly. The rest is child's play. "

COSTOLETTE DI AGNELLO RIPIENE
STUFFED LAMB CUTLETS

8 large (double) young lamb cutlets,
    French trimmed, fat removed
2 slices Parma ham or speck, quartered
8 sage leaves
8 small pieces Fontina cheese, sliced
salt and pepper
2 eggs, beaten
6 tbsp dried white breadcrumbs
olive oil, for shallow-frying

With a sharp knife, make an incision in the flesh of each cutlet, from the side opposite the bone, to make a pocket. Stuff the pockets with the ham, sage and cheese. Press the sides together to seal the cutlets. Season the meat. Dip the cutlets in the egg first, then coat well with breadcrumbs.

Pour enough olive oil into a large frying pan to cover the base generously and heat gently. Fry the cutlets until brown, about 5–6 minutes per side if you like them juicy as I do. Drain on kitchen paper and serve.

Serves 4

For this recipe the lamb cutlets have to be larger than usual, so that they can be stuffed. Get the butcher to cut eight cutlets on the bone, of 2.5–3cm thickness (which means a double cutlet with the meat of two bones, one of the bones removed). These lamb cutlets are wonderful hot, but are also great cold as part of a picnic.

BRACIOLINE DI ABBACCHIO E CARCIOFI
LAMB CUTLETS AND ARTICHOKES

12 young artichokes
50g lard
2 tbsp olive oil
12 new season's lamb cutlets
1 garlic clove, finely chopped
1 small onion, finely chopped
2 tbsp coarsely chopped marjoram
100ml dry white wine
150ml chicken stock (p314)
salt and pepper

Remove the tough outer leaves from the artichokes and trim the base of the stems. With a sharp knife, trim the tips of the leaves, leaving only the tender parts of the artichokes. Cut into quarters and remove any choke.

Heat the lard and olive oil in a large frying pan. Add the cutlets and brown on each side. Add the garlic, onion, marjoram and wine and cook for 5 minutes.

Add the artichokes to the pan, then pour on the stock. Cover and cook for 10–12 minutes until the artichokes and lamb are tender. Season with salt and pepper to taste and serve.

Serves 4

" This combination is well known from Liguria to Sicily. The abbacchio, milk-fed lamb from Rome, offers good flavour despite its youth, though I also tried this with milk-fed goat which was equally delicious. In Rome, cutlets with the bone are called braciole or bracioline. "

PUNTA DI PETTO D'AGNELLO RIPIENO
STUFFED BREAST OF LAMB

1 piece of punta di petto of lamb (see below), about 1kg
3 eggs, beaten
8 tbsp soft fresh breadcrumbs
1 tbsp raisins
1 garlic clove, finely chopped
1 tbsp pine nuts
60g Parmesan, finely chopped
1 tbsp finely chopped parsley
salt and pepper
a little olive oil

Preheat the oven to 180°C/Gas 4. Slit open the breast of lamb along one side and made a pocket among the layers. Mix together the eggs, breadcrumbs, raisins, garlic, pine nuts, Parmesan, parsley and some salt and pepper. Stuff the pocket with this mixture and then sew it up with a needle and kitchen string. Brush with a little olive oil and bake in the oven for 1¼ hours.

Serves 4–6

" This specific cut, more often used for veal, is the extreme soft part of the breast of lamb, underneath the cutlets. The various layers of meat and fat are ideal for making a pocket, which is filled, sewn together and cooked. Naturally the younger the animal, the more tender will be the final dish, which resembles a small cushion. "

SPALLA DI AGNELLO CON FUNGHI
SHOULDER OF LAMB WITH MUSHROOMS

200g hen of the woods, cleaned weight
15g dried ceps
4 small shoulders of lamb, boned
   (get your butcher to do this for you)
1 tbsp each of chopped parsley and rosemary
1 tbsp chopped garlic
salt and pepper
plain flour, for dusting
8 tbsp olive oil
1 onion, finely chopped
1 celery stalk, trimmed and finely chopped
1 tbsp black peppercorns
500ml chicken or vegetable stock (p314)
300ml white wine
2 tbsp Worcestershire sauce

Clean the fresh mushrooms thoroughly, and separate into small lobes. Soak the dried ceps in warm water for 20 minutes, then drain, reserving the water, and finely chop. Remove most of the fat from the lamb shoulders, trimming them well. You want each piece to weigh about 200g. Lay the pieces, boned side up, on the work surface.

Mix the chopped herbs and garlic together, season with salt and pepper, and divide between the pieces of lamb, spreading the mixture evenly on the meat. Fold each piece of lamb over, then roll and tie into an even shape with kitchen string. Dust with flour and fry in a casserole dish in the olive oil until brown on all sides, turning every few minutes. Add the onion, celery and peppercorns to the casserole dish and sauté briefly, then add the stock, wine and Worcestershire sauce. Cover and cook on top of the stove over a gentle heat for 1 hour. Turn occasionally.

After an hour, much of the liquid will have evaporated, but there should still be enough to serve as a sauce. Add the mushrooms, fresh and dried, plus a little of the soaking water if necessary, and cook for a further 30 minutes. Check the seasoning before serving.

Serves 6

“ This was one of the most loved recipes at the Neal Street Restaurant.
My chef, Andrea Cavaliere, developed the lamb side, while I took charge
of the mushroom accompaniment. In the restaurant we used to serve
this with polenta flavoured with Parmesan and butter. ”

IL GRAN BOLLITO MISTO
MIXED BOILED MEATS

600g pork skin, without fat
cayenne pepper
freshly grated nutmeg
finely chopped flat-leaf parsley
finely chopped rosemary
salt and pepper
2 uncooked cotechino sausages, 300g each
4 celery stalks, trimmed and cut into chunks
2 large onions, 1 spiked with 4 or 5 cloves
few black peppercorns
4 bay leaves
beef brisket, about 1.5kg
1 salted veal tongue, about 600–800g
veal brisket, about 1kg
1 chicken, about 1.5–2kg

Lay the pork skin flat on a surface and sprinkle with cayenne, nutmeg, parsley, rosemary, salt and pepper. Roll up and tie with string. Put into a saucepan with the cotechino and cover with cold water. Bring to the boil, then lower the heat and simmer for about 3 hours.

Meanwhile, put 3 of the celery stalks, the clove-spiked onion, peppercorns and bay leaves in a large pot of lightly salted water and bring to the boil. Add the beef and cook gently for 30 minutes. Add the tongue and veal brisket to the beef and simmer for 2 hours, skimming regularly to remove any scum from the surface. Top up with boiling water to cover.

Cook the chicken separately in water to cover, with the remaining celery and onion, for 1–1½ hours, depending on age. When all the meats are cooked and tender, remove them from the liquor. Peel and trim the tongue. Slice the meats and arrange them on a large serving plate. Serve hot, accompanied by salsa verde, a little of the stock, and some mostarda di Cremona.

Serves 10–12

" This is a great winter celebration dish for a large gathering. It is found in other regions, but this version is very typical of Piedmont. **"**

CUTTURIDDE
SOUPY LAMB OR MUTTON STEW

mixed pieces of lamb (medium fat, some
    on the bone), about 1kg
300g pomodorini (cherry tomatoes), halved
1 onion, finely chopped
200g mature pecorino cheese, diced
2 tbsp finely chopped flat-leaf parsley
salt and pepper

Put the lamb, tomatoes and onion in a pot, cover with water and cook with the lid on, very slowly and gently, for an hour.

Add the pecorino, parsley and some seasoning, and cook for a further hour, or until the meat is tender. Check the seasoning.

Serve the stew with good country bread, for mopping up the juices.

Serves 4

" I always like curious or less well-known recipes, and this one from the southern regions that make up the foot of Italy intrigued me. Mutton, with its full flavour, is ideal for this rustic dish. **"**

LA COSTOLETTA DEL CURATO
VEAL CHOP OF THE PRIEST
Illustrated on previous page

3–4 tbsp olive oil
4 veal cutlets, about 180g each

Sauce
150g mixed fresh herbs
4 tbsp extra virgin olive oil
50g mild mustard
juice of ½ lemon
salt and pepper

To prepare the sauce, put the herbs in a mortar and pound with the pestle, dribbling in the extra virgin olive oil gradually as you reduce the herbs to a paste. Add the mustard, lemon juice, and salt and pepper to taste; mix well.

Heat the olive oil in a large frying pan, add the veal cutlets and fry for about 6–8 minutes on each side until cooked. Spread the cold herb sauce on top of the cutlets and serve at once.

Serves 4

" In Italy, as we know, the clergy treat themselves proverbially well. You will find this recipe on the restaurant menus in Orvieto during May, when wild herbs are available in the fields.**"**

It was a challenge for me because the exact herb mixture is apparently a secret. The only known fact is that there should be at least 18 herbs. Gather together as many as you can find, but go easy on the more pungent varieties.

VITELLO TONNATO
VEAL IN TUNA SAUCE

1 litre dry white wine
2 celery stalks, trimmed and chopped
1 carrot, chopped
1 onion, chopped
1 garlic clove, chopped
a few bay leaves
1kg veal topside or eye of silverside, tied with
    kitchen string to make a large, longish 'sausage'
salt and pepper
a few parsley leaves, to decorate
salted capers, soaked and drained, to decorate

Sauce
350g mayonnaise
45g salted capers, soaked, drained
    and very finely chopped
60g pickled gherkins, very finely chopped
250g canned tuna in oil, drained
2 tbsp finely chopped flat-leaf parsley

Put the wine, celery, carrot, onion, garlic and bay leaves in a large pan with the meat and add enough water to cover. Season with salt and pepper, bring to the boil, then reduce the heat and simmer for 1½ hours, until the meat is tender.

Meanwhile, mix together all the ingredients for the sauce and purée in a blender or food processor. Season to taste with salt and pepper if necessary.

Remove the meat from the pan, take off the string and cut the meat into very thin slices. Spread them over a large serving place and cover with the sauce. Decorate with parsley leaves and capers.

Serves 6

" Fish and meat are very seldom combined, but in this recipe they make a perfect and delicate antipasto that was once typical of Piedmont and Lombardy but is now found all over Italy. "

PICCATA MILANESE
VEAL WITH PARMA HAM MILANESE-STYLE

4 thin slices of veal, about 125g each
65g butter
55g speck or Parma ham, cut into small strips
salt and pepper
flour, for dusting
4 tbsp stock
1 tbsp finely chopped flat-leaf parsley
juice of 1 lemon

Trim the slices of veal to a uniform shape. Heat 45g of the butter in a large pan and fry the speck or Parma ham for a few minutes. Season the veal and dust with flour, then fry in the same pan until golden on each side. Remove from the pan and keep warm.

Add the rest of the butter to the pan, then stir in the stock to loosen the bits on the base of the pan. Add the parsley and lemon juice, bring to the boil, then pour over the meat and serve immediately.

Serves 4

You can use chicken or turkey breast here instead of veal if you prefer. What these meats have in common is that they cook very quickly and absorb the flavouring, which can also be wine.

CARNE ALL'ALBESE
ALBA-STYLE RAW BEEF WITH PARMESAN AND WHITE TRUFFLE

400g beef fillet, cut into very thin slices
salt and pepper
4 tbsp extra virgin olive oil
juice of 1 lemon
4 celery stalks, trimmed and thinly sliced
12 fresh asparagus tips, cooked until just al dente
85g Parmesan, thinly sliced
45g white truffle, cut into thin shavings

Put the slices of beef between 2 sheets of heavy-duty cling film and beat gently with a meat mallet or the end of a rolling pin until very thin. It should be about 1–2 mm thick. Spread the meat over 4 large serving plates without letting the slices overlap. Season with salt and pepper, then brush with the olive oil and lemon juice.

Distribute the slices of celery, asparagus tips, Parmesan and white truffle over the meat and serve with grissini.

Serves 4

TAGLIATA DI MANZO
SLICED BEEF

8 tbsp olive oil, for shallow-frying
salt
4 topside steaks, about 200g each

Sauce
12 tbsp extra virgin olive oil
2 tbsp green peppercorns
4 rosemary sprigs, divided into smaller sprigs

Pour enough olive oil into your frying pan to cover the base generously, and heat gently. Salt the steaks, add to the pan and shallow-fry for 5 minutes on each side, until browned but still rare.

In a separate small pan, warm up the extra virgin olive oil, peppercorns and rosemary over a low heat.

To serve, cut the steaks into 2cm strips. Arrange the steak slices onto 4 plates and drizzle over the peppery rosemary oil. *Buon appetito!*

Serves 4

" The attraction of this sophisticated dish from Piedmont lies in its simplicity and, naturally, in the unbeatable combination of the meat with truffles. Locally in Alba, not only rich people enjoy this dish. The truffle-hunters themselves are very fond of it. "

This dish reminds me of Tuscany, where the local meat of the Val di Chiana, a valley near Florence, makes for very worthwhile eating. It is important here that you do not overcook the meat, as you want it to retain all of its natural succulence.

CODEGHIN IN CAMISA
SAUSAGE EN CHEMISE

2 raw or cooked cotechino sausages, about 250g each
6 tbsp olive oil
1 garlic clove, finely sliced
500g fresh ceps, cleaned and sliced
1 tbsp chopped flat-leaf parsley
1 tbsp chopped basil
1 boned breast or loin of veal joint, about 2.2kg
salt and pepper
40g butter
150ml chicken stock (p314)
200ml white wine

Put the cotechino sausages into a saucepan and cover with cold water. Bring to the boil, then lower the heat and simmer, allowing 3 hours if raw, 20 minutes if pre-cooked. Drain and cool slightly.

Heat 4 tbsp of the olive oil in a large sauté pan with the garlic. Add the ceps and sauté until softened and the juices have evaporated. Remove from the heat and mix in the herbs. Leave to cool for 10 minutes or so.

Preheat the oven to 180°C/Gas 4. Using a sharp knife, cut a deep pocket in the veal from one side, between the layers of fat and meat. Season the inside of the pocket with salt and pepper, then stuff with the cotechino. Put the mushrooms into the pocket too, pushing them all around the sausage. Sew up the opening with kitchen string.

Heat the remaining olive oil and the butter in a flameproof casserole dish and brown the veal on all sides. Add the stock and wine, cover and braise in the oven for 1½ hours. Skim off the fat from the surface of the liquor. Carve the veal into slices and serve with the liquor and potato purée or polenta.

Serves 6

This recipe originates from the Val Camonica, a source of many classic recipes. The idea is to make a pocket in a joint of veal and stuff it with the cooked pork sausage and sautéed ceps … intriguing and delicious! The cotechino (cooking sausages) of this area are made of 75 per cent pork and the rest beef. If you can't find fresh cotechino, you can use pre-cooked ones.

LIVER AND ONIONS

500g white onions, cut into thin strips
150ml olive oil
500g pork liver, cut into thin strips
plain white flour, for dusting
2 tbsp red wine vinegar
salt and pepper

Fry the onions in the olive oil in a pan with a lid on over a medium heat until soft.

Toss the slices of liver in some flour, shaking off the surplus, and add to the onions. Stir-fry on a high heat for a few minutes until the liver is cooked, then add the vinegar, salt and pepper. Stir-fry for a couple more minutes to let the acid in the vinegar evaporate, and serve immediately. Eat with country bread or potatoes.

Serves 4

" Virtually every Italian has a recipe or two for liver of various animals cooked in different ways. The fegato e cipolle from Naples is not dissimilar to fegato alla Veneziana, although in Venice they use white wine instead of vinegar and calves liver instead of pigs liver. I have also tried this recipe with chicken livers, and it is excellent. In Naples it used to be cooked with coagulated pork blood! "

MEATLOAF IN TOMATO SAUCE

750g lean minced beef
750g lean minced pork
6 eggs, beaten
100g Parmesan, grated
150g fresh white breadcrumbs
2 garlic cloves, finely puréed
salt and pepper
8 tbsp olive oil
2 large onions, finely chopped
800g polpa di pomodoro and chunky passata
10 basil leaves
500g rigatoni or penne (optional)

Preheat the oven to 180°C/Gas 4.

Put both minces in a large bowl and add the eggs, cheese, breadcrumbs, garlic, salt and pepper. Mix very well together, then shape with your hands into a nice oval shape, rather like a loaf of bread.

In a large 3-litre casserole dish, which should be big enough to hold the loaf and its sauce, heat the olive oil and gently fry the loaf until brown all over. Turn it gently so as not to break it. Now add the onions and fry until soft, about 10 minutes. Add the tomato pulp and basil to the casserole until the loaf is covered (add water if necessary). Cover with the lid or some foil.

Now let it cook in the preheated oven for 2 hours. Check from time to time: if it looks as if it needs additional moisture, add a little water. Taste for salt and pepper.

Let the meatloaf rest for 10 minutes. (If you wish to serve the meatloaf with pasta you should cook it in plenty of boiling salted water for about 8–10 minutes during this time). Lift the meatloaf – carefully! – from the sauce, cut into slices and serve with the sauce and pasta, if you like.

Serves 6

RAGU NAPOLETANO CON BRACIOLA
NEAPOLITAN BEEF OLIVE STEW

6 beef escalopes, quite thinly cut
3 tbsp fresh white breadcrumbs
40g raisins, soaked in water and drained
80g pine kernels
1 garlic clove, puréed
100g Parmesan, grated
4 tbsp coarsely chopped flat-leaf parsley
salt and pepper

Pasta
500g durum wheat flour, plus extra for dusting
1 egg, beaten

Sauce
2 large onions, sliced
6 tbsp olive oil
100ml dry white wine
800g polpa di pomodoro or chunky passata
2 tbsp concentrated tomato paste,
    diluted with 2 tbsp water
a few basil leaves, shredded

To make the beef olives, line up the escalopes side by side on your work surface. Make a stuffing mixture by combining the breadcrumbs, drained raisins, pine kernels, garlic, half the Parmesan and parsley, seasoning to taste. Divide the mixture evenly between the centres of the escalopes. Roll up each of the escalopes to enclose the stuffing and secure with a couple of wooden toothpicks.

Meanwhile, start to prepare the sauce by frying the onions in the olive oil in a large pan. When the onions are soft, after about 6–7 minutes, add the beef olives, and brown on each side. Add the wine and boil to evaporate the alcohol. Add the tomato pulp and the tomato paste and bring to the boil.

Reduce the heat, cover and let it bubble gently for 2 hours, turning the beef olives occasionally. When ready, add salt and pepper to taste and stir in the basil. Keep the beef olives separate from the sauce.

To make the pasta, pile the flour into a mound on a work surface and make a well in the middle. Add the egg and a splash of water. Gradually mix into the flour, adding enough water to bind the dough. Knead until smooth, then cover with a cloth and leave to rest for about 30 minutes.

Dust your work surface with a little flour and shape the dough a little at a time. Take a little piece of dough and roll it under the palm of your hand to make a baton, about 10cm long and 3mm in diameter. With a thin skewer, press the little baton around the skewer to make a spiral shape. Let the pasta spiral run down and off the skewer, then put on a cloth. Repeat to shape the rest of the dough.

Cook the pasta in boiling salted water until al dente, about 3–4 minutes. Drain and dress with the sauce.

Cut the beef olives into slices and arrange on top of the pasta. Scatter the remaining Parmesan over to serve.

Serves 4–6

" This classic Sunday dish of the Neapolitans is a piatto unico – an all-in-one dish that is served as a main course. The braciola is a sort of beef olive with a special filling, reminiscent of Arab cooking. These are relatively complicated to produce, but on Sundays everybody has time to prepare something so delicious. "

ARROSTO DI VITELLO AL LATTE
MILK-ROASTED VEAL

55g butter
lean silverside or topside of veal, about 1.5kg
100g Parma ham, cut into small strips
freshly grated nutmeg
salt and pepper
2 litres milk

Place the butter in a large pan into which the veal will just fit snugly. Add the meat and brown on all sides. Add the Parma ham strips, a pinch of nutmeg and season with salt and pepper. Then pour in just enough of the milk to cover the meat by two-thirds. Cover and simmer gently for about 2–2½ hours, until tender, topping up with more milk from time to time to prevent the meat from becoming dry.

Serves 6–8

This is a very delicate dish, which should be served in thin slices with green beans, Swiss chard or spinach.

STRACOTTO
BRAISED BEEF

4 tbsp olive oil
a nice piece of beef such as rump or brisket,
    with a little fat, about 1.5kg
2 carrots, cut into very small cubes
1 large onion, finely chopped
3 celery stalks, trimmed and cut into small cubes
10 juniper berries
20 peppercorns
a few bay leaves
100g fatty Parma ham, cut into thin strips
1 litre dry white wine
1 litre beef stock (p314)
salt
45g butter

Heat the olive oil in a large, preferably cast-iron, pan, add the beef and brown on each side, then remove from the pan and set aside. Add the carrots, onion, celery, juniper berries, peppercorns, bay leaves and Parma ham and fry until the vegetables are soft.

Return the meat to the pan and add the wine, stock and a little salt. Bring to the boil, then reduce the heat, cover and cook slowly until the meat is very tender, about 2 hours. Pierce the meat with a skewer to check if it is well cooked; if necessary, cook for a little longer. By the end of the cooking time most of the liquid should have evaporated.

Remove the meat from the pan, whisk in the butter and add a little more stock or wine – enough to bring it to a velvety consistency. Pass the sauce through a fine sieve. Serve the meat thinly sliced, accompanied by the sauce.

Serves 6

" Literally translated this means 'overcooked', which reflects the way this dish is cooked very slowly for a long time. "

CODA DI BUE ALL'ANDREA
ANDREA'S BRAISED OXTAIL

2 large oxtails, boned into flat sheets (ask your butcher)
salt and pepper
2 tbsp finely chopped mixed sage, bay and rosemary
flour, for dusting
6 tbsp olive oil
2 carrots, finely diced
1 small onion, finely diced
1 celery stalk, trimmed and finely diced
1 litre red wine
3 cloves
2 bay leaves
1 cinnamon stick
4 black peppercorns
20g butter

Preheat the oven to 180°C/Gas 4. Lay the oxtail sheets out on a work surface, and sprinkle with salt, pepper and the chopped herbs. Roll up each one to make a sausage shape and secure with string. Dust lightly with flour.

Heat 4 tbsp olive oil in a large frying pan and fry the oxtail rolls, turning until golden brown. Remove to a plate. Add the remaining olive oil to the pan and sauté the carrots, onion and celery until softened.

Transfer the vegetables to a deep roasting pan and add the oxtail rolls. Pour over the wine, then add the cloves, bay leaves, cinnamon and peppercorns, and some salt and pepper. Bake in the oven for at least 2 hours. Once cooked, transfer the oxtail rolls to a plate and leave to cool, so they firm up.

Meanwhile, skim the cooking liquor, boil to reduce by about half and then strain. Remove the string from the oxtail rolls, then cut into thick slices, about 4cm thick. Warm through in the reduced cooking juices with the butter added. Serve the oxtail with the cooking juices spooned over. Carciofi alla Romana (p248) make a delicious accompaniment.

Serves 4

" This dish was created by my former head chef, Andrea Cavaliere, and it is one that he should be immensely proud of. Although it might require a little more work than usual, the result is stunning. "

OSSOBUCO ALLA MILANESE
BRAISED VEAL SHANKS

1 shin of veal, about 1.25kg, cut into 4cm lengths,
    with the marrow bone in the centre
salt and pepper
flour, for dusting
4 tbsp olive oil, plus extra if needed
1 onion, diced
2 celery stalks, diced
1 carrot, diced
2 glasses of dry white wine
300ml veal stock

Dust the veal with seasoned flour. Heat the olive oil in a large pan, add the meat and fry until browned on all sides. Remove from the pan and set aside.

Add more oil if necessary, then gently fry the onion, celery and carrot in the same pan until lightly browned. Return the meat to the pan, pour in the wine and stock and bring gently to the boil. Cover and cook for about 1½ hours, until the meat is tender, removing the lid towards the end of cooking. Check from time to time and add a little more stock if the mixture is getting too dry. Adjust the seasoning and serve with Risotto Milanese (p140) and gremolata, a mixture of finely chopped lemon rind, garlic and parsley.

Serves 4

ROAST VENISON WITH PINE NEEDLES

1 venison fillet (or boneless leg joint), about 1kg
4 tbsp olive oil
50g butter
6 tbsp soured cream

Marinade
1 litre strong red wine
500ml chicken stock (p314)
2 celery stalks
2 large carrots, peeled
1 bouquet garni (rosemary, bay leaves, marjoram, sage)
freshly grated nutmeg
freshly ground cinnamon
1 sprig of pine needles (from the end of a branch)
1 lemon, halved
salt and pepper

For the marinade, put the wine, stock, vegetables, bouquet garni, a pinch of nutmeg and cinnamon and the pine needles into a saucepan. Squeeze the juice from the lemon and add to the pan with the spent halves and some salt and pepper. Bring to the boil and simmer for 5 minutes, then allow to cool. When cold, add the meat and leave to marinate in a cool place for 24 hours, turning from time to time.

Preheat the oven to 220°C/Gas 7. Drain the venison; strain and reserve the marinade. Put the olive oil in a roasting pan on the hob over a medium heat. Add the venison fillet and sear on all sides, about 8–10 minutes in total. Add 8 tbsp of the reserved marinade and the butter, stir, then put into the oven. Roast, basting from time to time with more marinade, for 20–25 minutes or longer, depending on the thickness of the fillet and how pink you like your venison.

Transfer the venison to a warm platter and rest for about 15 minutes. Meanwhile, add the soured cream to the juices in the roasting pan, stir well and heat. Carve the venison and serve with the sauce. If you dare, garnish each plate with a little sprig of pine needles! The dish may be served with polenta, canederli (p221), polenta or mashed potato.

Serves 6

VENISON CARPACCIO WITH RAW CEPS

300g small ceps, cleaned weight
250g venison fillet, very finely sliced
juice of 1½ lemons
3 tbsp extra virgin olive oil
salt and pepper
8 tbsp finely chopped parsley

Clean the mushrooms well and slice them finely.

Divide the very thin slices of venison fillet between 4 plates, spreading them out to the rim.

Make a vinaigrette with the lemon juice, oil and some salt and pepper, and sprinkle some of this onto the meat. Arrange the sliced mushrooms on top. Sprinkle on the remaining vinaigrette, then sprinkle with parsley and coarsely ground pepper. Eat as a starter with bread or grissini.

Serves 4

For this dish you need fillet of venison, the most tender part. Thin slices of fillet about 5mm thick are put between two sheets of cling film and then beaten gently to make them paper-thin.

" The name 'carpaccio' today is generally used to describe raw meat or fish very thinly cut and cured instantly with lemon juice and oil, plus some additions. I introduced a carpaccio of venison, one of the healthiest red meats, to my restaurant, with enormous success. It is wonderful served with raw ceps, also thinly cut from small, tender specimens. As a dish it is very easy to make. **"**

CAPRETTO CON PISELLI ALL'UOVO
KID WITH PEAS AND EGG

meaty kid or lamb, about 1kg, cut into 5cm pieces
50ml olive oil
1 large onion, very finely chopped
50ml dry white wine
400g tender garden peas
4 eggs, beaten
3 tbsp finely chopped flat-leaf parsley,
    plus sprigs to garnish
60g Parmesan, grated
salt and pepper

Put the kid or lamb in a pan with the olive oil and onion and cook slowly to brown the meat on all sides, about 10 minutes. Add the white wine and cook for a further 10–15 minutes. Add the peas and cook for another 10 minutes.

Just before serving, beat the eggs in a bowl with the parsley and cheese. Season the meat with salt and pepper to taste, then remove the pan from the heat. Slowly add the beaten egg mixture, stirring well – the heat of the meat should be enough to turn the egg into a lovely thick sauce. Serve at once, scattered with a few parsley sprigs.

Serves 4–6

This wonderful springtime dish is traditionally eaten at Easter, when young lamb and kid are very much in demand. Making egg function as a sauce for meat is quite widespread in the Mediterranean. If fresh peas are unavailable, you can use frozen ones.

SPEZZATINO DI CERVO CON POLENTA E FUNGHI
VENISON STEW WITH POLENTA AND CEPS

1.8kg venison, preferably from the haunch
salt and pepper
plain flour, for dusting
100ml olive oil
55g dried ceps, soaked and liquid reserved, then chopped
100g speck, cut into strips
½ tsp freshly ground nutmeg
100g concentrated tomato paste

Marinade

1 litre strong red wine
1 tbsp juniper berries, crushed
1 tsp black peppercorns, coarsely crushed
4 bay leaves
1 rosemary sprig
2 garlic cloves, crushed
zest of 1 lemon, coarsely chopped
2 carrots, finely chopped
1 onion, finely chopped

Polenta

3 litres water
salt
600g polenta flour (or pre-cooked polenta)
100g Parmesan, grated
100g unsalted butter

Put all the ingredients for the marinade into a stainless-steel bowl. Cut the meat into chunks and place in the marinade. Season to taste with salt and pepper, then leave for 24 hours, covered in a cool place. Pick out the meat, and put to one side. Strain the marinade and reserve the liquid.

Dry the meat, then dust with flour. Heat the olive oil in a large pan and fry the venison on all sides until golden. Remove the meat. Add the chopped ceps and speck, and fry briefly. Add the nutmeg and tomato paste along with 100ml of the reserved cep water and all the marinade (except for the lemon zest and rosemary). Then bring to the boil. Add the meat, reduce the heat, cover, and simmer for an hour. Add more of the soaking water from the ceps if necessary and cook for another hour or until the meat is tender. The venison should be very moist with plenty of sauce.

Meanwhile, cook the polenta. (If using the quick polenta, then follow the instructions on the packet.) Bring the water to the boil, add plenty of salt, then gradually add the polenta flour, stirring continuously with a wooden spoon. Incorporate all the flour without any lumps forming. Continue to stir until smooth and the polenta is starting to come away from the side of the pan, which should take about 30–40 minutes.

Mix the Parmesan and butter into the polenta. Serve the stew in deep plates, with a few spoonfuls of polenta.

Serves 8–10

" A venison or hare stew is best accompanied by wet polenta, the famous 'porridge' made with yellow or white maize. Any dish with a sauce needs something to absorb the juices (usually rice or potatoes), but game needs a stronger accompaniment like polenta to match the flavours. "

VERDURE

CARCIOFI ALLA GIUDIA
ARTICHOKES THE JEWISH WAY

12 Romanesco artichokes (make sure they are big but
  still young and tender, without a fully formed choke)
juice of ½ lemon or 1 tbsp white wine vinegar
salt and pepper
1 litre olive oil, plus extra for frying

Clean the artichokes of tough outer leaves, leaving
a little of the stem on, which is very tender. Peel the
latter. Put the artichokes in a bowl of water with
the lemon or vinegar for 30 minutes to stop them
discolouring. Drain. Beat them gently, one against
the other, to aid the loosening of the internal leaves.

Add salt and pepper to the centre of the artichoke, and
put them in a pan with the olive oil and a little water,
which must almost cover them. Cover and cook gently
for 20 minutes; the oil has to produce small bubbles.
Lift from the oil and open the leaves very gently with a
fork to form the shape of a rose. Place the artichokes on
a plate with the stem upwards until just before serving.

To finish the artichokes off, put about 1cm of fresh
olive oil in a pan and fry them gently on each side
so that the leaves and the stem start to turn golden.
A little sprinkling of hot water will make them turn
golden more quickly (but be very careful with the
hot oil). Drain off the excess oil and serve.

Serves 4

CARCIOFI, CIPOLLE E PATATE AL FORNO
BAKED ARTICHOKES, ONIONS AND POTATOES

salt and pepper
400g whole flat onions
600g young artichokes, trimmed of all tough stems
  and leaves (cleaned weight)
600g new potatoes, scraped and cut into half
150g Taggiasca olives
  (they are small and blackish)
20 whole cherry tomatoes
150ml extra virgin olive oil
1 litre chicken or vegetable stock (p314)
bunch of flat-leaf parsley, coarsely chopped

Preheat the oven to 180°C/Gas 4.

Put some boiling salted water over the onions and
blanch them on the heat for 6 minutes.

In a large ovenproof dish, assemble the drained onions,
the artichokes, potatoes, olives and tomatoes. Pour
over the olive oil, add salt and pepper to taste, and mix
thoroughly. Add the stock and bake in the preheated
oven for 30 minutes, stirring a little, and then cook for a
further 10–15 minutes at 200°C/Gas 6 to produce a little
crust. Take out of the oven, sprinkle with the parsley
and serve.

Serves 6–8

❝ For most of my life I have eaten carciofi alla Giudia,
always supposing they were cooked the proper Jewish
way. It was only in 1997 when I was filming in Rome for the
BBC, that I met Donatella Limentani Pavoncello, one of the
most respected members of the Roman Jewish community.
A precious little book of her family recipes since 1880
revealed to me finally how artichokes the Jewish way really
ought to be. Here is her simple but wonderful recipe, which
is always served during the celebration of Pesach, the
Jewish equivalent of Easter. ❞

TORTA DI SPINACI E CARCIOFI
SPINACH AND ARTICHOKE TART

olive oil, for oiling
flour, for dusting
675g frozen shortcrust pastry

Filling
1kg spinach leaves, cleaned, washed
    and any tough stalks removed
salt and pepper
6 tbsp olive oil
2 onions, thinly sliced
100ml water
6 baby artichoke hearts, trimmed and sliced
300g ricotta cheese
6 eggs, beaten
70g Parmesan, grated
freshly grated nutmeg

Preheat the oven to 180°C/Gas 4. Use a little olive oil to oil a 25cm tart tin, then dust with a little flour.

Blanch the spinach in boiling salted water for about 3 minutes, then drain well. Using your hands, squeeze the spinach leaves to extract as much liquid as possible. Chop finely.

Heat the olive oil and fry the onions briefly in a large saucepan. Add the water and artichokes, cover and cook until tender, about 20 minutes.

In a bowl, put the spinach, ricotta, eggs, 50g of the Parmesan, a little nutmeg and some salt and pepper to taste. Mix together well.

Roll the pastry out until thin and use it to line the prepared tart tin. Pour the filling into the tin, sprinkle with the remaining Parmesan and bake in the preheated oven for 30 minutes. Leave to cool a little and serve.

Serves 6

" This is not dissimilar to the French quiche which, although most known for its Lorraine connections, is actually made all over France. In Liguria, a similar egg tart is made, the torta pasqualina (Easter tart), of which this vegetarian tart is a variant. "

CARCIOFI ALLA ROMANA
ARTICHOKES ROMAN-STYLE

8 young Roman artichokes
1 egg, beaten
2 tbsp fresh breadcrums
1 garlic clove, very finely chopped
1 tbsp chopped mint
salt and pepper
2 tbsp olive oil, plus extra to cook the artichokes

Trim the top 2cm off the artichokes, pull away the tough outer leaves and cut the bottom 4cm off the stem. With a sharp knife, trim the tougher tops of the leaves, leaving only the tender parts of the artichokes – you will have cup-like containers. Make an aperture in the centre of each artichoke and excavate the choke if this has already grown; if the artichoke is young, this may not be necessary.

Peel the reserved artichoke stems and chop finely. Mix with the beaten egg, breadcrumbs, garlic, mint, salt and pepper, and 2 tbsp olive oil. Spoon the stuffing into the centre of the artichokes.

Put the artichokes head-down in a pan, in which they fit quite tightly together, and cover with half water and half olive oil. Bring to a simmer and cook gently for 15–20 minutes, or until very tender. To check, pierce one with a fine skewer – it should feel perfectly soft. The artichokes can be eaten hot or cold.

Serves 4–6

" The Romans adore artichokes, the best of which are cultivated near Ladispoli. These are violet in colour, oval not round, and much smaller than their French counterparts, which accounts for their tenderness. "

SCAROLA IMBUTTUNATA
STUFFED CURLY ENDIVE

4 heads of curly endive
salt and pepper
6 tbsp olive oil
30g dried breadcrumbs

Stuffing
1 garlic clove, finely chopped
20g salted capers, soaked and drained
8 anchovy fillets in oil, drained and chopped
20g raisins
20g pine nuts
50g pitted black olives, chopped
80g sun-dried tomatoes, chopped

Preheat the oven to 200°C/Gas 6. Blanch the endive heads in boiling salted water for 3–4 minutes, then drain. Pick off the tough, very green outer leaves so that only the hearts remain. Drain thoroughly, then open out each endive heart to make a cavity in the middle.

To make the stuffing, mix all the ingredients together, seasoning with salt and pepper to taste. Stuff the endive hearts with the mixture and sprinkle with a little olive oil. Fold the leaves together to enclose the stuffing in the shape of a ball, pressing with your hands, and tie up the tops with string to make a parcel.

Place the stuffed endive on a baking tray, bases uppermost. Drizzle with the remaining olive oil and sprinkle with the breadcrumbs, then bake in the preheated oven for 20–30 minutes. Serve hot or cold.

Serves 4

" This unusual dish, probably of Jewish origin, is likely to appeal to vegetarians if they omit the anchovies. It is typically served as a first course. "

SPINACI AL BURRO AGRO
SPINACH WITH 'SOUR' BUTTER

1kg curly spinach
salt and pepper
100g butter
juice of 1 lemon
50g Parmesan, grated

After you have thoroughly cleaned the spinach, bring a pot of lightly salted water to the boil. Blanch the spinach for 4–5 minutes. Drain but do not squeeze out any additional liquid.

Put the butter in a pan and melt until it is foaming. Add the lemon juice and some salt and pepper. Put the spinach on to plates, pour the butter on top and sprinkle with Parmesan.

Serves 4

This is an excellent dish, which I like to eat as a starter. You need to use the Continental curly variety of spinach, with very substantial deep green leaves. This kind of spinach requires several washes in water because sand or grit may lurk in the curls of the leaves.

ROTOLINI DI SPINACI AL SUGO
LITTLE SPINACH ROLLS

Pancakes
150g Italian '00' flour
250ml milk
2 eggs
salt and pepper
40g butter, melted, plus extra for greasing

Filling
800g spinach, washed
85g pecorino cheese, grated
200g ricotta cheese
100g cooked ham, cut into very small cubes
a pinch of freshly grated nutmeg

To serve
50g butter
1 recipe basic tomato sauce (p315)
50g Parmesan, grated

Preheat the oven to 190°C/Gas 5.

For the pancakes, make a batter. Put the flour in a bowl and make a well in the centre. Mix the milk and eggs together, and add salt and pepper to taste. Pour into the well and gradually mix in the flour until you have a smooth batter. Brush a 15cm pancake pan with some of the melted butter, and pour 1 tbsp of the mixture into it. Make a pancake, cooking it on both sides. Keep warm. Repeat, brushing the pan again with the butter, until you finish all the mixture. You should have about twelve pancakes.

For the filling, boil the spinach in lightly salted water for 3–4 minutes, then drain, squeeze dry and roughly chop. Mix with the pecorino and ricotta, ham, nutmeg and season to taste. Spread the filling mixture equally on each of the pancakes and roll up to obtain a cylindrical shape.

Lightly butter a baking dish, and line the rolls up next to each other in it. Cover with tomato sauce, sprinkle with Parmesan, and dot the rest of the butter on top. Bake in the preheated oven for 15 minutes.

Serves 6

RADICCHIO GRIGLIATO
GRILLED AND BAKED RADICCHIO

4 whole radicchio from Treviso (firm to the touch),
 with a nice pointed root (this is also edible)
8 tbsp extra virgin olive oil
salt and pepper
8 slices speck
125g fontina cheese, very thinly cut

Preheat the grill to medium and the oven to 190°C/Gas 5.

Remove the old outer leaves from the radicchio, and
trim the stems. Cut into two equal parts lengthways.
(The radicchio should be at least 20cm long, including
the root.) Brush the halves with olive oil, salt and
pepper, put under the preheated grill (make sure it's
not too hot), and cook gently for 15 minutes. Brush
with more oil and check that the leaves are not burning.

Remove from the grill, lay a slice of speck and fontina
on each half and sprinkle on some pepper. Put in the
preheated oven for 5–8 minutes or until the cheese has
melted. Serve as an antipasto.

Serves 4

GRIGLIATA DI VEGETALI
GRILLED VEGETABLES

1 aubergine, thinly sliced lengthways
2 courgettes, thinly sliced lengthways
1 red pepper, de-seeded and cut into strips
1 yellow pepper, de-seeded and cut into strips
4 tomatoes, halved

The marinade
5 tbsp extra virgin olive oil
2 tbsp very finely chopped mint
2 tbsp very finely chopped basil
2 tbsp white wine vinegar
salt and pepper

Preheat a charcoal grill or ridged grill pan.

Prepare the marinade by mixing together all the
ingredients. Dip the vegetables one by one into the
marinade, place on the hot grill and cook for a few
minutes each side. You will have to do this in batches.
Leave the cooking of the tomatoes until last as they
will make the grill wet. When turning the vegetables
on to the other side, baste with the rest of the marinade.

Eat either as accompaniment to main dishes, or as a
first course.

Serves 4

" Probably the best-known radicchio dish is
grilled radicchio, and this is my variation on
it. Thanks to the popularity of this vegetable,
which is often used in salads, we can also
appreciate its culinary versatility, for a huge
number of dishes in the last 20 years have
been based on it. "

At home you could either
charcoal grill these vegetables
on a barbecue or use a special
cast-iron ridged grill pan.
The most important thing to
remember is to add flavour with
a marinade into which you dip
the vegetables and which you
use for basting as well.

MEDAGLIONI DI MELANZANE
AUBERGINE MEDALLIONS

POLPETTE DI MELANZANE
AUBERGINE RISSOLES

8 x 15mm-thick round slices (from the middle section)
    of the aubergine
olive oil, for frying
60g pesto
125g pecorino cheese, cut into thin slices
125g polpa di pomodoro or chunky passata
85g Parmesan, grated
salt and pepper
8 basil leaves

400g aubergines, peeled and sliced
salt and pepper
350g minced veal
1 egg, beaten
½ garlic clove, extremely finely chopped
4 tbsp freshly grated Parmesan
¼ tbsp freshly grated nutmeg
1 tbsp finely chopped parsley
1 tbsp dried breadcrumbs
plain white flour, for dusting
olive oil, for frying

Preheat the oven to 200°C/Gas 6.

Fry the aubergine slices for 5 minutes on each side in
a pan with a little olive oil. Spread a little pesto on each
slice and top with some pecorino, tomato pulp and
Parmesan, adding salt and pepper to taste. Bake in the
preheated oven for 8–10 minutes until the cheese has
melted and the Parmesan is golden. Serve with the
fresh basil leaves as a starter.

Serves 4

Boil the aubergine slices in salted water for 8 minutes,
then drain.

Squeeze all the water you can from the aubergine,
and chop finely. In a bowl, mix the meat, egg, garlic,
Parmesan, nutmeg, parsley, breadcrumbs and salt
and pepper. Mix well with the aubergine until smooth.
With your hands, form 12 balls and shape them into flat
rounds. Dust them with flour and fry in medium-hot
olive oil for 5 minutes on each side. Put on some kitchen
paper to remove any excess oil, and serve.

Makes 12 rissoles

“ It is such a pleasure to be able to obtain
so many different dishes from the aubergine.
Its versatility is really rewarding, as is
illustrated in this recipe, where slices
of aubergine act magnificently as a base
or 'carrier' for other ingredients. ”

SICILIAN VEGETABLE STEW

800g aubergine
1 large onion, chopped
2 tbsp olive oil
3 ripe tomatoes, cut into chunks
1 tbsp tomato purée, diluted with a little water
1 tbsp caster sugar
1 tbsp salted capers, soaked and drained
20 pitted green olives
1 tbsp white wine vinegar
chopped leaves and stalks of 1 head celery
1 tbsp raisins
salt and pepper
1 tbsp pine kernels (optional)

Cut the aubergine into 3cm chunks, soak in cold water for 5 minutes, then drain. This will stop the aubergine from absorbing too much oil.

Fry the onion in the olive oil in a large pan for a few minutes to soften. Put the aubergine chunks into the pan and fry until soft and tender, about 10 minutes. Add the tomatoes, diluted tomato purée, sugar, capers, olives, vinegar, celery leaves and stalks, raisins and some salt and pepper and stew slowly until everything is melted together, about 30 minutes.

Stir in the pine kernels, if desired, and serve either cold or warm as a side dish, or by itself with good country bread.

Serves 4–6

" Versatile, delicious and easy to make, caponata is probably Sicily's best-known dish. Throughout the centuries Sicily has been invaded and colonised by many other nations, and many Sicilian recipes show influences from other cuisines. Here you will see that there are some hints of the French ratatouille, while the inclusion of raisins and pine kernels suggests some Arabic influences, too. "

MELANZANE ALL'ISCHITANA
AUBERGINE ISCHIA-STYLE

4 large or 8 small aubergines
3 garlic cloves, chopped
3 tbsp chopped parsley
60g salted capers, soaked and drained
125g Parma ham, finely diced
125g cooked ham, finely diced
salt and pepper

Sauce
1 small onion, finely sliced
50ml olive oil
1kg ripe tomatoes, finely chopped
8 large basil leaves, shredded

Make the tomato sauce first. Fry the onion gently in the olive oil until soft, then add the remaining ingredients. Season to taste with salt and pepper. Stir and heat through for a few minutes.

Top and tail the aubergines. Make three deep incisions with a pointed knife along each aubergine, without piercing the other side. Wash and pat them dry. Mix all the remaining ingredients together to produce a smooth mixture, seasoning it to taste. Fill every pocket in the aubergines with this mixture, and put them in the pan along with the sauce. Slowly cook for about 40 minutes, or until the aubergine is soft.

Serves 4

MILINCIANI ALLA PARMIGIANA
TIMBALE OF AUBERGINES WITH PARMESAN AND TOMATO
Illustrated overleaf

3 large, meaty aubergines
3 eggs, beaten
salt and pepper
flour, for dusting
olive oil, for frying
15 basil leaves
250g Parmesan, grated

Sauce
1 garlic clove, finely chopped
5 tbsp olive oil
800g polpa di pomodoro or chunky passata
4–5 basil leaves, torn

Cut the aubergines into 1cm slices and immerse in cold water for 1 minute, then drain and pat dry. Season the eggs with salt.

Dust the aubergine slices with flour and then dip into the beaten eggs. Heat a film of olive oil in a large frying pan and fry the aubergine slices until golden on each side. Drain on kitchen paper and set aside. Preheat the oven to 200°C/Gas 6.

To make the sauce, fry the garlic in the olive oil, then add the tomato pulp and basil. Simmer for 15–20 minutes, then season with salt to taste.

To assemble the timbale, spread 2–3 tbsp of the tomato sauce over the bottom of a suitable baking dish. Cover with a layer of aubergine slices, some more sauce, a little basil and plenty of Parmesan. Repeat until the ingredients are used up, finishing with tomato sauce and Parmesan. Bake in the oven for 20 minutes until golden and bubbling. Leave to stand for 5 minutes or so, then serve cut into squares.

Serves 6

" Aubergines and peppers have pride of place in the cuisine of the entire south of Italy. This curious but excellent and easy-to-make recipe comes from the island of Ischia. The filling can vary from family to family, but this one is the most popular. **"**

Many people believe this simple recipe originates from Emilia-Romagna, but it was born in Sicily. It appears in various guises and is often simply called parmigiana di melanzane. Serve as a starter or a vegetarian main course.

PEPERONI MANDORLATI
PAN-ROASTED PEPPERS WITH ALMONDS

4–6 fleshy yellow peppers
6 tbsp olive oil
2 garlic cloves, finely chopped
20g caster sugar
40g raisins
30g slivered almonds
3 tbsp white wine vinegar
salt and pepper

Halve, core and de-seed the peppers, then cut into strips. Heat the olive oil in a pan and fry the pepper strips, stirring from time to time, until they are soft and beginning to caramelise at the edges, about 20–25 minutes.

Add the garlic, sugar, raisins and almonds. Stir-fry for a few minutes longer, then add the wine vinegar and let it evaporate. Season with salt and pepper to taste. Serve hot or cold.

Serves 4

I like to eat peppers like this as part of an antipasto or as a side dish to grilled lamb. My mother cooked peppers in a similar way, but without the raisins and almonds. Sweet, meaty peppers are essential for this dish.

PEPERONI ARROTOLATI
STUFFED ROLLED PEPPERS

4 large, fleshy red and/or yellow peppers
20g dried breadcrumbs
olive oil

Filling
1 tbsp pine nuts
4 tbsp fresh breadcrumbs
1 tbsp finely chopped flat-leaf parsley
1 tsp salted capers, soaked and drained
3 tsp raisins
8 anchovy fillets in oil, drained and finely chopped
2 tbsp olive oil
salt and pepper

Preheat the oven to 200°C/Gas 6. Roast or grill the peppers for about 10 minutes until the skin is charred and can be peeled off easily.

Meanwhile, mix all the ingredients together for the filling, seasoning with salt and pepper to taste. Set aside.

Peel away the skin from the peppers, then halve or quarter lengthways, depending on size. Remove the seeds.

Lay the pepper pieces on a surface and divide the filling between them. Roll up to enclose and secure with a wooden toothpick or cocktail stick. Place on a baking tray, sprinkle with the dried breadcrumbs and drizzle with a little olive oil. Bake in the preheated oven for 15–20 minutes.

Serve the stuffed peppers warm or cold, with a bowl of olives on the side if you like.

Serves 4–8

“ Peppers and aubergines are the main players in the Pugliese cuisine. Peppers are fried, dried, regenerated, roasted, cooked with tomatoes, stuffed, grilled, preserved in vinegar … there's no limit to their versatility. I ate this dish for lunch in a trattoria in Lecce. It was so exhilaratingly good that I decided to make it for myself. ”

POMODORI FARCITI AL FORNO
STUFFED BAKED TOMATOES

4 large ripe tomatoes
50g risotto rice
salt and pepper
2 tbsp coarsely chopped mint, plus extra leaves to
    garnish
8 anchovy fillets in oil, drained and finely chopped
4 tbsp olive oil
1 garlic clove, very finely chopped

Preheat the oven to 180°C/Gas 4. Cut off the tops of
the tomatoes, keeping the lids. Scoop out the seeds
and liquid into a sieve over a bowl, to save the juice.

Cook the rice in salted water for 7 minutes, then drain
and cool. Add to the tomato juice with the chopped
mint, anchovies, olive oil and garlic. Season the
stuffing with salt and pepper to taste.

Spoon the stuffing into the tomato cavities and put the
lids on top. Place the tomatoes on a baking tray. Bake in
the oven for about 20 minutes, depending on size, until
the skin has wrinkled and the tomatoes are soft. Serve
garnished with mint leaves.

Serves 4

PEPERONI AL POMODORO
PEPPERS AND TOMATOES

90ml olive oil
600g peperoncini dolci (small sweet peppers)
    stems trimmed
1 garlic clove, finely chopped
400g ripe tomatoes, peeled, de-seeded and chopped
6 basil leaves
salt

Heat the oil in a pan and fry the whole peppers (the
little seeds inside are edible) for 10 minutes, stirring
constantly. Add the garlic and fry for a minute, then
stir in the tomatoes, basil and salt. Cover and cook
for about 15–20 minutes, until the peppers are soft.

My mother used to add some new potatoes and serve
these as a first course accompanied by country bread.

Serves 4

" In some parts of the South these small
sweet peppers are also called friarielli –
confusingly, since cime di rapa (rape tops)
are given the same name. This is a common
way of eating the very small peppers that
look like chillies but taste sweet. When
buying them you have to be sure to get
the real thing. "

ZUCCHINI ALLA SCAPECE
FRIED MARINATED COURGETTES

olive oil, for frying
6 courgettes, trimmed and cut into 7–8cm sticks,
	excess seeds removed
4 tbsp extra virgin olive oil
bunch of mint leaves, chopped
2 garlic cloves, cut into quarters
1 tbsp white wine vinegar
salt

Heat a little of the plain olive oil in a pan and fry the courgettes in batches so that they are separate rather than crowded together. Fry until brown, then drain on kitchen paper.

Put the courgette batons in a dish, and add the extra virgin olive oil, mint, garlic, vinegar and salt, and leave for the flavours to combine before eating.

Serves 4

FIORI DI ZUCCHINI RIPIENI
STUFFED COURGETTE FLOWERS

12 courgette flowers
275g ricotta cheese
freshly grated nutmeg
bunch of chives, chopped
1 egg, beaten
4 tbsp freshly grated Parmesan
salt and pepper
4 tbsp olive oil

Batter
2 eggs
55g plain flour
4 tbsp cold water

First make the batter, beat the eggs lightly in a bowl, then stir in the flour evenly. Gradually add the water to make a smooth consistency. Set aside.

Clean the courgette flowers carefully. Gently wash and dry the outside and make sure there are no insects inside. Prepare the filling by mixing together the ricotta, a pinch of nutmeg, chives, egg, Parmesan and some salt and pepper. Fill the flowers with spoonfuls of this mixture.

Heat the olive oil in a large frying pan. Dip the flowers in the batter and fry them, a few at a time, in the hot oil until golden brown, turning from time to time. Drain on kitchen paper before serving.

Serves 4

" Should you come home after work feeling peckish, then this little dish will induce a feeling of relaxation. Eaten with grissini, and a nice glass of wine, life will appear much more pleasurable! Typical of Naples, this dish is usually eaten as part of an antipasto, but can also be served to accompany meat and fish dishes. It is better to make a bigger quantity, which you can keep in the fridge for two or three days. "

❝ The Italians pay special attention to the flowers of the courgette and pumpkin. They are sold in bunches at the street markets and in good shops, when they are in season and are also used to make risottos or to prepare a sauce for pasta. ❞

PARMIGIANA DI ZUCCHINI
BAKED COURGETTES WITH TOMATO AND TALEGGIO

100g plain flour
4 eggs, beaten
freshly grated nutmeg
salt and pepper
olive oil, for shallow-frying
700g courgettes, trimmed and cut into 5mm-thick
   slices lengthways
400g Taleggio cheese, cubed
100g Parmesan, grated

Sauce
2 garlic cloves, finely sliced
6 tbsp olive oil
800g polpa di pomodoro or chunky passata
10 basil leaves

Preheat the oven to 200°C/Gas 6.

Make the tomato sauce by frying the garlic in the olive oil in a pan until soft, about 5 minutes. Add the tomato pulp and basil, some salt and pepper to taste and cook gently for 20–30 minutes.

To make the batter, put the flour in a bowl, make a well in the centre and pour in the beaten eggs. Season with a little nutmeg and some salt and pepper, and mix well to a thickish batter.

In a frying pan, gently heat a little olive oil. Dip the courgette slices into the batter, and fry in batches in the hot oil until golden, about 3–4 minutes per side. Drain on kitchen paper and set aside.

Now to assemble the dish. Put a layer of courgette slices on the base of a baking dish. Pour over a little tomato sauce, and some of the cheeses and then get on with the next layer. Finish with the sauce and Parmesan.

Bake for 30 minutes in the preheated oven. Leave to cool before cutting into portions to serve.

Serves 6–8

" This is a variation on the well-known parmigiana melanzane, the baked dish of aubergines with tomato and mozzarella. By using Taleggio instead of mozzarella and courgette in place of aubergine, I've made this dish a little lighter, but no less wonderful! "

ZUCCHINI CACIO E UOVA
COURGETTES WITH CHEESE AND EGG

1kg young courgettes
1 onion, finely sliced
85g butter
100ml olive oil
4 eggs, beaten
60g Parmesan, grated
2 tbsp coarsely chopped flat-leaf parsley
1 tbsp chopped mint leaves
salt and pepper

Clean and top and tail the courgettes. Cut them in half lengthways and, if they are very large, take away a little of the white pulp and seeds. Cut the rest into strips first and then little cubes.

Fry the onion in the butter and oil until soft, then add the courgette cubes and allow them to sweat a little over the low heat. When tender, add the beaten eggs into which you have mixed the Parmesan, parsley, mint and salt and pepper to taste. Do not let it become an omelette, and do not turn over as you would a frittata.

As soon as the eggs have solidified, serve warm accompanied by good country bread and a little salad for a light summer lunch.

Serves 4 as a starter

The cacio e uova (cheese and eggs) combination used in this Neapolitan recipe is also used in sauces for pasta and many other dishes. If you like strong flavours, replace the Parmesan with caciocavallo, a cheese similar to aged provolone.

ZUCCA AL FORNO
OVEN-BAKED PUMPKIN

1 pumpkin, about 3kg (preferably Marina di Choggia)
100g butter
2 garlic cloves, finely sliced
1 tbsp very finely chopped rosemary
salt and pepper
Parmesan, grated (optional)

Preheat the oven to 200°C/Gas 6.

Cut the pumpkin in half and remove the seeds. Cut each half into 3 wedges. Bake the pumpkin wedges for 50–60 minutes, depending on the size of the wedges. They should be slightly caramelised, and the flesh will be soft.

Melt the butter in a pan and fry the garlic slices and rosemary for a few minutes. Make an incision in the middle of the flesh on each pumpkin wedge, and pour in some garlic butter. Season to taste with salt and pepper. You eat it by spooning the buttery flesh out of the skin. Alternatively, you could sprinkle some Parmesan on top. It is an excellent first course. Pumpkin cooked in this way can be used for various other preparations such as Gnocchi di Zucca (p160) and Tortelli di Zucca (p121).

Serves 6

" When my mother was short of ingredients and also of time (we were six children!) then pumpkin was a welcome food. It didn't require a great deal of attention, but it fully satisfied our permanent hunger. At the time we loathed it – I wish I could have it now. "

BEANS BRAISED IN WHITE WINE

200g dried borlotti beans soaked for 12 hours
2 bay leaves
60g butter
30g speck, finely chopped
125ml Pinot Grigio or equivalent dry white wine
salt and pepper

Discard the soaking water and boil the beans in fresh water with the bay leaves for at least 2 hours, or until soft. In another pan, melt the butter and fry the speck until brown, then add the drained beans and stir for a few minutes. Add the wine and let it evaporate. Adjust with salt and pepper to taste.

Serves 4

BEANS AND RICE

300g dried borlotti beans
4 tbsp olive oil
1 large onion, finely sliced
100g pancetta, cut into small cubes
55g Parma ham, cut into small cubes
400g risotto rice such as carnaroli or arborio
100ml red wine, preferably Nebbiolo or Spanna
2 litres chicken stock (p314)

Soak the beans in plenty of water overnight, then drain. Put them in a saucepan, cover with fresh water and simmer for about 2 hours or until tender. Drain.

Heat the olive oil in a pan, add the onion, pancetta and Parma ham and fry for 5–6 minutes. Add the rice and beans and stir well. Add the red wine and then add the hot stock, ladle by ladle, stirring continuously. Wait until each ladleful has absorbed before you add the next. After 15–20 minutes the rice should be cooked al dente. Serve hot, without Parmesan.

Serves 6

" While I was visiting a wine company in Veneto, I ate in a small unknown restaurant or osteria. Some beans came to the table cooked as a side dish. They didn't look special but their flavour was unbelievable. I asked for the recipe and the answer was cotti con il Pinot, cooked with Pinot wine from the latest harvest. "

Originally from Vercelli, this is a risotto with beans, not to be confused with paniscia, a similar but much more complicated dish from the town of Novara. Ideally it should be made with fresh borlotti beans but because they are hard to come by, especially outside Italy, you could use the dried ones.

FAGIOLI GRASSI
'FAT' BEANS

10 pieces of pork skin, about 8 x 12cm
1 tbsp rosemary needles
1 tbsp roughly chopped parsley
1 red chilli
2 garlic cloves
salt and pepper
1kg fresh cannellini beans, or 450g dried,
   soaked for 12 hours
1 pigs trotter, cut in two
1 onion, pricked with cloves
1 carrot, diced
1 celery stalk, trimmed and diced
1 bouquet garni
   (bay leaves, rosemary, sage and parsley)
1 tbsp olive oil

Preheat the oven to 160°C/Gas 3.

To prepare the pork skins, finely chop the rosemary, parsley, chilli and garlic together. Lay the pieces of pork skin on the work surface and spread the herbs equally over them. Season well. Roll each up and bind like a sausage with kitchen string.

Put all the ingredients into a large pot of about 6–8 litres capacity with a lid. Cover well with water and cook in the preheated oven for 10–12 hours (you can do this overnight).

When cooked, remove and discard the bouquet garni and the onion, and serve. Should the dish be too liquid, you may take some of the beans and purée them before returning to the bulk of the beans.

Serves 10

66 This Piedmontese pièce de résistance comes specifically from Canavese, where I was brought up. Although the translation of the name doesn't make it sound very inviting, it is actually very tasty. This dish is called tofeja in the Canavese, from the name of a terracotta pot used in its cooking. It is eaten around carnival time in February, but is welcome throughout the winter months. Invite a few friends to share it with you. It's worth it! 99

FAVE NOVELLE IN PADELLA
BRAISED BROAD BEANS IN THEIR PODS

100ml olive oil
100g fatty pancetta, cut into strips
2 onions, finely sliced
1kg baby broad beans, with the bean just formed inside
200ml water
20 mint leaves, chopped
100g hot pork sausage (salsiccia piccante), cut into cubes
salt and pepper

Put the olive oil in a pan and fry the pancetta with the onions. Let the onions become soft, about 5 minutes, and then add the broad beans and the water (add more if required). Cook for 25 minutes, then add the mint and the sausage cubes. Cook for a further 10 minutes, then add salt and pepper to taste.

Serve as a first course.

Serves 4

The idea of eating whole broad beans, including the pods, comes from Sardinia. To do this you need to do a little 'cradle snatching'. Sadly, unless you have your own garden or you ask a neighbouring farmer with a broad bean field to help you, it will be difficult to cook this interesting dish.

MACCU
BROAD BEAN MASH

800g dried broad beans, without skins, in halves
1.5 litres water
salt and pepper
150ml extra virgin olive oil
2 garlic cloves, coarsely chopped
1 small chilli (not too hot), chopped
1kg cime di rapa, washed

Soak the beans overnight in the water with a little salt added. Next day, put the beans and water over a not too high heat and boil until the beans are dissolved and mix quickly to a fine mash. Add a little of the olive oil and some salt and pepper, and set aside.

Meanwhile, in another pan with a lid, heat 4 tbsp of the olive oil and gently fry the garlic and chilli. Add the cime di rapa, along with a little water, and braise until the vegetable is tender, about 15–20 minutes. Add a little salt and serve with the warm mash. Drizzle the rest of the olive oil over the top and enjoy.

Serves 4–6

" What polenta, the maize porridge, used to be for poor northerners, maccù was for southerners. It is a real peasant dish, you can find maccù on the menus of the best restaurants in the whole of southern Italy, but especially in Puglia and Sicily, the main areas of broad-bean cultivation. "

CIPOLLE DI TROPEA, PECORINO E FAVE
TROPEA ONIONS, PECORINO AND BROAD BEANS

2 large Tropea onions
300g pecorino cheese
800g young and tender broad beans
4–8 slices of good country bread
1 garlic clove, halved
extra virgin olive oil, for brushing

Slice the onions and cheese. Pod the broad beans. Rub the bread with the halved garlic clove and brush with a little olive oil.

There is no further cooking involved! Arrange the ingredients on 4 plates. Eat a piece of this and a piece of that and so on. A good Ciró wine from Calabria will accompany this very well.

Serves 4

In Calabria, more precisely in Tropea, there is a cultivated onion which is very special. It is not sharp at all in flavour, but slightly sweet. Unfortunately it has one handicap: it doesn't travel well. To mimic the 'sweetness' of Tropea onions, soak normal onions, cut into slices, in fresh water for a few hours. This takes away the sharpness.

PANELLE CON FRITTELLA
CHICKPEA FRITTERS
Illustrated overleaf

Panelle
300g chickpea flour
1 tsp aniseed
salt and pepper
500ml water
3 tbsp coarsely chopped parsley
olive oil, for oiling and frying

Frittella
4 tbsp olive oil
200g onions, finely sliced
300g fresh young and tender artichoke hearts, halved
275g podded tender garden peas
300g podded broad beans
100ml water
3 tbsp chopped flat-leaf parsley
1 tbsp salted capers, soaked and drained

To make the panelle, in a saucepan, mix the chickpea flour with the aniseed, some salt and pepper and water until smooth. Slowly bring to the boil, stirring, and cook, stirring, for 8–10 minutes until the mixture thickens, then mix in the parsley. Pour on to an oiled baking sheet or marble surface and flatten to a 1cm thickness. Leave until cool and set.

In the meantime, prepare the frittella. Heat the olive oil in a large saucepan and fry the onions until soft. Add the artichoke hearts, peas, broad beans and water.

Cover and cook for 15–20 minutes until all the vegetables are soft. Add the parsley and capers, and season with salt and pepper to taste.

Cut the set chickpea mixture into rounds or diamonds and shallow-fry in olive oil until golden on each side. Drain on kitchen paper, then serve the fritters with the vegetable stew.

Serves 4

❝ Panelle are a speciality of Palermo, where the fritters are often eaten in a panino (roll). Here they are served with a fresh vegetable stew, comprising artichokes, peas and broad beans – the perfect Sicilian complement. ❞

ASPARAGI CON LO SPECK
ASPARAGUS WITH SPECK

800g tender green asparagus spears, prepared
500g waxy new potatoes
salt and pepper
85g unsalted butter
300g speck, cut into thick slices and then into strips

Prepare the asparagus. If the skin of the new potatoes is nice and clean, leave it on and boil the potatoes in salted water until soft, about 20–25 minutes. Boil the asparagus in salted water until tender, about 10–15 minutes (pierce with a sharp knife to check.)

Melt the butter in a small pan but don't let it brown. Drain the potatoes and asparagus well and place the spears and a few cooked potatoes on each serving plate. Pour the melted butter on top, and season with salt and pepper. Add the strips of speck, sprinkled over if you prefer, and serve.

Serves 4

This dish would regularly make an appearance on the menu at my restaurant. You could substitute Parma ham for the speck, though I particularly enjoy the latter's delicate flavour here.

ASPARAGI BASSANESI
ASPARAGUS BASSANO STYLE

1kg white asparagus spears
  (green will do also), prepared
salt and pepper
85g butter, melted
1 tbsp very finely chopped parsley
a few drops of lemon juice
4 hard-boiled eggs, shelled and very finely chopped

Cook the asparagus spears in slightly salted water for 10–15 minutes, depending on their thickness.

Meanwhile, mix the melted butter with a pinch of salt and pepper to taste, the parsley, lemon juice and chopped eggs to make a smooth sauce. Serve the asparagus hot with the sauce poured over the middle.

Serves 4

" In the Veneto, people love asparagus when it is in season, and the white asparagus from Bassano del Grappa is famous. The Venetians are particularly fond of this recipe, which is quite simple. "

PISELLI AL PROSCIUTTO
PEAS AND HAM

a bunch of spring onions (white part only)
60g butter
150g good cooked ham (not the shoulder),
   cut into small cubes
500g frozen garden peas (petit pois)
2 tbsp water
salt and pepper
1 tbsp very finely chopped chives

Cut the white part of the spring onions very finely and fry in the butter, along with the ham, until the onions are soft. Add the frozen peas and the water. It will take a few minutes for the peas to defrost. Give it a good stir and cook for another 8–10 minutes. Test that the peas are tender, add some salt and pepper, and serve with a sprinkling of chives.

Serves 4

" This is a lovely dish for any occasion, and it's economical and very easy to prepare. I like to eat these peas just with bread as a starter, but they can be a good dish to accompany chicken, rabbit, lamb and also roast fish. I use cooked ham which doesn't give lots of taste and flavour to the dish, but it complements the subtlety of the peas. **"**

Frozen petit pois are good for this dish because the tenderness you want is very difficult to achieve unless you have your own garden. Whatever you do, don't use tinned peas.

ASPARAGUS EN CHEMISE

16 large green asparagus spears, prepared
16 whole eggs
4 tbsp milk
1 tbsp each of finely chopped fresh mint, parsley,
    thyme and chives
50g Parmesan, freshly grated
salt and pepper
olive oil
a few chive stalks

Cook the asparagus until al dente. Cool and set aside.

Mix the eggs, milk, herbs, cheese and seasoning well.
Using a little oil each time, make 8 very thin omelettes,
about 16cm in diameter.

Wrap 2 asparagus spears in each omelette, and bind
with a chive stalk to secure.

Makes 8 'parcels'

ASPARAGUS TIMBALE

1kg fresh green asparagus spears, prepared
salt and pepper
75g butter, melted
1 loaf of white sliced bread, crusts removed
2 eggs, beaten
200ml double cream
75g Parmesan, grated
60g Parma ham, very finely minced
freshly grated nutmeg

Preheat the oven to 200°C/Gas 6.

Cook the asparagus in salted water until al dente, about
7–8 minutes.

Butter a tin about 5–6cm deep and 30cm in diameter,
using a little of the butter, then line it with the sliced
bread, allowing it to go up the sides, and overlapping
slightly. Place half of the asparagus on the bread. Mix
together the eggs, cream, cheese, ham and remaining
melted butter. Season with salt, pepper and nutmeg to
taste, and pour half of it over the top of the asparagus.
Add the remaining asparagus and pour over the rest
of the mixture.

Bake in the preheated oven for 45 minutes, leave for a
few minutes to set, then invert onto a large plate. Serve
it like this, turned out 'upside down'. Cut it carefully
into wedges using a serrated knife.

Serves 8 as a starter, 4 as a main course

" I cooked this recipe for the first time for
a rather posh picnic at Glyndebourne. Our
guests were some Indian friends who are
both vegetarians, and I had to rack my brains
for an appropriate series of dishes. We very
much enjoyed the opera, the company
of our friends and, of course, the food! "

❝ Some good friends of mine from Cremona gave me a few wonderful and original local recipes. This is one of them, and it made me think again about the usefulness of sliced bread. ❞

BARBA DI FRATE CON AGLIO, OLIO E PEPERONCINO
FRIAR'S BEARD WITH GARLIC, OIL AND CHILLI

600g barba di frate, just attached to the root
salt
6 tbsp extra virgin olive oil
2 garlic cloves, sliced
1 chilli pepper, finely chopped

Put the barba di frate in boiling salted water and blanch until it reaches your desired crunchiness, about 4–5 minutes. Drain and put on a serving plate.

Put the olive oil in a pan and fry the garlic and chilli. Just before the garlic starts to colour, remove from the heat and pour on top of the warm vegetable.

Serves 4

CAVOLFIORE AFFOGATO
DROWNED CAULIFLOWER

1 cauliflower, about 1kg
150ml olive oil
2–3 saffron strands, soaked in a little hot water
3 garlic cloves, halved
30g pine kernels
30g raisins
salt and pepper

Cut small florets from the cauliflower, discarding only the tough stem and any leaves. Put the oil into a pan with a lid and heat gently. Add the florets, the saffron, garlic and a little water, cover and cook very gently until soft, about 25 minutes in total. After about 15 minutes, add pine kernels, raisins and salt and pepper to taste. This is a delicious accompaniment to chicken or fish.

Serves 4

Barba di Frate is also called barba di cappuccino, because it has nothing to do with coffee, but because it has connections with the Capuchin monks, a Franciscan order. This vegetable has become more popular in the last twenty years. I very much like to eat it prepared as in this recipe, though it is also good dressed simply with lemon and oil.

"Although most Neapolitan cooking is very simple, here is a recipe which leans towards the Arabic influences of further south. Pine kernels and raisins, two ingredients that appear more commonly in Middle-Eastern dishes, are seen quite often in the dishes of Campania, Calabria, Puglia and, naturally Sicily."

TORTA DI CICORIA
DANDELION PIE

300g Italian '00' flour
200g lard or unsalted butter at room temperature,
    cut into small cubes, plus extra for greasing
salt
water, as required
1 egg yolk, for glazing

Filling
700g dandelion leaves, washed and roughly chopped
salt
6 tbsp extra virgin olive oil
3 garlic cloves, finely chopped
1 tbsp salted capers, soaked and drained
1 chilli, finely chopped
55g pitted green or black olives
2 tbsp raisins
2 tbsp pine kernels
4 anchovy fillets in oil, drained and roughly chopped

For the pastry, mix the flour with the lard or butter,
a pinch of salt and enough water – about 6 tbsp – to
produce a pliable dough. Knead it well, then cover
and let it rest in the fridge for 20–30 minutes.

For the filling, blanch the dandelion leaves in slightly
salted water for 15–20 minutes. Drain and squeeze
out excess liquid. Put the olive oil into a large pan and
add the garlic, capers, chilli and olives, and fry briefly.
Add the dandelion leaves, raisins, pine kernels and
anchovies, and stir-fry until the anchovies are cooked.

Meanwhile, preheat the oven to 200°C/Gas 6.

Grease a tart ring of about 25cm in diameter with
a little extra lard. Roll half the pastry out to 3mm
thickness, and then transfer to the tart ring, trimming
off any excess. Roll out the rest of the pastry to a circle
of the same size. Fill the ring with the filling mixture,
and then cover with the circle of pastry to form a lid.
Seal by pinching the dough together around the rim.
Pierce a hole in the top to let the steam out. Brush
with the egg yolk, then bake in the preheated oven
for 25–30 minutes. Serve hot or cold.

Serves 4

TORTA DI ORTICHE
NETTLE TART

350g nettle leaves
salt and pepper
12 quails eggs
20g lard, melted
10 sheets of filo pastry
4 eggs, beaten
150g Parmesan or Cheddar cheese, grated
½ tsp freshly grated nutmeg
15g dried breadcrumbs
15g unsalted butter

Preheat the oven to 200°C/Gas 6.

Cook the cleaned nettle leaves in salted water for 5–8
minutes, depending on their toughness. Strain and
squeeze out the excess water. Leave to cool and then
chop roughly. Cook the quails eggs for approximately
7–8 minutes, then cool and remove their shells.

Brush a round baking tin of 25cm in diameter and
5cm high with a little lard, then place a sheet of filo
pastry on the base. Brush with lard, and then continue
to layer the sheets one by one, overlapping slightly,
until the whole inside of the tin is covered.

Mix the chopped nettle leaves in a bowl with the eggs,
Parmesan or Cheddar, nutmeg and salt and pepper
to taste. Place the quails eggs on the filo pastry, then
cover with the nettle mixture to fill the tin. Trim any
excess filo pastry from around the edge of the tin,
leaving 2.5cm overlapping. Fold the pastry over the
filling, taking care to leave the middle uncovered.
Sprinkle the tart with breadcrumbs and small dabs
of butter. Bake for 15 minutes in the preheated oven
until golden brown. Serve hot in wedges.

Serves 4

Be careful to wear gloves
when collecting nettles and
be sure to put them in a
plastic bag in the fridge
before preparation, it
reduces the sting!

" Why use nettles, when this dish could easily be made with any other type of greens? The reason is that nettles, while probably being the most scorned vegetable on earth, also have a delightful nutty taste, contain lots of natural goodness, and on top of that, cost nothing. "

CAPONATA DI FUNGHI
CAPONATA OF MUSHROOMS

300g mixed fresh ceps
2 large aubergines, cut into large cubes
8 tbsp olive oil
1 hot red chilli, sliced
8 garlic cloves, sliced
2 tbsp white wine vinegar
3 tbsp finely chopped celery leaves
2 tbsp finely chopped parsley
1 tsp caster sugar
salt and pepper

Clean the ceps thoroughly, and if large, cut to an appropriate size.

Aubergines absorb quite a lot of oil, so to avoid that, first dip the cubes in water, then pat dry. Fry them in the olive oil until brown on each side, drain well and set aside.

Fry the chilli and garlic in the same pan for 1–2 minutes, then add the ceps. Stir-fry for a few minutes, then add the aubergine, vinegar, celery leaves, parsley and sugar, and cook everything slowly together for 10 minutes. Add salt and pepper to taste.

Serve with toast, as a light dish, or to accompany meat or fish main dishes.

Serves 4

" This typical Sicilian dish is the epitome of all that is fresh in that part of the world, where it is often served with the Arabic touch of raisins and pine kernels.
This variation of mine – inevitably to accommodate mushrooms – looks at first glance to be a little artificial. The end result is, however, a side dish that goes with anything, and it's also good by itself as a light dish. "

CALZONE PUGLIESE
ONION PIE

CIPOLLINE IN AGRODOLCE
SWEET-AND-SOUR ONIONS

400g plain flour, plus extra for dusting
100ml olive oil, plus extra for oiling
1 egg, beaten
100ml dry white wine
salt

Filling
3 tbsp olive oil
1kg red onions, sliced
160g salty ricotta cheese
50g pecorino cheese, freshly grated
4 eggs, beaten

To make the pastry, put the flour in a bowl and make
a well in the centre. Add the olive oil, egg and white
wine, and gradually mix into the flour to make a dough,
adding water if necessary, and a pinch of salt. Wrap
in cling film and chill for 30 minutes before rolling.
Meanwhile, preheat heat the oven to 200°C/Gas 6.

For the filling, heat the oil in a pan and cook the onions
until soft. Leave to cool, then mix with the ricotta,
pecorino and most of the eggs (save a little for glazing).

Roll out the pastry on a lightly floured surface to a 3mm
thick round and place on an oiled baking tray. Pile the
filling onto the centre of the pastry, and fold over to
enclose the filling in a half-moon shape. Press the edges
together to seal and brush with the reserved egg. Bake
in the preheated oven for about 20 minutes.

This pie can be eaten warm or cold.

Serves 4–6

3 tbsp olive oil
800g cipolline (small onions), peeled and soaked
   in water for 20 minutes
4 tbsp strong white wine vinegar
4 tbsp dry white wine
2 tbsp plain white flour
2 tbsp caster sugar
salt and pepper
1 litre chicken or vegetable stock (p314)

Preheat the oven to 160°C/Gas 3.

Pour the oil into an ovenproof dish and then fry the
onions until they start to colour. Add the vinegar and
wine and leave for a few minutes to allow some of the
vinegar to evaporate. Sprinkle in the flour and mix well,
then add the sugar and some salt and pepper. Add the
stock, mix again, then put in the preheated oven for
2 hours. A thick sauce will be produced and the onions
will be brown, shiny and cooked.

Serves 4

" The calzone of Puglia is quite different
from the more familiar calzone of Naples,
which is essentially a folded pizza. The
Puglian version looks more like a pie
or giant pasty. Also known as pizza di
acqua viva, they are traditionally eaten
to celebrate the feast days of the two
saints, Dottori Cosimo and Damiano. "

My mother used to prepare
these onions, which were
avidly consumed by our
family, either in antipasto or
with boiled chicken and
meats. To make this dish, you
need the special small flat
onions so common in Italy,
called borretane (but I have
also seen them being sold
outside Italy). You could use
pickling onions instead.

POTATO CAKE

1kg floury potatoes
55g prosciutto cotto, cut into cubes
25g buffalo mozzarella, cut into small cubes
100g provola cheese (smoked mozzarella),
    cut into small cubes
55g Parmesan, grated
4 eggs, beaten
2 tbsp finely chopped flat-leaf parsley
salt and pepper
butter, for greasing
4 tbsp dried breadcrumbs
4 tbsp olive oil

Preheat the oven to 180°C/Gas 4. Boil the potatoes until tender, then drain and peel them. Pass them through a sieve to make a purée. Mix the potato purée with the prosciutto, mozzarella, provola, Parmesan, eggs, parsley and some salt and pepper.

Butter a round 25cm cake tin, and dust with some of the breadcrumbs. Pour the potato mixture into it and press gently with a fork to give some shape. Sprinkle with the remaining breadcrumbs and then trickle over the olive oil. Bake for 30 minutes, until browned on top.

The cake is very good warm but also excellent cold.

Serves 6

POTATOES AND CEPS

200g fresh ceps
600g waxy firm potatoes
salt and pepper
85g butter
6 tbsp olive oil
12 sage leaves

Clean, trim and finely slice the ceps, and peel the potatoes. Boil the potatoes in salted water until soft. Drain and leave them to cool, then slice thickly.

Fry the cep slices in half the butter and half the oil until brown, then set aside. Fry the potatoes and two-thirds of the sage leaves in the rest of the butter and oil.

Mix the ceps and potatoes together in a large dish and season to taste. Scatter the remaining sage leaves over. Serve either as a starter or a side dish with meat or fish.

Serves 4

" Gattò is derived from the French gâteau, which this resembles in shape when baked. It is very common in Naples, where many French-influenced recipes are cooked even today – a legacy of the Bourbon occupation in the 18th century. "

" An excellent combination of two natural ingredients, which are almost made for each other. As with many things in life, sometimes simplicity can most nearly approach perfection. In this Italian recipe, texture, flavour and looks blend superbly. "

TORTINO DI SEDANO RAPA
CELERIAC CAKE

1 celeriac, about 1.25kg, peeled and cut in half
salt and pepper
800g spinach, well washed
2 egg yolks
200g mascarpone cheese
¼ whole nutmeg, freshly grated
100g Parmesan, freshly grated
50g butter
¼ garlic clove, finely chopped
20g dried breadcrumbs

Preheat the oven to 200°C/Gas 6.

Cook the peeled celeriac in salted water until tender, about 30 minutes. Drain and cut into very thin slices. Cook the spinach for 4 minutes in boiling salted water, then drain, squeeze and roughly chop. Mix the egg yolks with the mascarpone, nutmeg, salt, pepper and grated Parmesan.

Take a single large ovenproof dish or four individual ovenproof ramekins, and use a little of the butter to grease them. Melt the remaining butter in a small pan, and gently fry the garlic. Lay some slices of celeriac, some spinach and a 1cm thick layer of mascarpone mixture in the container(s). Repeat and finish with the celeriac. Pour the foaming garlic butter on top and sprinkle with breadcrumbs. (Incidentally, should you forget to buy or make breadcrumbs, just mince some grissini, as I did). Bake in the preheated oven for 15 minutes or until a golden crust develops.

Serves 4

" It is fascinating to create a brand-new recipe. For me, the rules to follow are: first, a good combination of taste and flavour; secondly, to be simple, to choose down-to-earth ingredients and not to be too clever or outrageous. In other words, make culinary sense while playing with food. This is one of those recipes. **"**

CUORI DI SEDANO GRATINATI
CELERY HEART GRATIN

4 small, white, tender heads of celery,
   or 2 medium-sized ones
salt and pepper
60g butter, melted, plus extra for greasing
40g fresh country bread, preferably Pugliese,
   made into crumbs
½ garlic clove, extremely finely chopped
1 tsp very finely chopped parsley
30g Parmesan, grated
½ tsp freshly grated nutmeg

Preheat the oven to 200°C/Gas 6.

Cut the tops off the celery so that you have hearts of 15cm long. Cut these in half and boil them in salted water for 8 minutes. Drain and arrange them next to one another on a buttered baking tray.

Put the breadcrumbs into a blender along with the garlic, and blend to make garlic-scented breadcrumbs. Mix with the parsley. Sprinkle the melted butter equally over the celery, then the Parmesan, nutmeg, salt and pepper, and finally the breadcrumbs. Put in the preheated oven and bake for 10–12 minutes, or until a nice crust is formed.

Serves 4

Of the two kinds of celery, the white is normally used raw, and the green is used more in cooking or to flavour other preparations. Here I use the white hearts of small celery, boiled first and then baked. It is utterly delicious treated this way, and can be served as a small starter, or to accompany other delicate dishes.

FINOCCHI GRATINATI
FENNEL GRATIN

4 large fennel bulbs
salt and pepper
80g unsalted butter, cut into cubes
100g fresh white breadcrumbs
freshly grated nutmeg

Preheat the oven to 200°C/Gas 6.

Cook the whole fennel bulbs in salted water until the point of a sharp knife enters easily, about 20–25 minutes. Drain and leave to cool.

Cut the fennel into 5mm slices and arrange them like roof tiles on a baking tray. Sprinkle with the cubed butter and the breadcrumbs, plus a little nutmeg, salt and pepper and bake in the preheated oven until the crust is golden, about another 20 minutes.

Serve hot.

Serves 4

" I love fennel, either raw or cooked, and sometimes I eat it as a digestive. When buying your fennel, be sure to check the outer layer – it should be shiny, fresh and not too tough. This dish can be eaten either with bread or on its own as a starter, or served as an accompaniment to a main course – fish or meat. "

DOLCI

MANGO CON SCIROPPO DI LIME
MANGO WITH LIME SYRUP

MELECOTOGNE IN COMPOSTA
QUINCE COMPOTE

2 large ripe mangoes
4 small mint sprigs

Syrup
3 limes
100g caster sugar

To peel the mangoes, cut close to the large, narrow stone along the length of the fruit on either side. You will have two rounded bits, and the stone. Cut the peel off the rounded bits and place the 4 pieces on a large plate.

To prepare the syrup, first cut the zest off the limes, leaving behind any pith. Slice this zest into thin strips. Squeeze the juice from the limes into a small pan and add the sugar. Simmer until the sugar has melted, then boil to reduce this liquid by half. Add the strips of zest and continue to simmer for a few minutes, until caramelised. Leave to cool.

Pour the cooled lime syrup over the mango halves and decorate with the mint sprigs.

Serves 4

" This extremely simple recipe is full of lots of fresh flavour. The best mango to use here would be the Alfonso variety from India, but this recipe will be a success whatever type you use, provided the mangoes are ripe and soft. "

1kg quinces, quartered, peeled and de-seeded
400g caster sugar
1 lemon
1 cinnamon stick (optional)

Put the quinces in a large pan and add enough water to reach a third of the way up the fruit. Add the sugar and squeeze in the juice from the lemon, then add the squeezed-out lemon halves and the cinnamon stick, if using.

Bring to the boil, cover and simmer for about 15 minutes, until the quinces are soft but still hold their shape. Check by inserting the knife from time to time. Remove the lemon halves and leave to cool. Serve chilled with some double cream, mascarpone, or even with plain yoghurt.

Serves 4

LAMPONI E MORE AL LIMONE
RASPBERRIES AND BLACKBERRIES WITH SUGAR AND LEMON

300g mixed ripe raspberries and blackberries
juice of 1 lemon
100g caster sugar
mascarpone, to serve (optional)

Put the berries into a non-reactive bowl and sprinkle with the lemon juice and sugar. Mix very carefully and gently to amalgamate.

Serve the berries with mascarpone if you like.

Serves 4

" I have often said that Italians have a sweet tooth, but not necessarily after meals. Day-to-day, fresh, ripe seasonal fruit is the usual way to round off a meal. As a young boy, fruit became my responsibility and I became expert in monitoring farmers' fruit crops. During the autumn, I would obtain wonderful raspberries and pick wild blackberries to complement them. "

GRANITA DI PANTELLERIA
RASPBERRY AND BLACKBERRY GRANITA

1.5kg very ripe mixed raspberries and blackberries
juice of 2 lemons
finely grated zest of 1 lemon
1.5kg caster sugar

Put the berries in a stainless-steel pot over a medium heat and let them burst and release their juices, stirring from time to time. Add the lemon juice and zest, followed by the sugar, and cook for 15 minutes, still stirring. When the sugar has melted, leave the mixture to cool. The berries will have almost dissolved, so there should be no need to strain, but if you are sensitive to texture, you can do so.

To make the granita, take the berry mixture and dilute with half its volume of water. Mix well and then place in a suitable container in the freezer. When the mixture starts to set, remove from the freezer and stir well to break up the ice crystals. Repeat this process a couple of times, or until the crystals have been completely dispersed and the granita is evenly grainy. Spoon into glasses and serve immediately.

Makes about 3kg

I once had a granita like this (though made of mulberries) on a holiday in Pantelleria, a small island in the middle of the Mediterranean. Ripe strawberries can be used in the same way, as indeed can any other soft fruit.

❝ Calabria holds many memories for me, not least the
wonderful baked dried figs. They were called crucette
('little crosses'), because the figs were cut open and twisted
together in pairs to make a little cross. ❞

CROCETTE DI FICHI AL FORNO
BAKED HONEY FIGS

juice of 2 oranges
75ml water
3 tbsp honey
30 large, soft dried figs
30 half walnuts or whole blanched almonds
30 small pieces tangerine, orange or citron zest

Put the orange juice in a pan and dilute with the water. Add the honey and bring to the boil. Add the figs to the pan and cook gently for about 15 minutes until they begin to swell. Drain, reserving any liquor, and spread the figs out on a tray. Leave to dry for a day.

Preheat the oven to 200°C/Gas 6. Make an incision in each fig, and insert a nut and a piece of tangerine, orange or citron zest in each slit. Close tightly and bake for about 25 minutes, until caramelised and brown.

At the end, I drizzle the reserved orange and honey syrup over … delicious.

Makes 30

This great classic dessert is made with very simple ingredients indeed. For it to work, however, the figs have to be impeccably ripe and of good quality.

FRUTTA SCIROPPATA
FRUITS IN SYRUP

1kg fruit (see below)
800g caster sugar
1 litre water
1 vanilla pod

If using peaches, blanch them briefly in boiling water, then skin and halve them and remove the stone.

Put the sugar, water and vanilla pod ina large pan and heat gently until the sugar has completely dissolved. Add the fruit and cook gently until just tender – anything from 25 minutes for the softest fruit to 40 minutes for the harder ones. Remove the fruit with a slotted spoon and set aside.

Increase the heat and boil the liquid until reduced in volume by a third. Reduce the heat again, put the fruit back in the pan and cook over a very low heat for another 30 minutes. Transfer to a sterilised jar, seal and store in a cool place until needed.

Makes enough to fill a 1.5kg jar

" This is halfway between a compote and crystallized fruit. The secret is to achieve a degree of sugar concentration in the liquid so that it functions as a preservative. The fruit should keep its shape. Ripe peaches, plums or kumquats are all ideal. It is often served with ice-cream or pannacotta."

PERE AL VINO ROSSO
WILLIAMS PEARS IN RED WINE SAUCE

6 ripe Williams pears
400ml red wine
zest of 1 lemon, in pieces
150g caster sugar
whipped double cream, to serve (optional)

Preheat the oven to 200°C/Gas 6.

Wash and put the pears upright in a suitably sized ovenproof container. You want them to fit snugly, without too much space between them.

Bake in the preheated oven for 30–40 minutes.

Remove the pears from the oven and pour over the wine. Sprinkle over the lemon zest and most of the sugar, reserving a small amount to spoon on top of the pears. Bake for another 20 minutes, by which time the wine will have reduced and thickened in consistency.

Put the pears in a glass bowl, cover with the red wine syrup and chill.

Divide between 6 plates and serve with the syrup and some whipped double cream, if desired.

Serves 6

" An autumnal recipe using ripe pears and
an uncomplicated red wine. This simple dish
is very Italian, and has loads of flavour. "

CANEDERLI CON PRUGNE
DUMPLINGS WITH PLUMS

8 ripe plums, about 500g, pitted
8 sugar cubes
2 tbsp dried breadcrumbs
50g butter
ground cinnamon
icing sugar, for dusting

Dough
500g floury potatoes
salt
4 tbsp caster sugar
100g plain flour
1 egg yolk

To make the dough, boil the potatoes in salted water until tender, then drain and remove the skins. Pass through a sieve or potato ricer into a bowl. Add the sugar, flour, egg yolk and a pinch of salt to the potato purée and mix to a smooth, pliable dough.

Take a small handful of dough (enough to coat a plum), and flatten it in your hand. Place a plum in the middle, and put a sugar cube into the plum cavity. Fold the dough around the plum to enclose and form a dumpling, making sure it's sealed all around. Do the same with the remaining plums, sugar cubes and dough.

Cook the dumplings in 2 or 3 batches. Bring a large pan of water to the boil, plunge the dumplings in and cook for a few minutes, just until they rise to the surface. Scoop them out with a slotted spoon and keep warm while you cook the rest.

Fry the breadcrumbs in the butter until golden brown, then flavour with a large pinch of cinnamon to taste. Sprinkle this spicy mixture on top of the dumplings and serve hot, dusted with icing sugar.

Makes 8

" This recipe, which comes from near the Slovene border, is in fact Austrian in origin. Ripe, fresh apricots can be used instead of plums; I have also had excellent results with prunes. Serve as a dessert or sweet snack. "

PRESNIZ
FRIULIAN PASTRY WITH RUM-SOAKED FRUIT AND NUTS

100g raisins
100ml dark rum
40g butter, diced and softened, plus extra for greasing
140g biscuits (such as digestives)
70g pine nuts, toasted
70g walnut halves, toasted
70g blanched almonds, toasted
80g dark chocolate, finely chopped
60g candied orange and citron peel, diced
grated zest and juice of 1 lemon
1 egg, beaten
500g ready-made puff pastry
flour, for dusting
3–4 tbsp icing sugar

Soak the raisins in the rum for 1–2 hours. Preheat the oven to 180°C/Gas 4 and lightly grease a baking tray. Drain the raisins, reserving the rum.

Crush the biscuits, using a pestle and mortar, then tip the crumbs into a bowl. Add the butter and mix until evenly combined. Add the raisins, pine nuts, walnuts, almonds, chocolate, candied peel and lemon zest and juice. Stir well, then mix in the beaten egg and some of the rum to make a moist filling.

Roll out the pastry on a lightly floured surface to a 60 x 40cm rectangle, about 2mm thick. Spoon the filling along the middle and brush the pastry edges with water. Fold one long side over the filling to enclose it and make a sausage, then press the edges together to seal. Coil into a circle and place on the prepared baking tray. Bake in the oven for 50 minutes.

Carefully transfer the pastry to a wire rack to cool. Serve warm or cold, sprinkled generously with icing sugar. A good glass of Picolit or Torcolato wine alongside would do very nicely.

Serves 6–8

FETTUCCINE WITH POPPY SEEDS

20g black poppy seeds
200g fettuccine, pappardelle or tagliatelle
80g unsalted butter
½ tbsp grated nutmeg
¼ tbsp ground cloves
pepper
80g vanilla sugar

Roast the poppy seeds in a very hot oven for 10 minutes. Cook the pasta in unsalted water until al dente.

Heat the butter in a pan and add the poppy seeds, nutmeg, cloves and a pinch of pepper.

Drain the pasta, divide onto plates and sprinkle with the vanilla sugar.

Serves 4

" From my student times spent in Vienna one of the most memorable desserts was a Mohnnudeln or poppy pasta. I made my own adaptation to create this recipe, which I believe has Bohemian origins. "

GIANT RAVIOLI WITH PECORINO AND HONEY

4 rounds fresh pecorino cheese, 10cm in diameter, 5mm thick
olive oil, for deep-frying
120g orange-blossom honey, warmed

Dough
150g Italian '00' flour, plus extra for dusting
1 egg, plus 1 extra yolk
salt
1 tbsp caster sugar

To make the pasta dough, pile the flour into a mound on a surface and make a large well in the centre. Put the egg, egg yolk, pinch of salt and sugar in the well and beat lightly with a fork. With your hands, gradually mix in the flour. When the mixture has formed a dough, knead it well with the palms of your hands for about 10 minutes, until it is very smooth and elastic. Cover and leave to rest for 20 minutes.

Roll out the pasta dough on a lightly floured surface to a 2mm thickness and cut out 8 rounds, each 15cm in diameter. Put a cheese round on each of 4 pasta rounds, brush the pasta edges with a little water, then top with the other pasta rounds. Press the edges together to seal.

Heat the olive oil in a suitable pan and deep-fry the ravioli until golden, about 7–8 minutes. Remove and drain well on kitchen paper. Serve hot, drizzled with the warm honey.

Serves 4

" Of the many Sardinian sweet specialities, these sweet ravioli
(also known as seadas) are something out of the ordinary.
They bring together two typical and excellent regional products,
fresh pecorino cheese and orange-blossom honey. A good
glass of Monica di Sardegna is the perfect complement. "

POLENTA BISCUITS

200g unsalted butter, softened,
 plus extra for greasing
200g granulated sugar
300g quick polenta
100g plain flour
½ tsp baking powder
4 eggs, beaten
finely grated zest of 1 lemon

Preheat the oven to 200°C/Gas 6.

Mix all the ingredients together in a large bowl. Take a piping bag and fill it with the mixture. Pipe the mixture onto a greased baking tray in either little dots or S shapes. Leave a generous amount of space between the shapes as the biscuits will spread while cooking.

Bake in the preheated oven for 15 minutes, until golden.

Cool on a wire rack, and store in an airtight container.

Makes about 50 biscuits

" I love polenta in every guise. In Piedmont, where I spent my youth, there are many polenta biscuits, but none with the crispness I achieved by using polenta svelta, the quick polenta flour. These biscuits are wonderful as accompaniments to fresh fruit salads, or dipped into zabaglione. "

STRUFFOLI NAPOLETANI
NEAPOLITAN FRIED PASTRIES

5 eggs
3 tbsp granulated sugar
500g plain flour
grated zest of 1 lemon and 1 orange
salt
1 tbsp pure alcohol (if not available use strong vodka)
oil, for deep-frying
50g cedro (candied citron peel), chopped
25g edible silver balls, to decorate

Caramel
100g sugar
250g honey
2 tbsp water

In a large bowl, beat the eggs with the sugar, then gradually mix in the flour to make a smooth dough. Add the citrus zest, a pinch of salt and the alcohol. Knead well for 3–4 minutes and roll into a ball. Cover and leave to rest for 2 hours in a cool place.

Taking a little bit of dough at a time, roll it with your hand into sausage shapes about 1cm in diameter. Cut the sausage shapes into small pieces about 1cm long. It is quite laborious rolling out these sausages and will take you some time.

In a small pan, pour in the oil to a depth of 2–3cm and heat until moderately hot. Deep-fry the pieces of dough in the hot oil in batches until lightly browned. Remove and drain on kitchen paper.

To make the caramel, in a large heavy-based pan, heat the sugar and honey with the water until the liquid becomes clear. Add the fried struffoli and the chopped peel. Stir carefully until all the struffoli are coated with caramel.

Arrange in the form of a crown on a serving plate, decorate with a few silver balls and leave to cool.

Serves 10

TORTA DI NOCCIOLE
HAZELNUT CAKE

100g unsalted butter
150g Piedmontese hazelnuts, shelled
125g caster sugar
4 large eggs, separated
30g plain flour
300g fresh ricotta cheese
1 tbsp finely grated lemon zest
200g apricot jam, slightly diluted with water
30g dark, bitter chocolate, grated

Preheat the oven to 200°C/Gas 6. Use a little of the butter to grease a 25cm flan tin.

Toast the hazelnuts on a baking tray in the preheated oven until a golden colour, a few minutes only. Leave to cool and chop finely.

Soften the rest of the butter and beat together with 70g of the sugar in a large bowl. Add the egg yolks and beat until smooth, then add the flour and mix well.

In another bowl, stir the ricotta with a fork until smooth. Add the cooled, chopped hazelnuts and the grated lemon zest.

Beat the egg whites separately in another bowl until stiff, then add the remaining sugar, beating until completely blended. Gently fold the yolk mixture into the whites using a large metal spoon until even, being careful to lose as little air from the whites as possible.

Spoon or pour the mixture into the prepared tin and bake in the preheated oven for 30 minutes. Take out and leave the cake to cool in the tin.

When cool, remove the cake from the tin, and place on a cake plate. Spread the jam on top and sprinkle over the grated chocolate to finish.

Serves 8

The most intensive taste of hazelnuts comes from the tonda gentile delle Langhe, a hazelnut grown in the Langhe region of Piedmont. The hazelnut itself is full of flavour, but becomes even more special after a gentle toasting.

CASTAGNACCIO
CHESTNUT CAKE

750g fresh chestnut flour
salt
6 tbsp caster sugar
6 tbsp extra virgin olive oil
3–4 rosemary sprigs
150g raisins (preferably zibibbo)

Preheat the oven to 180°C/Gas 4. Mix the flour, a pinch of salt and the sugar with enough cold water to obtain a soft but not too runny mixture. Put the oil in a deep 30 x 40cm baking tray and spread evenly, then pour in the batter. Sprinkle with the rosemary and raisins and bake for 20 minutes, until golden. Cut into squares to serve. It's best served hot but can also be eaten cold.

Serves 8–10

There exist various versions of this seasonal dish, which is made with the flour of new autumn chestnuts. Chestnut flour tends to become stale quite quickly, which is why it is best used fresh.

TORTA PARADISO CON MASCARPONE
SPONGE CAKE WITH MASCARPONE

250g butter, just melted, for greasing
250g caster sugar
4 large eggs, beaten
1 tsp vanilla extract
225g self-raising flour
25g cornflour
1 tsp baking powder

To serve
300g mascarpone cheese
50g caster sugar
vanilla extract
3–4 tbsp raspberry jam
icing sugar, for dusting

Preheat the oven to 180°C/Gas 4. Line a 25cm shallow round cake tin with baking parchment and grease with a little butter.

Using a balloon whisk, whip the melted butter into the sugar until light and fluffy, then slowly beat in the eggs and vanilla. Gradually sift the flour, cornflour and baking powder together over the mixture, carefully folding it in with the balloon whisk. Pour into the prepared tin and bake for 20–25 minutes until golden and springy to the touch.

Turn out and cool on a wire rack, then cut horizontally into two layers. Beat the mascarpone with the caster sugar and a few drops of vanilla extract until smooth. Spread the jam over the bottom cake layer, then cover with the mascarpone mixture. Top with the other cake layer, sprinkle with icing sugar and serve. A glass of Moscato or Malvasia di Pavia is the perfect complement.

Serves 4–6

"Rich, creamy mascarpone comes from southern Lombardy and it is the ideal filling for this wonderfully light sponge."

TORTA DI RICOTTA
RICOTTA TART

50g butter
3–4 sheets of filo pastry (frozen)
500g fresh ricotta cheese
120g caster sugar
5 eggs, separated
150g mix of orange and lemon zest, cut into small cubes
finely grated zest of 1 lemon
50g bitter chocolate, broken into small pieces

Preheat the oven to 180°C/Gas 4. Grease the inside of a 25cm flan tin with a little of the butter, melting the remainder in a pan over a low heat.

Line the tin with the filo pastry, brushing each sheet with some of the melted butter.

Put the ricotta in a bowl and loosen the texture with a fork. Mix in 100g of the sugar and the egg yolks, followed by the cubes of zest, the grated zest and the chocolate. Mix well together.

In another bowl, beat the egg whites until stiff, then add the remaining sugar. Fold this carefully into the ricotta mixture using a large metal spoon, taking care not to lose the airiness of the whipped whites.

Spread this filling onto the filo pastry on the base of the tin. Brush melted butter over the remaining sheet or sheets of filo. With scissors, cut ribbons of buttered filo pastry and spread these decoratively on the tart.

Bake in the preheated oven for 30 minutes and leave to cool before serving.

Serves 6–8

CROSTATA DI CUGNA
MIXED FRUIT JAM TART

500g Italian '00' flour, plus extra for dusting
200g butter, cut into small cubes, plus extra for greasing
5 egg yolks
200g caster sugar
1 tbsp vanilla sugar
grated zest of ½ lemon
salt
350g favourite jam

Pile the flour up on a work surface into a volcano shape, made a well in the centre and add the butter, 4 of the egg yolks, caster sugar, vanilla sugar, lemon zest and a pinch of salt. Gradually draw in the flour, and then with the palm of your hand, knead quickly and lightly to obtain a smooth dough. Wrap in cling film and leave to rest in the refrigerator for 1 hour.

Preheat the oven to 180°C/Gas 4. Take three-quarters of the pastry and roll it out on a lightly floured board until it is large enough to fit a 25cm round flan tin or a rectangular baking tray. Butter the tin or baking tray and line with the pastry, trimming off the excess. Fill with the jam, then roll out the remaining pastry and cut it into long strips with a pastry wheel or a sharp knife to make a lattice for the tart. Brush with the remaining egg yolk and bake in the preheated oven for 30 minutes. Leave to cool and then serve.

Serves 6–8

Italians love ricotta – a by-product of the cheese-making process – and use it to produce both savoury and sweet dishes. The most important thing to remember about ricotta is that it must always be very fresh: if there is even the tiniest hint of sourness, the ricotta is off.

" The Italian equivalent of English tea at 4 or 5 o'clock in the afternoon is the merenda, when most children eat a slice of what every Italian mother can make – jam tart. It is usually filled with a good homemade jam such as peach, apricot, cherry or prune. It can also be made with fresh or cooked fruit on a blind-baked shortcrust pastry base. "

CREMA ALLA PANNA

PANNACOTTA FROM THE AOSTA VALLEY

750ml single cream
200ml full-fat milk
250g caster sugar
seeds from 1 vanilla pod
½ tsp vanilla extract
2 tbsp peach liqueur or dark rum
3 gelatine leaves

Put everything except the gelatine in a pan and very slowly bring to the boil.

Soften the gelatine leaves in a little warm water. Lift out, squeeze out the excess water and add to the hot cream mixture just before it comes to the boil. Stir with a wooden spoon until the gelatine has dissolved, then pour into 8 ramekins or dariole moulds.

Leave to cool, then refrigerate until set. To unmould, dip the base of each mould into warm water for a few seconds, then turn out onto small serving plates.

You might like to serve the pannacotta with crystallised fruit or a little fruit sauce; it is also good with some caramel poured on top.

Serves 8

ZABAIONE CON SALSA DI CIOCCOLATO AMARO

ZABAGLIONE WITH BITTER CHOCOLATE SAUCE

6 egg yolks
120g caster sugar
170ml Moscato Passito di Pantelleria, Marsala or Madeira

Sauce
200g bitter chocolate, broken into pieces
100ml double cream

Put the egg yolks and sugar in a heatproof bowl (preferably a copper pan with a rounded base) and whisk for a few minutes to obtain a smooth and pure foam. Add the chosen dessert wine and mix well.

Have ready a pan of boiling water, in which the bowl will fit, without the base touching the water. Put the bowl in place in the pan, and beat continuously over the simmering water until the mixture starts to thicken.

Divide the mixture between 6 glasses and chill.

In the same way – in a bowl over a pan of hot water, base not touching the water – melt the chocolate carefully. Add the cream and stir well until smooth.

Put this on the top of the zabaglione. You can eat this straightaway or chill it again before serving.

Serves 4

" This is the original pannacotta. According to the Aostani, the recipe originated in Savoy, and it is probably a derivative of the French crème caramel, except that there are no eggs in pannacotta, only a little gelatine to hold it altogether. "

This terrific dessert is easy to make, delicious warm or cold and can be used in many different ways. It can be either eaten as it is, accompanied by some polenta biscuits (p302), used as a filling for choux pastry buns, or made into a wonderful ice cream.

MARRONI AL MASCARPONE
CANDIED CHESTNUTS WITH MASCARPONE

2 egg yolks
100g caster sugar
1 tsp vanilla sugar
2 tbsp whisky
4 tbsp single cream
400g mascarpone cheese
12 whole chestnuts in syrup or marrons glacés
12 bay leaves

Beat the egg yolks with the caster sugar, vanilla sugar and whisky to obtain a smooth cream. Beat the single cream into the mascarpone to soften it and then carefully fold in the egg yolk mixture. Put the mixture into a piping bag and pipe 3 equal dollops onto each dessert plate. Top with the chestnuts and then decorate with the bay leaves.

Serves 4

TIRAMISU
TIRAMISU

2 egg yolks
100g caster sugar
½ tsp vanilla extract
400g mascarpone cheese
80ml single cream
milk, if needed
400ml strong espresso coffee
4 tbsp Kahlúa or Tia Maria
18 Savoyard biscuits or ladies' fingers
bitter cocoa powder, for dusting

In a small bowl, beat the egg yolks, 80g of the caster sugar and the vanilla extract together. In a second larger bowl, mix the mascarpone with the cream to make it thinner. Mix the mascarpone with the egg. Should the mixture be too dense, add a few drops of milk.

Mix the coffee, chosen liqueur and remaining caster sugar together in a third bowl. Dip the biscuits briefly into the coffee (don't let them absorb too much liquid) and use to line 4 individual ramekins, cutting them in half, if necessary, to fit. Put in a layer of the mascarpone mixture, then top with some more biscuits, finishing with mascarpone and filling the ramekins to the top. Dust the tops with a little bitter cocoa powder and chill until ready to serve.

Makes 4

❝ Tiramisu is now so internationally well known that it can be found absolutely everywhere. But this classic MOF, MOF (Minimum of Fuss, Maximum of Flavour) recipe, which I created 30 years ago, is both simple and delicious. Try it, and you will discover that you instantly become a dessert-maker! ❞

GELATO ALLO ZAFFERANO
SAFFRON ICE CREAM

600ml milk
pinch of saffron powder
8 egg yolks
125g caster sugar
175ml double cream

Bring the milk to the boil in a pan and add the saffron. Beat the egg yolks and sugar together in a bowl until foamy and then gradually pour in the milk, stirring all the time, to obtain a velvety mixture.

Pour the mixture into a bowl set over a pan of very hot water, making sure the water is not touching the bowl, and cook, stirring, until it begins to thicken.

Add the double cream, mix well, then transfer to an ice-cream maker and freeze. If you do not have an ice-cream maker, pour the mixture into a shallow bowl and place in the freezer for about 1 hour, until it is beginning to solidify around the edges. Whisk it well with a fork, then return to the freezer. Repeat this process 3 times and then freeze until firm.

Serves 6

CASSATA SEMIFREDDA
SICILIAN ICE CREAM

200g egg whites (about 4 eggs)
70g caster sugar
100g good-quality ricotta cheese
20ml milk, plus a little extra if needed
400ml double cream
100g thin honey, warmed
100g mixed candied citron and orange peel, chopped
50g pine nuts, toasted
50g dark, bitter chocolate, chopped
80g skinned pistachio nuts
8–10 red candied cherries

Whisk the egg whites until stiff, then gradually whisk in 50g of the sugar. In another bowl, fluff the ricotta with a fork, adding a little milk to soften if it is too firm. Whip the double cream in another bowl until thick.

Fold the honey into the whisked egg whites, followed by the whipped cream and ricotta. Then fold in the chopped candied peel, pine nuts and chocolate. Spoon into a 1.2 litre bowl or bombe mould, cover and chill in the freezer for 12 hours.

Before serving, whiz the pistachio nuts with the remaining 20g sugar and 20ml milk in a blender to make a sauce.

To unmould, dip the bowl into hot water for a few seconds to release the cassata, then turn out onto a plate. Cut into wedges, using a warm knife.

Put a little pistachio sauce on each plate, lay a wedge of cassata in the centre, decorate with a cherry and serve.

Serves 8–10

" This is the easier ice cream and candied fruit version of cassata, as opposed to the elaborate, rich sponge, which is more time-consuming. My former head chef, Andrea Cavaliere, perfected this cassata recipe – it is a semifreddo, with a superb soft texture. "

PANFORTE DI SIENA
SPICED FRUIT AND NUT CAKE

rice paper
240g figs or pitted dates
50g honey
100g soft brown sugar
½ tsp each of ground cinnamon, cardamom,
  cloves, nutmeg and pepper
250g candied fruit, such as cherries, citron,
  lemon and orange zest
50g blanched almonds
50g pine nuts
50g shelled hazelnuts, toasted
3–4 tbsp plain flour, sifted
50ml Vin Santo
icing sugar, for dusting

Preheat the oven to 150°C/Gas 2. Line a shallow 25cm round cake tin, or a 20cm square tin, with rice paper.

Mince the figs or dates and put them in a pan with enough water just to cover. Add the honey, brown sugar and all the spices. Cook gently for about 10 minutes, then tip into a bowl. The mixture should be soft and sticky, but not wet.

Add the candied fruit and nuts and mix well, then add the flour and Vin Santo and mix to a sticky mass. Spoon the mixture into the prepared tin and bake in the oven for 30–40 minutes.

Take out of the oven and leave to cool in the tin. Sprinkle generously with icing sugar and serve cut into thin wedges.

Serves 10

“ This is perhaps one of the oldest sweets in Italy, dating back through the centuries to the introduction of new spices from afar, via the naval port of Pisa. Panforte is sticky but irresistible, and is normally eaten in winter, perhaps with coffee and liqueurs after a meal. A small piece is sufficient to tell you about the complexity of the spices used at that time. ”

CROCCANTE DI NOCCIOLE
HAZELNUT CRUNCH

400g caster sugar
100g honey
zest of 2 tangerines, cut into strips,
   then into very small dice
500g hazelnuts, toasted and skinned
rice paper
1 lemon, cut in half

Melt the sugar and honey in a heavy-based pan over a gentle heat. Raise the heat slightly and, when the sugar begins to go a blondish-brown colour, add the tangerine zest. Stir for a minute with a wooden spoon, then add the hazelnuts. Heat a little, stirring, until the hazelnuts are coated with the sugar syrup.

Pour the very hot mixture onto the rice paper and use the lemon halves to spread it out to about 2.5cm thick (lemons are ideal for this because they do not stick to the mixture). As soon as it has cooled down, but is still warm, cut into cubes with a large knife. They will still be attached at the bottom. Wait until they are completely cold, then break the cubes apart. Put them in an airtight jar and enjoy them when you feel like it. At Christmas they are served at the end of the meal.

Makes 1kg

A popular sweet at every village festa (fête), especially in the South, and one that announces that Christmas is approaching, it can be made with almonds, pistachios or mixed nuts (though toasted hazelnuts are my favourite).

SALAME DI NOCI
CHOCOLATE AND WALNUT SALAMI WITH CANDIED FRUITS

300g shelled walnuts
200g caster sugar
2 tbsp water
100g dark, bitter chocolate, broken into small pieces
150g candied orange peel, finely diced
150g citron peel, finely diced
1 tsp ground cinnamon
½ tsp ground cloves
1 tbsp pepper
200g dried figs, roughly chopped
200g dates, pitted and minced
rice paper

Crush two-thirds of the walnuts, leaving the rest whole.

Put the sugar in a pan with the water and heat gently until the sugar has dissolved. Continue to heat until the sugar syrup just turns golden.

Meanwhile, combine all the other ingredients, including the crushed and whole walnuts, in a bowl. Add the sugar syrup and mix well. Divide the mixture in two and spoon each portion along the middle of a sheet of rice paper.

Roll up in the paper, shaping each into a 'salami'. Leave in a cool place until set.

Serve cut into thin slices, with coffee or Moscato, or wrap decoratively in cellophane for an edible Christmas gift.

Makes 2 x 750g salami

BASIC RECIPES

BRODO DI PESCE
FISH STOCK

1.2kg white fish heads and bones
3 litres water
salt and pepper
2–3 celery stalks, coarsely chopped
2 carrots, cut into chunks
bunch of flat-leaf parsley
1 onion, halved
2 garlic cloves, peeled
1 tsp fennel seeds

Wash the pieces of fish under cold running water, then place in a saucepan with the water and a little salt. Bring to the boil and skim away the froth from the surface. Add all the remaining ingredients and leave to simmer gently for 40 minutes. Strain the liquid through a sieve into a bowl, check the seasoning and allow to cool.

On cooling, this stock tends to set into a jelly. Chill and use as required within 1–2 days, or freeze.

Makes about 2.2 litres

BRODO DI GALLINA
CHICKEN STOCK

1 chicken, about 2kg
salt
4 litres water
2 carrots, cut into chunks
1 onion, halved
2–3 celery stalks, coarsely chopped
4 bay leaves
1 tbsp black peppercorns

Put the chicken in a large pan with a little salt and cover with the water. Bring to the boil and skim off the froth from the surface. Add the remaining ingredients and allow to simmer gently for 1½–2 hours, skimming occasionally. Strain the stock into a bowl, check the seasoning and allow to cool.

Remove the solidified fat from the surface. Keep the stock in the fridge and use within 4 days, or freeze.

Makes about 3 litres

BRODO DI CARNE
BEEF STOCK

1kg stewing beef and some bones
4 litres water
salt
2 carrots
1 onion, halved
2–3 celery stalks, coarsely chopped
4 bay leaves
1 tbsp black peppercorns

Put the meat in a large pan with a little salt and cover with the water. Bring to the boil and skim off the froth from the surface. Add the remaining ingredients and allow to simmer for 2–3 hours, skimming occasionally. Strain the stock into a bowl, check the seasoning and leave to cool.

Remove the solidified fat from the surface of the stock. Keep in the fridge and use within 4–5 days, or freeze.

Makes about 3 litres

BRODO DI VEGETALI
VEGETABLE STOCK

1.3kg mixed vegetables (carrot, celeriac, celery, fennel, onion, parsnip, etc.)
1 garlic clove, chopped
bunch of flat-leaf parsley
2 bay leaves
few thyme sprigs (or other herbs)
salt and pepper

Prepare and roughly chop the vegetables and put them into a pan with the garlic, herbs, seasoning and 1.7 litres water. (Keep the vitamin-rich water from cooking green vegetables to use here.) Bring to the boil and simmer for 20 minutes or so until the vegetables are tender.

Strain the stock into a bowl and allow to cool. Keep in the fridge and use within 3 days, or freeze

Makes about 1.2 litres

SALSA DI POMODORO BASE
BASIC TOMATO SAUCE

1.5kg ripe and meaty tomatoes (large or San Marzano)
4 tbsp olive oil
1 medium onion, very finely sliced
1 garlic clove, coarsely chopped
10 small, fresh basil leaves, shredded

Plunge the tomatoes into boiling water for 1 minute to loosen the skins. Remove the skins. Cut the tomatoes in half. Discard the inner liquid and seeds, leaving only the flesh, which you coarsely chop.

Heat the oil in a pan and fry the onion for 5 minutes. Add the garlic and fry for a further minute. Add the tomato and bring to the boil, reduce the heat and simmer for 30–40 minutes. Halfway through, add the shredded basil leaves. When it has finished cooking, add some salt to taste and liquidize. The sauce keeps for a few days in the fridge, but is best if eaten when freshly made.

Makes about 1kg

PASTA ALL'UOVO
EGG PASTA DOUGH

400g Italian '00' flour, plus extra to dust
4 large, very fresh eggs
large pinch of salt

Pile the flour in a mound on a surface and make a well in the middle. Break the eggs into the well and add the salt. Stir the eggs into the flour, with a fork at first, and then with your hands, until it forms a coarse paste. Add a little more flour if too moist.

Now knead the pasta dough, either using a pasta machine or by hand, until it is smooth and workable, not too soft but not too hard. To knead by hand, lightly flour the surface and your hands and knead the dough with the heel of one hand, pushing it away from you and folding it back towards you; do this for 10–15 minutes. Cover the dough with a cloth and rest for 15–30 minutes before rolling out. Divide the dough into 4 or 5 portions. If rolling by machine, pass the dough through the rollers, a portion at a time, decreasing the gap between the rollers each time, so that the dough becomes thinner and longer. Repeat this until you obtain the desired thickness: 3–4mm for lasagna and cannelloni;

1.5–2mm for stuffed pasta; even thinner for finer pasta. Then either pass through the cutting rollers to make various sizes of ribbon, or cut into sheets. If rolling by hand, gently roll out a portion at a time on a lightly floured surface to the required thickness, rolling away from you and giving the dough a quarter-turn after each rolling. To cut ribbons, fold the sheet of pasta into a loose roll and cut it into ribbons of the desired width.

For stuffed pasta, such as ravioli, use the pasta straightaway. If you are making lasagna or ribbon pasta, place on a floured cloth to dry for 10 minutes or so before cooking.

Cook fresh pasta in a large saucepan, allowing 1 litre water per 100g pasta, plus 2 tsp salt. When you put the pasta into the pan, give it a quick stir to prevent it from sticking together. (It is only with lasagne, which must be immersed one sheet at a time, that you need to add a few drops of oil to the water.) Cooking time varies according to the type of pasta, its thickness and whether it is stuffed, but homemade pasta will take about 3 minutes. Stir a few times during cooking, preferably with a long-handled wooden fork.

Test the pasta when you think it should be almost done: it is ready when it is al dente, and slightly resistant. A few moments before it reaches that stage, take the saucepan off the heat, add a glass of cold water, and leave for a couple of seconds. Then drain the pasta (perhaps saving a little of the water in case a sauce needs it) and return immediately to the saucepan or preheated dish. Mix it with a little sauce and perhaps some grated cheese. Serve immediately.

Makes about 600g

INDEX

Editorial director Jane O'Shea
Creative director Helen Lewis
Project editor Simon Davis
Editorial assistance Louise McKeever, Romilly Morgan
Design Claire Peters and Jim Smith
Photographer Alastair Hendy
Illustrator Katie Horwich
Production James Finan, Vincent Smith

This edition first published in 2018 by Quadrille,
an imprint of Hardie Grant Publishing

Quadrille
52–54 Southwark Street
London SE1 1UN
quadrille.com

ISBN 978 1 78713 356 3

Printed in China